www.wadsworth.com

www.wadsworth.com is the World Wide Web site for Thomson Wadsworth and is your direct source to dozens of online resources.

At *www.wadsworth.com* you can find out about supplements, demonstration software, and student resources. You can also send email to many of our authors and preview new publications and exciting new technologies.

www.wadsworth.com
Changing the way the world learns®

Performing Literary Texts

Concepts and Skills

CLELLA JAFFE
George Fox University

THOMSON ™

WADSWORTH

Australia • Canada • Mexico • Singapore • Spain
United Kingdom • United States

THOMSON

TM

WADSWORTH

Performing Literary Texts: Concepts and Skills

Clella Jaffe

Publisher: *Holly Allen*
Acquisitions Editor: *Annie Mitchell*
Assistant Editor: *Aarti Jayaraman*
Editorial Assistant: *Trina Enriquez*
Senior Technology Project Manager:
  Jeanette Wiseman
Associate Technology Project Manager:
  Inna Fedoseyeva
Senior Marketing Manager: *Kimberly Russell*
Marketing Assistant: *Alexandra Tran*
Marketing Communications Manager:
  Shemika Britt
Project Manager, Editorial Production:
  Matt Ballantyne

Art Director: *Maria Epes*
Print Buyer: *Judy Inouye*
Permissions Editor: *Sarah Harkrader*
Production Service: *Matrix Productions*
Copy Editor: *Janet McCartney*
Illustrator: *Cadmus*
Compositor: *Cadmus*
Cover Designer: *Janet Wood*
Cover Image: *"Saint Phil Reading Aloud,"* by
  David-Glen Smith
Text and Cover Printer: *Transcontinental
  Printing – Louiseville*

Printed in Canada
1 2 3 4 5 6 7 09 08 07 06 05

For more information about our products,
contact us at:
**Thomson Learning Academic Resource Center
1-800-423-0563**

For permission to use material from this text
or product, submit a request online at
http://www.thomsonrights.com.

Any additional questions about permissions
can be submitted by email to
thomsonrights@thomson.com.

Library of Congress Control Number:
  2005922292

ISBN 0-534-62001-9

**Thomson Higher Education
10 Davis Drive
Belmont, CA 94002-3098
USA**

Asia (including India)
Thomson Learning
5 Shenton Way
#01-01 UIC Building
Singapore 068808

Australia/New Zealand
Thomson Learning Australia
102 Dodds Street
Southbank, Victoria 3006
Australia

Canada
Thomson Nelson
1120 Birchmount Road
Toronto, Ontario M1K 5G4
Canada

UK/Europe/Middle East/Africa
Thomson Learning
High Holborn House
50–51 Bedford Row
London WC1R 4LR
United Kingdom

Latin America
Thomson Learning
Seneca, 53
Colonia Polanco
11560 Mexico
D.F. Mexico

Spain (including Portugal)
Thomson Paraninfo
Calle Magallanes, 25
28015 Madrid, Spain

Contents

Preface

Welcome to the exciting world of performance studies. Throughout the term, you will learn concepts and skills that will enable you to succeed in one of the oldest of all communication activities: oral performances of cultural or literary texts. In both historical and contemporary settings, performers throughout the world have used their skills to transmit, maintain, and sometimes challenge their cultures.

This is a practical course. Students at my university apply performance skills in real-life situations such as reading to children, participating in religious services, performing in open mike sessions at local coffeehouses, and creating on-campus performance events. They also use what they learn about audiences to be more effective participants in the hundreds of performances they attend.

I decided to write this book one summer when I was trying to choose a text for the Oral Interpretation of Literature course I would teach in the fall. I originally inherited the class, along with an accompanying textbook, from a retiring professor in the theater department. My students complained about that text, so I began to search for a book that emphasized skills and included a cultural perspective. Several semesters later, I sat down at my word processor, typed out a table of contents, and began to draft some chapters of this text. My goal was to create a book that balanced theory and practice, used contemporary and classic texts, and integrated Western and non-Western traditions. After a summer of writing, I tested the draft on my students. They responded favorably, and I continued to refine and broaden this text so that it would appeal to an audience outside my classroom.

Because my major personal and scholarly interest is in the relationship between culture and communication, I weave cultural information throughout the entire book. As humans, we create, maintain, repair, and transform our cultures through our communication activities, including our performances. Consequently, I would argue that a text that ignores cultural performance traditions omits something essential.*

Authors have goals for their readers, and I am no exception. I hope that after you study this text you will be able to succeed in the following areas:

- *Overcoming performance-related anxiety.* Many students are initially daunted by the prospect of selecting and performing literature. They feel insecure about their abilities to prepare and perform a text. For this reason, I have included a section on overcoming anxiety in the first chapter. The practical tips there will provide you with tools for dealing constructively with nervousness.

- *Cocreating a performance with an audience.* Students often think long and hard about their role in performance, but they may fail to consider the audience's essential role in contributing to their success as a performer. Consequently, Chapter 2 discusses audience characteristics. I hope you use it to analyze your listeners and the situations in which you perform. I also hope it helps you become a better audience member yourself.

- *Developing critical thinking skills.* At first glance, you might not think of performance as a way to develop critical thinking skills. However, analyzing your audience, selecting and analyzing texts, and critiquing your classmates' performances are all critical thinking skills that you will develop throughout the term. As you analyze ways that your text perpetuates or confronts cultural norms, you will develop additional critical thinking skills.

- *Developing performance skills.* Of course, much of the material in this book provides guidelines intended to help you not just get up and read literature, but to perform a text in such a way that both you and your listeners find satisfactory.

- *Understanding the link between performance and culture.* Many students are almost entirely unaware of the variety and richness of global performance traditions. This text is unique in that it presents selected cultural traditions. My goal is to help you realize some ways that you are connected globally and historically with performers and audiences through all ages and within all cultures.

Last year I took a sabbatical from teaching so that I could finish this book and delve into literature that I neglect when I teach full time. During the year, I read close to 50 books, everything from biographies and scholarly works to poetry and fictional texts, by international and American authors, classic and contemporary works. I have enjoyed sharing some excerpts from these texts with you, and I wish you the joy of sharing fascinating texts with others.

---

*Carey, J.W. (1989). *Communication as Culture: Essays on Media and Society.* Boston: Unwin Hyman.

1

Introduction to Oral Performances

This chapter will help you:

- Define aesthetic communication

- Give reasons to perform aesthetic texts

- Describe some Western and non-Western performance traditions

- Explain four elements of performance: place, content, audience, and intention

- Compare and contrast oral performance with reading and acting

- Learn strategies for overcoming stage fright

Ms. Johnson gathers 22 first-graders around her chair. After three weeks of class, she has become familiar with her students' interests and attention spans. She carefully selects a picture book to interpret to them. Using a wide range of voices and facial expressions, she performs all the characters and keeps the children's interest in the story. When the story has ended, they sigh with delight. Ms. Johnson has done what you'll do in this class: select a text, analyze it, and plan ways to perform it, keeping in mind the audience and the situation.

Ms. Johnson illustrates just one way in which oral performances take place daily in communities across the world. Such performances are significant because, as the Kenyan scholar Ngugi wa Thiong'o[1] explains, communities learn and pass on their moral codes and aesthetic judgments through various types of performances. Here are a few examples that regularly occur in the United States:

- Authors make cross-country book tours to read from their latest works; poets perform at open mike sessions in local coffee shops.

- Coworkers tell jokes over lunch; friends regale one another with funny stories about daily happenings.

- Improvisation groups create humorous sketches on the spur of the moment in nightclubs.

- Participants in religious services listen to sacred texts and chant the rituals that reaffirm their faith—sometimes in unison, sometimes responsively.

As you can see, professional actors aren't the only performers. Millions of people perform as part of their daily routines. Those who are effective do more than simply read words or stagger through their stories or jokes. They add energy and nuanced interpretations so that their performances engage and interest their listeners. The purpose of this text is to provide you with the concepts and skills for creating more meaningful and effective oral performances.

This introductory chapter defines performance and aesthetic communication and describes some performance traditions, both Western and non-Western. It then explains elements of performances and provides guidelines you can use to plan your performances. Finally, because stage fright is common, it closes with a discussion of ways to overcome nervousness.

PERFORMANCE AND AESTHETIC COMMUNICATION

Performance is sometimes defined broadly to include the daily roles we play, the rituals we enact, the ways we perform gender, racial and ethnic identity, personal identity, and so on.[2] However, this text discusses a more narrowed definition of **performance** that focuses on presentations of artistic or aesthetic texts, both literary and nonliterary. **Aesthetic communication** includes utterances that are created to entertain or to express ideas creatively in interesting language. Aesthetic communication can be defined by use, qualities, and effect or response.[3]

- *Use.* Aesthetic texts are created and used *as* aesthetic texts. In oral cultures, this includes folklore, rituals, and other forms of communication that participants recognize as aesthetic.
- *Qualities.* The performance event has features that are generally considered aesthetic, regardless of the creator's intent.
- *Effect or Response.* The text has social, ethical, political, and/or aesthetic effects on the listeners or readers. The audience willingly takes the role of audience and responds to the performer as a performer.

In this text, you'll study oral performance of literary texts, which involves analyzing an audience and situation and then selecting and performing a text in an artistic, aesthetic manner.[4]

WHY PERFORM AESTHETIC TEXTS?

The chapter opening explains that cultures pass on their moral codes and aesthetic judgments through performance. But what does this mean to you? What will you personally gain from performing aesthetic texts? After all, you are going to put in a lot of time and effort, and the thought of performing in front of an audience may be nerve-racking. Here are a few of the many individual benefits of performance:

- First, performance is a method of studying a text. Giving voice and physical expression to a text enhances your understanding of its meanings. You can also appreciate and analyze the work for its emotional meanings.
- This course requires you to find, to select, and to hear some creative utterances of others that you might not otherwise experience. Thus, it contributes to your liberal arts education by inviting you to affirm or question the conventions and roles you may take for granted.[5]
- Participating in a performance class helps sharpen your critical thinking skills. You'll learn to analyze and evaluate the suitability of a specific text for a specific audience and to identify criteria for performances. You will evaluate performances based on these criteria. You will also evaluate the intentions and goals of the creators and the performers of various texts as you decide the value of the text for you personally.
- Performing can help build speaking and presentation skills you can use in other areas of your life. For example, an article available on InfoTrac® College Edition identifies the benefits of acting lessons for accountants, physicians, and others who do not normally see themselves as performers. The authors argue that learning to use your voice and body effectively, skills you'll hone in this class, helps you adjust to different audiences, avoid distracting mannerisms, and present your ideas clearly.[6]

In summary, studying others' performances and participating in performances yourself can enrich you mentally and socially. Throughout this course, you will be developing skills that are transferable to many other areas of your life.

PERFORMANCE TRADITIONS

Human beings have a natural propensity for participating in performances, whether as spectators or performers. In fact, some scholars refer to humankind as **homo performans** instead of *homo sapiens*.[7] They mean that in every culture and in every age, performers pass on their culture's explanations of human origins, historical memories, cultural values, and everyday practices. However, performances can also challenge or resist cultural beliefs and practices. Take, for example, performance artists who confront cultural assumptions about politics, sexuality, religion, and so on. Or consider the impact of lectors in Cuban cigar factories on the Cuban revolution, as described in the Performing Culture feature on page 7.

It would be impossible to write a history of performance in just a few pages, so this section simply highlights a few Western and non-Western performance traditions that span the centuries. For additional information, log onto the Internet and search for some of the performance traditions within your cultural heritage. (Suggestion: Use www.google.com and search for the exact phrase "performance traditions" plus a specific tradition, such as "Japanese" or "Muslim.")

Some Western Traditions

Although performances were part of the earliest human societies, historians who trace Western traditions often begin by describing Greek performers.[8] In classical Greece, the **rhapsodists** recited Homer's epics. Their symbolic gesturing and vocal variations added dramatic effects to their words, and they kept the rhythm with their staffs. In contests, the best rhapsodists showed off their abilities to improvise creatively on Homer's work. Remnants of this tradition persist in modern Greece; for example, contests in Cyprus feature poet-performers who present both prepared and improvised texts, like the ancient rhapsodists did.[9]

Ancient Roman performers, known as **recitatio**, recited Roman epics at prestigious, formal events held in recitation halls. These events were not merely entertaining; they also provided opportunities to reaffirm aristocratic values and expectations. Like many contemporary oral interpreters, the *recitato* kept the written text in hand. Other Roman poets and performers held forth on street corners and in theatres. They educated the young and comforted and entertained the adults. Performers were everywhere; in fact, the poet Horace complained that he couldn't avoid them, even in the baths![10]

As one era followed another, Western performance traditions evolved. Fast-forward to the medieval period, and you will find **troubadours,** the wandering

ILLUSTRATION 1.1 Diagrams from Elocution Manuals Showing Movements Used in Depicting Emotions and Moods.[13]

minstrels associated with the aristocratic class in southern France. They are best known for performing works relating to "courtly love," poems and songs that presented idealized notions of women and romantic relationships, which contrasted to the more masculine virtues featured in epic literature. Other performers throughout Europe, from Scandinavia to the Balkans, from southern Europe to the Baltic region, recited oral narrative poetry. They memorized the poems but improvised as they performed, resulting in dynamic, creative, and evolving epics. In Spain today, Judeo-Spanish performers carry on similar traditions.[11]

The **elocutionary movement** became popular in Britain and the United States in the 18th and 19th centuries. Thomas Sheridan, an actor turned writer and lecturer, produced manuals to standardize the pronunciation of English and to teach speakers how to emphasize, gesture, and use tones to communicate meanings. Elocution focused on delivery—on vocal qualities and bodily movements. (See Illustration 1.1.) Public as well as private recitations, especially of poetry, became popular forms of entertainment in the 1800s. Paying audiences gathered to hear professional elocutionists recite, and friends and families gathered in parlors and around hearths to encourage the amateur performers in their midst. Collections of suitable recitations included "serious, comic, patriotic, heroic, sublime, humorous, descriptive, didactic, and ridiculous" texts, to be used in homes, schools, churches, clubs, literary societies, and public and private recitals.[12]

Today, the definition of performance has broadened to include what occurs in everyday conversations and in rituals. A range of scholars contribute articles to the journal *Text and Performance Quarterly* that reflect this broader definition. Their articles discuss "the performance of childhood,"[14] the performance of "race, gender, and drag,"[15] and even lynchings as violent performances.[16] They examine festivals and parades, celebrations and religious rituals, exhibitions and photographs. Students who major in performance studies take courses in such diverse disciplines as acting, design, cultural studies, literature, history, dance, and gender studies.

Some Non-Western Traditions

The West is not unique. People the world over have distinctive performance traditions. African **griots** and **griottes** trace their roots back to 13th-century Malian speaking traditions. Thomas Hale writes of these performers, "No other profession in any part of the world had such wide-ranging and intimate involvement in people's lives."[17] These men and women functioned as village historians, royal advisors, diplomats, mediators, teachers, exhorters, witnesses, praise singers, and key participants in ceremonies. They memorized and performed their tribes' genealogies, tales, proverbs, songs, and poetry. Alex Haley's 1976 novel *Roots*[18] described *griots* for readers in the United States; some African Americans have adopted the term to identify themselves or their interests. For example, students at Michigan State University have titled their black studies journal *The Griot*.

Asian traditions include the **pansor'i performers** of Korea. These male and female performers chant traditional stories in a folk style that may last up to six hours. Traditionally, a single storyteller impersonated all the characters in the narrative, accompanied by a drummer. The audience was expected, even required, to participate.[19] Today, pansor'i performances are posted on the Internet; just click on the links at http://madang.ajou.ac.kr/~moon/pansori.htm to view some examples.

The **Ramayana tradition** can be found across South Asia, from India to Vietnam and into Indonesia. This storytelling practice, which is over 2,000 years old, relates the epic Hindu tale of Prince Rama and Princess Sita. The storytellers modify and embellish the tales, incorporating their personal insights as well as regional traditions. Modern film and video producers have joined traditional bards and singers as well as "countless grandmothers"[20] in passing along Hindu customs and traditions in this manner.

On the North American continent, Native Americans had many oral traditions. Among the Cree, some storytellers inherited the profession, others were chosen, and still others were recognized because of their natural talent. They refrained from telling fictional stories during the summertime; that was the season for work, not for entertainment, and snakes or toads might climb into bed with a storyteller who ignored this custom. Moreover, since dangerous animals might hear negative stories about themselves and take revenge, it was better to tell entertaining tales at their expense when they were safely tucked away, hibernating in their winter lairs.[21] The Lakota Sioux, like other groups, differentiated among types of stories. They told *Ehanni* (special stories from before time), *Ohunkskan* (stories of the great-great-great-grandfathers), and *Ehanni Wicowayake* (stories recounting important historical events of the Lakota people).[22]

These are just a few global performance traditions, but there are probably as many traditions as there are groups. Performers within each society support the culture in which they practice their art. Some of the exercises at the end of the chapter ask you to explore additional cultural traditions.

PERFORMING CULTURE: Cuban Cigar Factory Readers (Lectors)

To better understand how oral interpretation of literature can influence culture, consider the story of the Cuban lectors.

In the late 19th century, poet and cigar maker Saturino Martinez decided to publish a newspaper that would provide information and entertainment for workers in the cigar factories, colonial Cuba's major industry. However, Martinez discovered that many workers could not read, so he enlisted students from a local high school to act as **lectors** and read aloud to the workers as they hand rolled cigars. Lectors proved so successful that cigar factories throughout Cuba began employing them. They read all kinds of books and newspapers during working hours and, in time, Cuban cigar workers became the world's "best educated workforce."[23] The workers eventually began acting on their newfound knowledge by organizing and striking; soon thereafter, the Spanish government banned lectors as subversive, and the readings went underground. Their overall effect on Cuban society was profound. The most famous lector is Jose Marti, who led Cuba's fight for independence from Spain[24] using

funds donated from cigar workers in the United States. In the United States, lectors provided up-to-date information about the revolution.[25]

U.S. lectors modified the readings slightly by adding dramatic elements to increase their listeners' interest and understanding. (Nilo Cruz's play *Anna in the Tropics,* which won the 2003 Pulitzer Prize in Drama, is about a lector whose reading of Tolstoy's novel *Anna Karenina* changes the lives of a family that works in the factory. You'll find an excerpt in Chapter 4.)[26]

Today, lectors still read aloud in a few factories. Every day at noon in the Cuba Aliados Cigar Factory in Honduras, a lector ascends the platform in the middle of the rolling room and reads from newspapers and novels. As he reads, the PA system broadcasts his words throughout the entire factory.[27]

For additional information about lectors, log onto InfoTrac College Edition and search for the article "Guadalajara Book Fair Focuses Spotlight on Cuba's Cigarmakers." What type of literature did cigar makers typically like to have read? What cigars did they name after literary characters?

ELEMENTS OF PERFORMANCE

In his treatise *Penpoints, Gunpoints and Dreams: The Performance of Literature and Power in Post-Colonial Africa,*[28] Ngugi wa Thiong'o identifies the main ingredients of performance as place, content, audience, and goal (the end or purpose); goals include instruction, pleasure, or a combination of the two. Ngugi argues that performance is intentional, that it should have some reformative effect on the audience. This section discusses each of these elements in turn.

Place

According to Ngugi, performance spaces are sites of physical and social forces. The **physical setting** is the room or place in which the performance takes place—the theatres, street corners, homes, places of worship, and so on where performers create their art. You may perform in a variety of settings in the future, but most of your performances during this course will take place in your college classroom. Wherever you perform, consider the obstacles that might hinder your audience from seeing or hearing you. Look for the best place to stand to be seen and heard; you might need to ask some listeners to adjust their seats so you can maintain eye contact with everyone.

Performances also take place in specific **cultural settings** that are rooted in broader social situations. In all cultures, deeply embedded values and beliefs operate at an almost subconscious level, and these ingrained ideas or ideologies powerfully shape perceptions. For instance, independence and choice are American values. Can you imagine a government bureaucrat telling you that you must major in chemistry and be a chemist? In the United States this is almost unthinkable, but Chinese government officials look at students' test scores and assign them to a career; in China, the good of the group is more highly valued than individuality and choice. As you work with your piece, probe it for the values it represents, and think about how those values are reflected in the broader cultural discourse. (Chapter 3 lists other cultural values in the United States.)

Your college or university is another element of the social context. Consider the region of the country where you live, the type of students your school attracts, and the current political or national and international issues that might influence your performance. For example, how might the following incidents affect a classroom performance?

- The debate team wins a national title.
- Your campus receives national news coverage after student hecklers prematurely force a political speaker off the stage.
- A fraternity hazing incident results in the hospitalization of two students.
- Students boycott classes to protest a federal government policy.
- Hundreds of copies of a conservative campus newspaper are stolen before they can be distributed.
- A terrorist attack kills hundreds of U.S. citizens.

Incidents such as these form the social and cultural background for your performance. It is important to consider their impact on your audience as you choose your text and anticipate your listeners' responses to your performance.

Content

A current definition of **text** is "any human document."[29] This ranges from songs and physical movements to works of literature and to noncanonical and nonliterary texts, such as personal narratives, folklore, and oral histories.[30] In this broad sense, **literature** can be defined as:

a written, visual, and oral art form that represents cultural history and the human experience.... The study of literature expands experience, promotes critical thinking, and leads to an appreciation of the beauty and richness of language.[31]

In choosing texts, look for stories, ideas, and themes that interest and resonate with you. Narrow your choices down to those works you deem worthy of your time and of your listeners' attention.

Find a text that matches your interests and skills and is appropriate to your audience and the allotted time frame. Think back to books you've read, poetry, songs, or folklore you've memorized, plays you've seen or studied, films you've loved. Your enthusiasm about a text will be reflected in your performance, so you're better off selecting something you enjoy rather than trying to drum up fake energy for a ho-hum piece. Your instructor will probably ask you to perform material from three **genres of literature:** poetry, prose (short stories, diaries, essays), and drama (plays). (Each genre is covered in a later chapter.)

Because there are so many available texts from which to choose, you must use your judgment as you decide on a specific text for your specific audience. Here are a few things to consider at the outset (Chapter 3 provides more details on choosing texts):

- Search for a text that actively engages your audience in historical and/or social issues and events.

- Look for pieces that will help listeners interpret their surroundings, feelings, and ideas and understand human commonalities and bonds.

- Consider material from classic as well as contemporary sources; draw from diverse styles and points of view that reflect a wide range of ethnic, cultural, and gender concerns.[32]

Audience

Your relationship with your audience is so essential that all of Chapter 2 is devoted to it. In the last few decades, the **dialogical theory** has been influential in communication studies. This theory argues that conversation or dialogue forms the foundation for all communication.[33] Dialogue involves give and take. In a conversation, you expect the other person to pay attention, to consider your ideas, to give nonverbal feedback, and to contribute ideas of her or his own. Similarly, in a performance situation, good audience members pay attention, respond emotionally, consider their personal interpretations, contribute nonverbal feedback during the performance, and sometimes provide verbal insights afterward.

A major difference between a conversation and an oral interpretation of literature is the presence of the creator or author. In interpretation, although you are not the original source of the words you say, you are the voice and body through which an *other* (the creator or author) enters the conversation. In a real sense, you mediate or "go between" the creator and the listeners.

> **STOP AND CHECK: Create a List of Potential Texts**
>
> Start listing possible sources and pieces for performance. Make one list of "Authors I Enjoy," another of "Pieces I Enjoy," and a third of "Themes That Interest Me." Add to these lists throughout the course.
>
>   If you need help getting started, visit www.authorsontheweb.com or www.poets.org or go to www.yahoo.com and link to web directory → arts → humanities → literature. Follow links that interest you. If you need help with themes, check to see if your campus library has the *Dictionary of Literary Themes and Motifs.*

Furthermore, you yourself are also an audience member. Paul Campbell[34] argues that, in fact, you are the primary audience for the text; when you read to others, you also are reading to yourself. Campbell adds that when we listen to ourselves, we hear our own characters and our own enactments of the text. For example, if Lia decides to interpret O. Henry's story "The Gift of the Magi," she enters into a kind of dialogue with the text during her analysis and rehearsal period. Then, in her public performance, she hears herself create the characters and the mood; and she listens along with the audience as she performs the author's words. Because the performance is dialogical, she watches her audience's nonverbal feedback, and she adapts her performance as she proceeds. Afterward, her classmates' comments provide her with additional insights into O. Henry's piece as well as their responses to her interpretation of the text.

Intention or Goal

Creators of texts act intentionally; that is, they express themselves in order to create or evoke audience responses. Consequently, figuring out your **goals or purposes** will help you plan your performance more effectively. Literature has four general purposes that often overlap: to inform, to persuade, to entertain, and to express personal ideas and emotions.

The **informative purpose** aims at increasing the audience's understanding or knowledge about a topic. Informative texts emphasize factual information more than emotional coloration. Here's the opening paragraph in a well-written informative piece by Larissa MacFarquhar titled "Slim Chance."[35]

> We have tried, we humans, to do things Nature's way. We have retired the old man-conquers-Nature approach, and sidled up to Mama Earth with wheedling apologies. Can it have escaped anyone's notice, though, that Nature has responded, not with the *noblesse oblige* we might expect of her, but with nasty little passive-aggressive stabs at revenge? Cockroaches capable of surviving a nuclear war; humans made sick by tiny viruses. And which among these petty annoyances is a surer sign that Nature is determined to frustrate us to death than her mean refusal to allow us to shed

fat? In this matter, at least, we have been forced to take things into our own hands—with liposuction.

Authors whose aim is **to persuade** generally focus on one of several areas: They might hope to create, to maintain, or to change their audience's beliefs, behaviors, values, or attitudes. For example, parents tell stories to create ideas and values in very young children; Aesop told fables to maintain cultural values such as "Fine clothes may disguise, but silly words will disclose a fool"; inspirational stories encourage people to change—to forgive, to let go of the past, to do volunteer work.

The goal of some authors is to influence mental processes; they want **to convince** readers to believe a particular idea. For instance, scientific stories explain how the world began and how it works; religious stories bolster belief systems about ultimate realities such as our purpose on earth and what happens after death; editorial and opinion columnists argue that their opinions about political and social issues are valid.

Another persuasive goal is **to actuate** or motivate readers to behave in a specific way. Many children's stories are created with this purpose in mind; for instance, "Goldilocks and the Three Bears" aims at motivating children to stay out of other people's houses and to leave their property alone. Stories about the homeless, about people with AIDS, and about the environment try to inspire people to become involved in solving the problems.

A third type of persuader aims **to reinforce** or maintain readers' current beliefs, actions, or values. Think of the many ways that moviemakers—the great storytellers of this day and age—reinforce cultural beliefs and values: The screenwriter for *October Sky* reinforced the cultural value of perseverance; romantic comedies reinforce the cultural myth that romantic love transcends barriers of social class, ethnicity, and age.

Some of the most interesting and enjoyable texts are written **to entertain.** In spite of their overall intent, many entertaining pieces also have a point or moral. They are often distinguished by less somber or weighty themes and by interesting, creative language. Here's an example from Louise Rafkin's book, *Other People's Dirt: A Housecleaner's Curious Adventures:* [36]

> Alone in a house, I piece together strands of life stories as if I were an archeologist, the home a midden. . . . I know who has $1.2 million in just one stock portfolio. I know which wife is having an affair. I don't read diaries but I read clues. I see things and I hear things. I am there when the answering machine picks up. I have heard rendezvous arranged and indiscretions confessed. I dust birthday cards and fish behind headboards, all in the name of cleanliness. Disguised as a pleasant, competent housecleaner, I am invisible. Who needs the CIA?

Finally, consider the **expressive purpose,** which is especially common in poetry. Here, the creators' major purpose is to express or confess their thoughts, feelings, and opinions about topics as disparate as nature's beauty, love of country, family ties, religious sentiment, and experiences that evoke strong emotional

responses. Francis Scott Key expressed his delight at seeing the United States'
flag after 25 hours of battling against British bombs. His poem, which was
later set to music, became the U.S. national anthem:

> O say can you see,
> By the dawn's early light,
> What so proudly we hail'd
> At the twilight's last gleaming?
> Whose broad stripes and bright stars,
> Thro' the perilous fight,
> O'er the ramparts we watch'd,
> Were so gallantly streaming?
> And the rocket's red glare,
> The bombs bursting in air
> Gave proof thro' the night
> That our flag was still there.
> O say, does that star-spangled
> Banner yet wave
> O'er the land of the free
> And the home of the brave.[37]

In this course, you will probably choose persuasive, entertaining, or
expressive pieces more often than informative ones. However, many people
read informative material as an essential part of their careers. Among them
are newscasters who read from teleprompters and scholars and scientific
researchers who read papers at conventions. You can imagine how boring
this material can be unless it is performed in an engaging, conversational
manner!

READING, ACTING, AND PERFORMING LITERARY TEXTS

There are some noteworthy differences between reading, acting, and performing an interpretation of a literary text. For starters, the level of preparation
required to *perform* a literary text is considerably greater than the preparation
required to *read* it. Here are some additional differences for you to consider:

- A reader looks at the printed page much of the time; in contrast, an interpreter or performer knows the text well enough to look away from the
  words most of the time.

- Performers make more choices than readers do. When you read, you are
  voicing what the author has written, sometimes adding feeling to the
  words. However, when you interpret a text, you are making additional
  decisions about vocal variation and bodily movements. You weave these
  together to create an artistic, aesthetically pleasing performance that
  reveals the meanings you've gleaned from your analysis.

If you've had acting experience, you may be frustrated by differences between acting and the solo performance of aesthetic texts. Here are a few ways the two typically differ:

- Actors typically use makeup and clothing to look like the character; interpreters, in contrast, use vocal variation and body language to suggest the character with minimal use of props and costuming.

- Actors generally play one role; interpreters can perform a number of roles, including that of narrator.

- Actors memorize their lines; interpreters become very familiar with the text but don't always memorize it, and many hold a manuscript during their performances.

- Actors usually perform dramatic scripts, written to be staged; interpreters perform prose and poetry as well as dramatic texts.

In summary, you do not just read a text out loud; you analyze it, make performance decisions, and plan specific ways to communicate your interpretation to your audience. Your interpretation will differ from every other performer of the same text because your analysis and choices will inevitably differ from theirs. Your major goal, however, is to create a performance that makes sense to your audience, one that they will accept as a realistic, believable interpretation of the author's message.

OVERCOMING ANXIETY (STAGE FRIGHT)

The idea of standing in front of an audience and performing a piece of literature frightens many people, perhaps even you. You know that people will be looking at you, and you may feel reluctant to loosen up enough to portray the emotions required in your piece. This fear is called **stage fright.** It has many dimensions and results from both process anxiety and performance anxiety. Typically, your responses to fear will fall into both psychological and physiological categories.

Process Anxiety

Process anxiety happens when you don't know how to go about doing something. You are assigned to read a poem, but you think you don't know anything about choosing an appropriate piece, analyzing it, planning a performance, and so on. You do not know where to look during your performance, and you are unsure what to do with your hands. The thought of using a manuscript (often kept in a notebook) during your performance is daunting. The whole assignment seems overwhelming, and you don't know where to begin.

This usually results in a **psychological response,** in which your mind plays little games with you. This begins when you first get the assignment. Your mental monologue may sound something like this:

Oh no! I can't do this. I don't know what to read. How am I supposed to find a piece of literature that they'll like? I can't even find a piece *I* like half the time. And I'm supposed to portray the emotions?? No way. That's just not my personality; I'm basically shy, and I feel stupid showing my emotions. They'll think I'm dumb. I can't do this. And worse yet, the instructor just handed out the grade sheet. She's going to grade this! There goes my GPA.

On the other hand, some students will have a great deal of experience in acting and performing in a variety of situations. These people may feel pretty confident about their acting abilities but less so about interpreting literature in a solo performance. Nevertheless, their presence in the class can intimidate students who rarely or never perform publicly.

To overcome negative self-talk, psych yourself up by saying affirmations regarding your audience, your text, and yourself. Remind yourself that your listeners are all amateurs; none of them wants to see you fail. Then focus on your text. Think about the important theme of your piece, and remind yourself of its significance to you and to the audience. Finally, engage in some positive self-talk, and tell yourself that you'll succeed because you have carefully planned, prepared, and rehearsed your performance.

And, remember, the reason you're taking this class is to *learn* the process of oral performance; you're not expected to know how to interpret literature right away. That's why this text exists—to identify and explain the major skills required for good oral performances. The course itself also requires you to learn by doing; that is, you will learn the process by actually doing the skills.

Performance Anxiety

Performance anxiety revolves around what will happen during the performance itself. Again, your mind fears dire consequences, but they're related to the actual performance or delivery of the presentation. You're afraid you won't remember your piece well enough. You're pretty sure you can't portray the emotion adequately; you think you'll probably talk too fast and fidget with your manuscript. Besides that, you know yourself—you're the shaky-knees type. Performing makes you want to throw up!

To overcome these mental fears, rehearse by using a process that Ayers and Hopf[38] call *visualization.* Athletes use it before performances; musicians use it before they go onstage. It works like this: Set aside some time in a quiet place and mentally go through your performance from beginning to end, as if you were an audience member. Imagine that your name is called; imagine yourself calmly leaving your seat and walking to the front, where you pause slightly, then open your script book and begin to perform. Visualize yourself looking up and gesturing and smiling. Listen to your voice portray the meanings in the text. Go through the entire piece this way. Then visualize yourself coming to an end, closing your script book, pausing slightly, and walking back to your seat. Visualization is valuable for working out performance flaws, gaining confidence, anticipating problem areas, and, in general, operating as a troubleshooting technique.

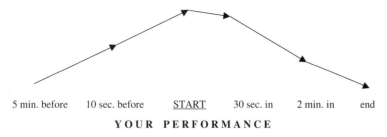

5 min. before   10 sec. before   <u>START</u>   30 sec. in   2 min. in   end

Y O U R   P E R F O R M A N C E

FIGURE 1.1 The Anxiety Process

It often helps to understand the anxiety process. You can expect some **physiological responses,** which are bodily reactions to frightening situations; they involve what is called the **fight-or-flight mechanism.** When faced with a threatening situation, your body goes into defense mode, whether the threat is real or imagined. Adrenaline pumps in and prepares you to either fight the danger or run away from it. This manifests itself in the shaky knees, butterflies in the stomach, rapid heartbeat, flushed feeling, and sweaty palms of stage fright. These are normal responses that all performers feel at one time or another.

Physiological responses, although intense, eventually peak and recede. Brownell and Katula[39] plotted the typical anxiety process by asking their speech students to report their anxiety levels at several points in their speech delivery. They found that anxiety is greatest just before the performance and during the introduction. It typically lessens during the speech itself and is almost gone by the end, as Figure 1.1 shows.

You can almost predict what will happen to you on performance day. You may have trouble sleeping the night before, so you may feel tired and decide to hit the caffeine. However, this may not be the best strategy, as caffeine may just intensify your nerves. It's better to jog or walk off some of your adrenaline. Do things that relieve your anxiety, such as listening to soothing music, meditating, or doing deep breathing exercises. All these things can minimize your fight-or-flight reaction.

When you do get to class, you're likely to be "up" but not panicky. It's a good strategy to consciously relax and breathe slowly and deeply. Settle into your seat as the instructor posts the order of the performances. If you are allowed to choose, you may want to go first to finish your performance early. Regardless of the speaking order, you can expect your heart to pound the hardest just as your name is called, as you walk to the front, and first open your mouth to speak. This is the time to say affirmations: "I can do this; this is a good piece; I'm really well prepared. . . ." Walk slowly, settle into your stance, pause and breathe deeply even before you look at the audience, then begin.

STOP AND CHECK: Assess Your Anxiety

Assess your personal anxiety regarding performance in this course. Use the Web resources that come with this text and take the Personal Report of Public Speaking Anxiety (PRPSA).

SUMMARY

Performance can be defined broadly to include everyday actions, or it can be defined more narrowly to include artistic, staged, or theatrical performances that are distinguished by use, qualities, or effects. This text focuses on one narrowed performance type: interpreting literary texts.

Performing literature is a part of a liberal arts education. Performance is a method of analysis, a way to understand texts. You'll have an opportunity to encounter ideas you might not otherwise, and you will hone your critical thinking skills as you evaluate your own work and that of others. Finally, performing helps you develop speaking and presentation skills you can use in other areas of your life.

Because performance is a global, historical phenomenon, you can think of *homo sapiens* as *homo performans*. On every continent, performers both reinforce and resist cultural values and practices. The example of Cuban cigar factory lectors illustrates how readers enlightened their audiences, who then helped to create social change.

Performance places include the physical as well as the cultural settings and social contexts in which the performers play out their roles. Performers select texts that are intended to evoke specific responses in their audiences. Their purposes are to inform, to persuade, to entertain, or to express their thoughts, feelings, and opinions.

Oral performances of aesthetic texts differ from both reading and acting in a number of ways. Interpreters usually keep the text in hand, but they are familiar enough with it that they can look up about 80% of the time. In contrast to acting, a single performer uses fewer actions and minimal props to portray all the characters.

Chances are you'll have some anxiety about your performance. To overcome stage fright, distinguish between process and performance anxiety. Process anxiety comes when you don't know what to do or how to do it. Learning specific performance techniques and skills will help you deal with this type of anxiety. Performance anxiety, the nervousness you typically feel when you actually stand up to perform, is based in the physiological "fight or flight" response that generally peaks just before and in the earliest part of the performance itself. You can use visualization and incorporate physical relaxation to help with your anxiety.

KEY TERMS

performance	physical setting	to reinforce
aesthetic communication	cultural setting	to entertain
homo performans	literature	expressive purpose
rhapsodists	text	process anxiety
recitatio	genres of literature	performance anxiety
troubadours	dialogical theory	visualization
elocutionary movement	goals or purposes	psychological response
griots/griottes	informative purpose	physiological response
pansor'i performers	to persuade	fight-or-flight mechanism
Ramayama tradition	to convince	stage fright
lectors	to actuate	

QUESTIONS AND EXERCISES

1. Make a list of oral performances that regularly occur in your school and your community. For instance, where do storytellers perform? What religious rituals take place regularly? Where do poets and authors read from their works? List the campus or community performances, if any, that you attended this week. Share your lists with your classmates.

2. For information about performance theory, do an InfoTrac College Edition advanced search for Dwight Conquergood's essay, "Of Caravans and Carnivals: Performance Studies in Motion." It's in the Winter 1995 issue of *TDR: The Drama Review*. Professor Conquergood is one of the best-known figures in the field of performance studies. What biographical information does this essay provide that helps you understand the field better?

3. Use InfoTrac College Edition to find additional information about performance traditions that you can discuss with your classmates. Here are some possible searches: To learn about Arab professional poetry reciters, do a text word search for "Arab AND *rawi*"; for Sikh reciters, search for "Punjab AND *dhaji*"; for Caribbean customs, search for "calypso AND Trinidad"; to discover more about modern and traditional characteristics of southern Bantu African traditions, search for "Bantu AND praise AND poetry."

4. Go to http://www.abcactionnews.com/stories/cubanconnection/revolution.shtml to discover some ways that cigar workers in the United States helped Cuba gain its independence from Spain. The site provides a photograph. For additional photographs, go to www.google.com and search in IMAGES for "lector" and "cigar factory."

5. To read a humorous example of elocution, go online to http://www.oddbooks.co.uk/edgerly/reviews/shaftesbury-recitations.html. There, you'll find "The

Weird Visitor," a poem reportedly "recited with a thrilling power that has produced effects upon an audience never caused by any other recital." This poem comes complete with instructions for when to kneel, when to raise the hand as if taking an oath, and when to use "a chilling, grave-like tone of the lowest pitch."

6. Divide a sheet of paper into two columns. Label the left column "Process Anxiety" and the right column "Performance Anxiety." Identify aspects of the process that create anxiety because you don't know what to do or how to do it. Then identify your concerns about your actual performance. Plan strategies to deal with both types of anxiety.

7. Find out if your school has a speech team (sometimes called a forensics team). When and where do they meet? At what type of events do students most typically perform? When and where do they compete? If possible, arrange to attend at least one oral interpretation round in a nearby tournament sometime during the term.

2

Performers
and Audiences

This chapter will help you:

- Create an audience-centered performance

- Consider your audience's demographic characteristics

- Evaluate your audience's psychological makeup

- Do an emotional analysis of your listeners

- Analyze the performance situation

- Consider your role as an audience member

- Describe four types of audiences: inactive, active, interactive, and proactive

- Consider your responsibilities to yourself as an audience member

- Be aware of your responsibilities to other listeners

- Provide nonverbal feedback during a performance

- Give the performer constructive verbal feedback

- Give written feedback after a performance

In a scene from Lucy Montgomery's classic novel *Anne of Green Gables*,[1] Anne has been chosen to represent her village in a public performance in a nearby town. Choosing her piece, "The Maiden's Vow," was easy; she would rather "make people cry than laugh." However, looking out over the crowd, she is intimidated:

> [Anne sat on the platform] between a stout lady in pink silk and a tall, scornful-looking girl in a white-lace dress. The stout lady occasionally turned her head squarely around and surveyed Anne . . . and the white-lace girl kept talking audibly to her next neighbor about the "country bumpkins" and "rustic belles" in the audience. . . .

> Unfortunately for Anne, a professional elocutionist was staying at the hotel and had consented to recite. . . . She had a marvelously flexible voice and wonderful power of expression; the audience went wild . . . [Anne] could never get up and recite after that—never. Had she ever thought she could recite? Oh, if she were only back at Green Gables!

> At this unpropitious moment her name was called. Somehow Anne . . . got on her feet, and moved dizzily out to the front. . . . Everything was so strange, so brilliant, so bewildering—the rows of ladies in evening dress, the critical faces, the whole atmosphere of wealth and culture about her. Very different this from the plain benches at the Debating Club, filled with the homely, sympathetic faces of friends and neighbors. These people, she thought, would be merciless critics. Perhaps, like the white-lace girl, they anticipated amusement from her "rustic" efforts. She felt hopelessly, helplessly ashamed and miserable. . . .

> But suddenly . . . she saw Gilbert Blythe away at the back of the room . . . Her fright and nervousness vanished; and she began her recitation, her clear, sweet voice reaching to the farthest corner of the room without a tremor or a break. Self-possession was fully restored to her, and in the reaction from that horrible moment of powerlessness she recited as she had never done before. When she finished there were bursts of honest applause. Anne, stepping back to her seat, . . . found her hand vigorously clasped and shaken by the stout lady in pink silk.

> "My dear, you did splendidly," she puffed. "I've been crying like a baby, actually I have. There, they're encoring you" . . . Smiling, blushing, limpid eyed, Anne tripped back and gave a quaint, funny little selection that captivated her audience still further. The rest of the evening was quite a little triumph for her.

Although the audience was initially frightening, Anne knew what response she wanted from her listeners. When she finally conquered her nervousness, she began to interact with her audience, and they with her. That is, she created a performance for a specific group; they listened, cocreated meanings, and provided positive feedback. This chapter describes performer-audience relationships. It first looks first at your relationship with your audience, and then it discusses your role as an audience member.

YOUR RELATIONSHIP
WITH YOUR AUDIENCE

Meanings are in people.[2]

This is a fundamental communication principle: The meanings in a message or text are not somehow located magically in the words themselves; they lie in our responses to those words. And we tend to be egocentric and to interpret things from our own vantage points and perspectives.

Take, for example, the word *epilepsy.* In Anne Fadiman's book *The Spirit Catches You and You Fall Down: A Hmong Child, Her American Doctors, and the Collision of Two Cultures,*[3] a girl's doctors define epilepsy differently than her Hmong parents do. The physicians consider epilepsy to be "a sporadic malfunction of the brain" (p. 29) that varies in severity and cause. It cannot be cured, but it can be controlled by anticonvulsant drugs. In contrast, the child's parents attribute their daughter's frequent seizures to soul loss; she has "the illness where the spirit catches you and you fall down" (p. 29). Each side proposes vastly different cures, with tragic results. Clearly, epilepsy means different things in these different cultures.

Read through the following poem and make as much sense as you can from it:

Bora Ring

BY JUDITH WRIGHT[4]

The song is gone; the dance
is secret with the dancers in the earth
the ritual useless, and the tribal story
lost in an alien tale.

Only the grass stands up
to mark the dancing-ring; the apple-gums
posture and mime a past corroboree
murmur a broken chant.

The hunter is gone: the spear
is splintered underground; the painted bodies
a dream the world breathed sleeping and forgot;
the nomad feet are still.

Only the rider's heart
halts at a sightless shadow, an unsaid word
that fastens in the blood the ancient curse,
the fear as old as Cain.

What does this poem mean? You must know several things about the culture it represents before you can understand it. For starters: What's a *bora ring?* (an Australian Aboriginal ritual circle) What does *corroboree* mean? (an Aboriginal word for *meeting,* which includes the physical gathering as well as the gathering of minds, thoughts, and philosophies)[5] And who is *Cain?* (one of Adam and Eve's sons, who killed his brother Abel and wandered the earth, cursed) Your experiences and attitudes also will affect your emotional response. What are your experiences with indigenous groups? What are your attitudes regarding "progress"? These questions and others like them will determine the personal meanings you draw from the poem.

Because meanings lie in people, think about the responses you hope listeners will have (**audience-centered** focus) instead of concentrating on the literature (**text-centered** focus) or on yourself (**speaker-centered** focus). In summary, when you perform, keep in mind that meanings are not in the words you say. Nor are they in your analysis of the text and the insights that inform your performance. The final meanings are those that the audience makes out of your performance. In order to be audience-centered and to focus on audience responses, analyze three aspects of your listeners: their demographic, psychological, and emotional factors.

Demographic Analysis

Demographic analysis considers the audience according to the groups or populations they represent. Demographic categories include ethnicity, age, religion, gender and sexual expression, socioeconomic status, occupation, and group affiliation, which can all influence a listener's responses to your performance. However, a person's identification with a category is more or less **salient,** meaning it varies in significance or importance, depending on the situation.[6] Let's say a woman in the audience is a middle-aged Democrat whose ancestors were Christians from Taiwan. Her identification with her gender, political affiliation, religion, or ethnicity will vary from topic to topic and from situation to situation. (See Performing Culture: Rudolfo Anaya.)

It's sometimes easier to perform for a **homogeneous** group comprised of similar people, such as 18- to 20-year-old students at a conservative college or relatively well-off Jewish senior citizens on an Elderhostel outing, than it is to have **heterogeneous** listeners who represent several demographic categories. (No audience is completely homogeneous, however, because every demographic category is comprised of individuals. For example, each "Sigma Chi member" or "lesbian" or "Jewish senior citizen" differs from all the others in that category.)

In summary, plan your performances with audience demographics in mind. Consider three variables: (1) the demographic categories your listeners represent; (2) their homogeneity or heterogeneity in relevant categories; and (3) the salience of a particular category as it might relate to your specific performance.

Psychological Analysis

Our beliefs, attitudes, and actions, which communication theorist Barnett Pearce calls our "core resources,"[9] are three aspects of our psychological makeup. These entities are not separate or static; they are dynamic and

PERFORMING CULTURE: Rudolfo Anaya, Chicano Author[7]

According to the New York Times,[8] Anaya is the most widely read author in Hispanic communities. He illustrates some ways that demographic categories combine to form one's identity. His gender and marital status (male, married), occupation (author, Professor Emeritus at the University of New Mexico), age (born in 1927), ethnicity (Chicano), and religion (Catholic upbringing) all contribute to his writings. This essay resulted from a trip he took to Spain when that country was reexamining its 500-year history with the Hispanic Americas.

I prefer the term "Nuevo Mexicano" to describe my cultural heritage. My parents and my grandparents of the Puerto de Luna Valley of New Mexico spoke only Spanish, and as I honor my ancestors, I keep up their language and folkways. "Hispano" to me means using the Spanish language of my ancestors. The term, like "Latino," also connects me to other Spanish-speaking groups in this country and in Latin America.

The great majority of the Mexicanos of the Southwest are Indo-Hispanos, part of La Raza of the New World, the fruit of the Spanish father and the Indian mother. We take pride in our Hispanic heritage; that is, we know the history of the Spanish father, his language, and his character. . . . [But] we have not known and honored the heritage of our mother, the Indian mothers of Mexico and the Southwest. . . . For the Mexicanos of the Southwest the mother is Malinche, the Mexican woman who was the first Indian woman of Mexico to bear children fathered by a Spaniard. But the mother figure is more real than the symbolic Malinche; our mothers embody the archetype of the indigenous Indian mother of the Americas. If we are to truly know

ourselves, it is her nature we must know. . . .

The Americas represent a wonderful experiment in the synthesis of divergent worldviews, and each one of us is a representative of that process. . . . To define ourselves as we really are and not as others wish us to be allows us to become authentic and that definition carries with it the potential of our humanism. . . . My generation of Hispanos, or Mexican-Americans . . . [named] ourselves Chicanos. For us, using the word "Chicano" was our declaration of independence, the first step toward our true identity. . . . We took the word "Chicano" from "Mexicano," dropping the first syllable and keeping the "xicano." We are proud of that heritage even though we are not Mexican citizens, and although we are citizens of the United States we are not Anglo-Americans. We have our own history rooted in this land. The word "Chicano" defined our *space in time*, that is our history and our identity. "Chicano" embraced our Native American heritage, an important element of our history. . . .

The definition of our identity . . . should encompass the multiple roots and histories of the Americans . . . We seek to know our roots, to know ourselves. When we encounter the taproots of our history we feel authentic and able to identify self, family, and community. Finding self should also mean finding humanity; declaring personal independence also means declaring that independence for all individuals.

Explore some ways that your demographic makeup figures into your personal identity. For instance, when is your ethnicity salient? Your age? Your religious background? How does your demographic makeup compare with that of others in your classroom?

STOP AND CHECK: Do a Demographic Analysis

What can you tell by observing your classmates? What ages are they? Do they wear wedding or engagement rings? Jewelry or clothing that indicates a specific religion? Clothing that indicates living quarters such as residence halls, sororities, or fraternities?

Ask your classmates about their majors or recreational interests. Then use this information to select literature, anticipate audience responses, and craft your performance in a way that is responsive to the demographic diversity in your class.

---

intertwined, as Figure 2.1 illustrates. For instance, what we believe generally influences our attitudes and behaviors; on the other hand, our attitudes can predispose us to belief. And, not surprisingly, our beliefs, attitudes, and behaviors change as we grow and become exposed to new ideas and experiences. Understanding the core resources your listeners bring to your performance can help you better anticipate their responses to your interpretation of the text.

- **Beliefs** are mental understandings or knowledge about a topic. Our beliefs can be relatively unimportant or so deeply held that they are elements of our worldview. We commonly have partial knowledge or hold misconceptions about many subjects.

- **Attitudes** are our tendencies to evaluate something positively or negatively. Attitudes are commonly assessed on a scale from strongly negative to neutral to strongly positive. To illustrate, most people have a strongly negative attitude toward death and a strongly positive attitude toward weddings.

- **Actions,** our behaviors or lifestyle choices, often reflect the depth of our beliefs or the strength of our attitudes. Do we really believe that people are using too many natural resources? What kind of cars do we drive? Do we really believe that good health is vital? What do we eat? How much do we exercise?

During your preparation, try to assess your listeners' knowledge about your text's topic and to gauge whether they are likely to have misconceptions or resistance to the text's perspective. Prepare accordingly. Audiences who are unfamiliar with customs or cultural allusions such as the bora ring will need background information before they can understand. Audiences familiar with your subject are likely to be bored if your text presents a trite or commonplace approach. People who hold misconceptions may become defensive or angry if you strongly challenge their beliefs.

Performing a positive piece about a topic to an audience who has a positive attitude toward that topic will reinforce or strengthen listeners' existing attitudes. The audience generally enjoys this, because showing support for

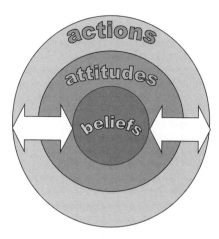

FIGURE 2.1 Beliefs, Attitudes, and Actions

their attitudes allows them to stay within their comfort zones. However, you may be drawn to a text that confronts or clashes with their attitudes and beliefs. Challenging selections will likely cause audience discomfort; if you threaten a deeply held belief, be prepared for negative responses. (Performing Culture: Performance as Affirmation or Resistance, develops this idea further.) If you want to change beliefs or attitudes, it is a good strategy to plan a series of performances across a span of time. Each performance should be increasingly positive (or negative, if applicable) toward your subject, because attitudes change only incrementally.

Finally, when preparing, consider how listeners *actually* behave in light of how you want to encourage them to behave. As Chapter 1 pointed out, you can use texts to persuade and to motivate, as these examples show:

- Matthew Shepard, a young gay college student, was brutally murdered in Wyoming in 1998. In response, Moisés Kaufman and members of the Tectonic Theater Project wrote the play *The Laramie Project*, later made into a movie. Their express purpose in writing it was to change people's beliefs and attitudes toward gay people and to motivate them to fight bias against homosexuals. As one reviewer wrote, "We must hope that this film reaches the people who haven't decided how they will treat those around them—who are not like themselves. . . ."[10]

- The Bellwether Prize for fiction was created by novelist Barbara Kingsolver. It recognizes socially responsible literature that invites readers to work for economic and social justice or for environmental accountability. Examples of this type of literature include David Guterson's *Snow Falling on Cedars* and Alice Walker's *The Color Purple*.[11]

As you might imagine, a particular audience may be more or less homogenous in beliefs, attitudes, and behaviors. But these core psychological resources will influence your listeners' responses to your performance.

PERFORMING CULTURE: Performance as Affirmation or Resistance

Performers commonly choose materials that affirm or reinforce a culture's core resources. For instance, parents who read *Beauty and the Beast* to their children are supporting the belief that one should not judge by appearances alone. *Charlotte's Web* teaches children about the power of friendship. Native American trickster figures (Raven, Rabbit, Fox, or Coyote) are humorous deceivers who are often deceived. In story after story, they fail to learn from their mistakes, but the audience discovers the outcome of inappropriate actions from hearing about their foibles.[12]

In contrast to texts that support cultural ideals, the French playwright-philosopher-theorist Antonin Artaud argued for a Theatre of Cruelty to confront social norms and release feelings that listeners usually repress in their unconscious minds. Artaud believed that such performances break the boundaries of performer/spectator and that they are difficult and cruel both to those who watch and to those who perform. Jerzy Grotowski, a highly influential theater theorist, elaborates:

> The spectator likes easy truths. But we are not there to please the spectator. We are there to tell the truth. . . . The spectator protests, but afterwards he will not forget what you have done. After a few years the same spectator will say, "He is the one who told the truth."[13]

Contemporary performers often resist or challenge cultural notions regarding "ethnic and religious identity, sexual orientation, homophobia, racism, globalization, postcolonialism, and so on."[14] In InfoTrac College Edition, find and read Ngugi wa Thiong'o's article "Enactment of Power: The Politics of Performance Space" to discover how Kenyan performers first resisted colonial powers and then the postcolonial elite, as the citizens and leaders negotiated the symbols that would represent postcolonial Kenya.

Alternatively, search the Internet for a description of James Luna, a performance and multimedia artist who lives on the La Jolla Reservation in North San Diego County. Luna deromanticizes the dominant culture's idealization of "Indians," presenting the realities of a colonized people and the conditions that plague them and highlighting the commercialization of Native cultures.

Come to class prepared to discuss Ngugi's or Luna's ideas with your classmates.

Emotional Analysis

Aristotle emphasized the importance of **pathos,** or emotional responses, as a type of proof in rhetoric. He argued that a listener who is indifferent to a subject will lack the motivation to spend time pondering that subject, much less doing something about it. Now, you may not associate oral interpretation of literature with rhetoric, but Aristotle defined **rhetoric** as "the faculty of observing in any given case the available means of persuasion."[15] Consequently, the short stories, plays, or poems that have influenced your attitudes, beliefs, or behaviors are rhetorical. Because pathos, or emotion, is an important element of persuasion, it is helpful to analyze your audience's emotions and needs.

- **Emotions** are all the feelings that change people in ways that affect their judgments.[16] **Positive emotions** are those we enjoy experiencing, including joy, peace, love, friendship, contentment, loyalty, approval, and generosity. **Negative emotions** are those we want to avoid because they aren't pleasurable. They include shame, guilt, fear, rage, insecurity, disgust, indignation, anxiety, envy, and hatred.

- An additional way to understand an audience better is to consider their **needs.** Abraham Maslow[17] identified five levels of needs, each building on previous levels: (1) **basic needs,** such as food, water, sex, and air; (2) **security,** or feeling safe and in control of one's circumstances; (3) **love and belonging,** or having meaningful, stable, and dependable relationships; (4) **esteem,** or feeling important and competent in the larger society; and (5) **self-actualization,** which includes the desire to have peak experiences and to reach one's highest potential. Vance Packard[18] added the **need for roots,** or the desire to know where one has come from, and the **need for immortality,** or the desire to believe that death will not be the end.

During your preparation, anticipate the impact your text will have on your listeners' feelings and how their aroused emotions might move them to accept or reject your presentation of your text's ideas. But treat emotions with care, because emotional appeals are easily overdone. "Shock" pieces about horrifying cruelty or sexual violence can so repulse listeners that they miss the point entirely. On the other hand, positive emotions can be presented in an embarrassingly syrupy manner that also turns listeners away. A fundamental way to avoid overblown emotions is to choose texts that suggest a point, rather than hammer it home.

Situational Analysis

As Chapter 1 pointed out, the performance situation is important. Your challenge is one thing if your listeners are crowded into a hot room and seated on uncomfortable chairs at the end of a long, tiring day. It's quite another if they are comfortably seated and wide awake in an air-conditioned room. Here are some questions to ask regarding the situation:

- *What time of day will the performance take place?* Will listeners be sleepy or alert? What precedes the performance? What follows it? For example, will you tell a story to a group of children just before lunch? Are you scheduled at the end of a long day at a retreat, when the participants have been in workshops and lectures most of the day and are ready to relax and socialize?

- *What's the occasion?* Is it formal or informal? Do listeners expect a serious or a humorous performance? How long should your performance last, given the occasion?

> ### STOP AND CHECK: Analyze Your Audience's Psychological Makeup
>
> Select four or five representative audience members; then, one by one, consider each person's interests, needs, wants, worries, challenges, and so on. Use your ideas to analyze your piece by asking yourself the following questions:
>
> - What particular theme in this piece relates to this person?
> - What images may be similar to her experiences?
>
> - Which character(s) will probably be a lot like someone he already knows? Which will be less familiar to him?
> - What does she already know or believe about my subject?
> - What's his attitude toward it?
> - What emotional reactions might she have?
> - If this classmate were to find himself in the text's setting, how might he react?

- *What's the physical setting?* Will you perform in a room or outside? What's the space like? Is it well lit? How large is it? How large is the group? What's the seating arrangement? Is there a platform? A lectern? How much interaction can you have with audience members? Are there any potentially distracting objects or room decorations? What sounds or sights might distract your listeners?
- *How's the sound system?* Is a microphone available? Are outside noises (traffic or sirens) audible? Are there distracting sounds (radiators or air conditioners) in the room itself?

Knowing information such as this before you even begin planning your performance will help you make wiser choices all along the way.

In a classroom setting, you may want to create an **artificial audience** by defining your classmates in a particular way and then gearing your performance to the imaginary group you defined. For example, if you perform a children's book, you might tell your fellow students, "Let's say you are fourth-graders." Then perform the story as if you were facing a group of 9- and 10-year-olds.

YOUR ROLE AS AN AUDIENCE MEMBER

Although you will perform several times during this course, most of your class time will be spent listening to your classmates' performances. And outside of the classroom, you will be part of many audiences. Consequently, it's to your advantage to be a thoughtful audience member.

Audience Roles

Ronald Pelias and James Van Oosting[19] envisioned audience participation as existing along a continuum in which the listeners' involvement increases and the performers' authority decreases. They identified four types of audiences: inactive, active, interactive, and proactive.

STOP AND CHECK: Analyze Your Performance Situation

Analyze your classroom setting.

- What time of day is your class held? How might this affect your performance or the audience's predisposition to listen?
- What time limitations constrain your performance?
- What's the room like? The seating? The possibility for interaction? The decorations? The furnishings?

- Does the room have good acoustics? What external or internal noises might affect your performance?
- Do you need to create an artificial audience? If so, decide exactly who the imaginary audience for your text should be, and then plan how you will communicate this artificial identity to your actual audience.

Inactive Audiences When performing for an inactive audience, you will notice a clear difference between the performers and the audience. These audience members know and enact the norms or conventions for "good" listening behavior. They sit quietly, refrain from whispering, pay attention to the entire performance, and applaud at the end. The performers do most of the work. They select the materials, analyze and rehearse them, and deliver their interpretations. Many, even most, classroom audiences are inactive.

Active Audiences Active audiences differ from inactive because they respond actively within the artistic event. Instead of sitting quietly, audience members interact with the performers, but only at the direction of the performer, who provides cues to which they may (or may not) respond. One example is a call-and-response sermon; a preacher asks, "Can I get a witness?" to which the audience responds, "Amen!" If the audience fails to respond to the performer's invitations, the performance falls flat.

Interactive Audiences Interactive audiences are much more involved than the previous two types, so much so that the audience coproduces the artistic event with the performer. Each contributes to the performance, and there is less distinction between the onstage and offstage regions. Although the performers select the subject and initiate the interaction sequence, the listeners codetermine the direction the performance eventually takes. Improvisational theatre is interactional: Performers take suggestions from audience members and sometimes incorporate listeners into the performance itself.

Proactive Audiences In a proactive audience, everyone has the status of performer; all who are involved determine the outcome of the performance. One example is a "flash mob," a short-term performance organized through e-mails and text messages, in which a group of people make a sudden appearance and then disappear. You can read about this phenomenon at www.flash-mob.com. Another example is the Madres de la Plaza de Mayo, a demonstration comprised of Argentine women who have been gathering

Do to others as you would have them do to you.

The Golden Rule

weekly on the Plaza de Mayo in Buenos Aires since 1977 to remember and seek justice for the 30,000 *desaparecidos* (the "Disappeared")—their sons and husbands who vanished when Argentina was under rule of a military junta from 1976 to 1983.[20]

Audience Responsibilities

Because you are so frequently an audience member, you should take your role seriously. Let the Golden Rule of "Do to others as you would have them do to you" be your guide. To enact this ideal, consider your responsibilities in three areas: to yourself, to other audience members, and to the performers.

Responsibilities to Yourself One of your educational tasks is to grow in your understandings of yourself and of your world. With this goal in mind, do your best to enter a dialogical relationship with both the text and the performer. Approach each text with an open mind, probing for personal meanings and applications, and try to empathize with the characters and emotions you encounter in the performance. Of course, you must understand the meanings of the words and the cultural context represented in the text. If you are unclear about something, ask questions afterward, when appropriate, or continue to explore the topic at a later time.

As noted earlier, your classmates' performances may confront and challenge your most cherished attitudes, beliefs, and behaviors. In fact, literature often "comforts the afflicted and afflicts the comfortable," as the old saying goes. So approach the performance aware that you may feel defensive or angry, pleased or vindicated by what you see and hear—and that the author and the performer may *intend* for you to experience these feelings.

Because performances are often both powerful and moving, you owe it to yourself to exercise critical thinking skills as you discern the meanings in the text and in the performance. Here are some questions you can use to guide your thinking:

- What was the author's goal in creating the text? What might have been the performer's goal in selecting the piece? Was it to inform, to persuade, or to entertain? Let this purpose guide your responses.

- Is the emotion presented honestly and authentically, or is it overblown or manipulative? How does this affect your responses?

- Is the literature honest and truthful? Does it have integrity? Or does it twist or manipulate facts? How should this influence your appreciation of the text?

- What are the ethical implications of the piece? Does it demean a group's ethnicity, gender, religion, and so on? Does it promote understanding among different people? How should you respond to the values and behaviors it presents? Is it worth your time to consider it further?

Because meanings are neither in the text nor in the artistic event itself, the ultimate meanings of a performance lie within you. Consequently, take seriously your part in creating meanings by entering into a dialogical relationship with both the text and the performer.

Responsibilities to Other Listeners Regardless of your reaction to a performance event, you should give other listeners the opportunity to experience it for themselves. Use some basic rules of courtesy. Don't deflect other people's attention or impair their ability to listen by making distracting movements or sounds. Leave your cell phone at home, or turn it off before the performance begins. Arrive on time so that you do not interrupt a performance in progress. Give the gift of your attention. These simple rules, and others like them, show respect to the performers and enable the entire audience to see and hear what the performers have worked so hard to produce.

Responsibilities to Performers Chapter 1 pointed out the dialogical nature of performance, emphasizing that a dialogue or conversation requires at least two persons who mutually cocreate meanings. As part of an inactive audience, you will be relatively quiet, but you still will have an important role to play. Each performer counts on your attentiveness and your responses to the aesthetic event. Your feedback, both nonverbal and verbal, whether spoken or written, will help the performers improve their interpretive skills.

Providing Nonverbal Feedback All of your bodily movements communicate. Imagine, for instance, facing a roomful of people, half of whom slump in their chairs, eyes closed; others look out the window; still others roll their eyes in boredom throughout your presentation. That's the stuff of nightmares!

To avoid being someone's bad dream, assume a receptive, alert posture as you listen. (When you're really "into" a performance, you almost literally sit on the edge of your seat.) Make eye contact; this both helps the performer and keeps your attention focused on what you're seeing and hearing. Respond emotionally; when appropriate, smile, laugh, or be somber. Clap at the end to support the performer and show your appreciation for the performance. In the opening story, the audience's nonverbal reactions encouraged and emboldened Anne of Green Gables to give her best performance.

Providing Verbal Feedback Actors work with directors, and speech team competitors work with coaches who listen to their performance ideas and suggest additional possibilities. Your instructor may ask you to pair up with a classmate to coach one another and give constructive verbal feedback before your actual performances. This type of **partner work**[21] requires you to listen to one another and work as a team to craft more effective individual presentations. Talk over your literary choices with your partner, and try out your performance ideas on her. Note what she thinks is effective, and listen carefully to her suggestions for improvement. Do your final rehearsal for your partner— an audience of one. Be honest with one another; it's much better to have one person point out obvious problems than to discover them during your performance.

If your class is typical, you will be asked to verbally describe your reactions to at least one classmate's performance. When your time comes to comment, focus on two or three specific aspects of the event by describing what you saw and how you responded to the performance. Talk about what was well done and what could be improved. Phrase the comments as objectively and positively as you can. (Often, I ask students to give only positive comments aloud; they can write out their suggestions for improvement.) Here are some sample comments:

- Description: "I noticed that your page turns often corresponded with the transitions in the flow of ideas." Or, "You used halting speech, darting glances, and a facial tic for your nervous character."

- Personal response: "I was nervous along with your character." Or, "I felt emotionally drained by the intensity of the courtroom scene."

- Evaluation: "I thought your page turns were effective in communicating changes in mood." Or, "I thought you communicated the character's nervousness well. You appropriately distinguished him from the other two characters, and you presented him consistently throughout."

Comments such as these are specific enough to be useful, and they give the performer an idea of the overall impression his or her interpretation left on at least one listener.

Providing Written Feedback Chances are you will also be asked to provide written performance critiques. In general, your critique should do two things: establish the criteria for judging the performance; and make judgments on how well the performance met the criteria.

Although different types of literature require different evaluative criteria, there are some basic considerations you can apply to almost any performance:

STOP AND CHECK: Write a Critique

View a performance on the Web resources that accompany this text. Jot down some observations about effective and ineffective things you see the performer do, and then write a critique that describes, responds, and evaluates the overall performance. Discuss your critique with your classmates.

- How well was the text suited to the audience, the situation, and the performer's skill level?

- How well did the performer's nonverbal expressions (body movements, facial expressions, vocal variation, and so on) communicate the characters and moods in the literature?

- Was there evidence of adequate preparation and rehearsal? Was it apparent that the performer had analyzed the literature carefully? Did she or he know the piece well enough to look up about 80% of the time? If there was a manuscript, how effectively was it handled?

- If there were characters, were they believable? Was their portrayal consistent throughout the performance?

In your written critique, write enough to make your feedback useful to the performer; don't just say "good job." Follow the guidelines for verbal feedback. Describe specific things you observed, and jot down your personal responses to the performance. Point out as many positive things as you can, and then evaluate the performance by identifying a few things that could be improved.

SUMMARY

Because meanings lie in people, it's important to be audience-centered and to consider audience characteristics at every stage of your preparation.

One way to approach your audience is to consider its demographic characteristics. These include ethnicity, religion, gender and sexual expression, age, socioeconomic status, and occupation and group affiliation. Demographic influences vary in salience; that is, they are more significant in some situations than in others. It's often easier to perform before an audience that is relatively homogeneous or similar than before a heterogeneous or diverse group.

Also consider a psychological analysis of your listeners. What do they believe? Do they have misconceptions or gaps in their knowledge about your topic? What attitudes do they hold toward your subject? What behaviors might influence their reception of your material? Good literature often confronts people's assumptions, attitudes, and behaviors, so if you present challenging material, you can expect some resistance as listeners struggle psychologically to deal with the challenges you present.

Finally, analyze the situation in which you will perform by factoring in how the time and place for your performance might affect your audience and their reaction.

Throughout the term, you'll listen more often than you perform. Classroom audiences are commonly inactive or active, but you may find yourself in an audience where your participation is interactive or proactive. As the audience moves along this range of participation, they progressively take more responsibility and the performers take less for the outcome of the performance itself.

As an audience member, you owe it to yourself to pay attention and to listen with an open mind to learn as much as you can from the literature you hear and from the performance techniques you see. However, use your critical thinking skills to discern the goal of the performance and the integrity and merit of the literature.

You owe to other listeners the opportunity to experience the performance without distractions. Consequently, minimize or eliminate things that might blunt their focus on the performer.

Finally, when you provide nonverbal, verbal, and written feedback to the performers, follow the Golden Rule and treat the performer as you want to be treated. Give the gift of your attention. Be honest but kind in your feedback. Describe, personalize, and evaluate what you see and hear. And do it in an educational way that will help the individual become a more effective performer in the future.

KEY TERMS

audience-centered	pathos	self-actualization
text-centered	rhetoric	need for roots
speaker-centered	emotions	need for immortality
demographic analysis	positive emotions	artificial audience
salient	negative emotions	inactive audience
homogeneous	needs	active audience
heterogeneous	basic needs	interactive audience
beliefs	security	proactive audience
attitudes	love and belonging	partner work
actions	esteem	

QUESTIONS AND EXERCISES

1. List some ways that being audience-centered, rather than performer-centered, might help you conquer stage fright.

2. To explore your ethnic heritage further, log onto the Internet and go to http:directory.google.com/ Top/Society/Ethnicity/. Follow links to one or more ethnic groups in your background. List some ways your ethnic identification might influence your role as a performer or as a spectator.

3. Select two demographic categories and describe how they might influence your participation in this class. For example, if you are a 27-year-old married parent in a classroom with mostly 20-year-old singles, how might you respond differently from them? If you are a gay Latino in a classroom that is comprised mostly of heterosexual Anglos, how might you respond differently?

4. What cultural beliefs and attitudes do you want to affirm? To resist? To challenge? How might listeners in your specific classroom respond to your affirming performance? To your resistance or challenge?

5. Log onto the Internet, and search using the phrase "performance artist." Read about at least one artist who challenges cultural norms in some way. Come to class prepared to share your findings with your classmates.

6. Write down the five levels of Maslow's hierarchy plus the additional needs Packard identifies. Then beside each need, write at least one example of literature related to that type of need.

7. To find out more about Maslow's hierarchy, log onto the Internet and use the search engine www. google.com. Search for the exact phrase "Abraham Maslow." Locate at least one additional need that has been added to his taxonomy.

8. Watch one performer on the Web resources that go with this text. Analyze your responses to the characters and/or emotions in the presentation. What do you think was the goal of the performance? What overall effect did it have on you?

9. Find someone in your class who might be a good partner or coach for you throughout the semester. Discuss your lists of authors, themes, and texts from Chapter 1. Which ones sound interesting to your partner? Which are less interesting? Provide feedback about your partner's lists.

3

Selecting Literary Texts
for Performance

This chapter will help you:

- Consider the merits of a literary text

- Evaluate a work for universality, uniqueness, and significance

- Compare and contrast typical U.S. values with other value systems

- Consider how the text evokes emotions

- Consider your interests and skills

- Factor in the time allotted for the performance

- Choose a text from resources on the Internet

- Identify ethical considerations for selecting a text

- List ethical principles for cutting and adapting literary works

- Observe the laws for performing copyrighted pieces

Throughout the term, you will analyze and interpret several literary texts. But how do you choose just a few works to perform from among the millions of possibilities? What criteria have others used to help them narrow their choices? In her memoir, *Reading Lolita in Tehran*,[1] Azir Nafisi explains some of the reasons she chose specific works to teach in her literature course at the University of Tehran:

> I asked my students what they thought fiction should accomplish, why one should bother to read fiction at all. It was an odd way to start, but I did succeed in getting their attention. . . . I explained that most great works of the imagination were meant to make you feel like a stranger in your own home. The best fiction always forced us to question what we took for granted. It questioned traditions and expectations when they seemed too immutable. I told my students I wanted them in their readings to consider in what ways these works unsettled them, made them a little uneasy, made them look around and consider the world, like Alice in Wonderland, through different eyes. . . .

Nafisi selected texts that present ideas in ways that evoke critical inquiry; that they were imaginative and crafted in aesthetic language was also important.

For many decades, the type of course you are taking was called "Oral Interpretation of Literature"; in fact, many colleges and universities still use that title. Course goals stated that students would gain experiential knowledge of a text through performance of literature, which was defined as a special kind of humanizing *writing* with aesthetic or formal properties, values, and insights. As Chapter 1 points out, however, in the 20th century the term **text** broadened in meanings and uses to include noncanonical and nonliterary texts such as personal narratives, folklore, and oral histories.[2] Consequently, *text* is currently defined more dialogically and inclusively, so that the voices of new text creators and new forms of aesthetic communication can be heard and experienced. The term **literature** now includes whatever a community accepts as literature.

Although *text* can be defined broadly, you will be asked to perform written literature, so this chapter discusses principles commonly used to select literary texts. It first describes ways to evaluate works for distinctive qualities. Then it guides you to think about the audience, the situation, and your capabilities in light of the text. Finally, it explains some ethical issues relating to your choices.

CONSIDER THE MERITS OF THE TEXT

Courtney, one of my students, summarized in her final self-evaluation what performance taught her about the importance of discriminating among literary texts:

> Initially . . . I just assumed that as long as my piece applied to the audience in some way so that they could relate to it, then it must have merit. I failed to take into account the author's unique approach to a subject, mainly

Table 3.1 Core Values in the United States

Every culture embraces a few core values. Milton Rokeach[3] puts them in two categories: (1) terminal values or ends such as world peace and success and (2) instrumental values or means such as ambition, tolerance, and cleanliness. Here are some fundamental values in the United States.

ambition	privacy	tolerance	honesty	science and rationality
individuality	equality	freedom	choice	achievement and success
change	democracy	orderliness	courage	efficiency and practicality
family	education	creativity	self-control	helping others
self-help	loyalty	friendship	world peace	prosperity
happiness	inner peace	pleasure	self-esteem	competition

Which values would you classify as ends? Which are means to those ends? Which are especially important to you?

through use of creative, applicable language. My poetry piece was an appropriate example of my ignorance, as it tended to be very generic and clichéd. As I continued with prose and drama, I focused more attention on finding pieces that utilized more complex, descriptive language with applicable allusions. . . . I became receptive to the audience's responses to the literary styles I was choosing . . . they liked things that were not merely a straight account of an event, but something that was out of the ordinary.

Throughout the term, she learned to apply four criteria that helped her choose one text over another: universality, uniqueness, significance, and the presentation of emotion within the text.

Universality

Universal literature deals with themes or with life experiences that are relevant to large numbers of people. For example, people from every culture wonder about life, death, love, and loss. We all experience sickness and health, good weather and storms, birth and death. Universal emotions include jealousy, anger, fear of rejection, hope, and generosity. And we all share basic human needs. Chapter 2 points out our physiological needs, as well as our needs for security, love and belonging, esteem, self-actualization, roots, and immortality (a sense that death is not the end).

Values are our ideas about what is fundamentally important and worthy. Table 3.1 presents some core American values. Each is the basis for many pieces of literature; each relates in some way to your fellow students. Read through the list and make note of the values that are especially important to you and ones you might like to emphasize in the pieces you present. For each value you identify, think of a text that illustrates that value. (For example, a text might illustrate the need for tolerance, the importance of world peace, or the value of courage under hardship.)

PERFORMING CULTURE: Diversity in Cultural Values

Individuality is one of the most important values in the United States, one that is essential to other typically American values such as privacy, choice, self-reliance, and freedom. Other cultures, however, stress group connections or family interests above individual expression.[4] For instance, traditional Chinese culture emphasizes "filial piety," or respect for parents and elders as a dominant value. Differences in cultural values result in different literatures; thus, many Chinese folktales praise sons and daughters who put their parents' well-being above their own.

To explore this topic further, log onto the Internet and look for James Huang's article "Filial Piety in America" at http:www.taoism.net/articles/xiao.htm. How does he explain the concept of filial piety? How does he explain its lack in American teens? How important is filial piety to your peer group?

To identify Hispanic core values, the Denver Public Schools developed the ALMA Project (from *el alma de la raza*—the soul of the people); its goal is to provide multicultural information to teachers in the Denver public schools, which are 80% minority. ALMA researchers identified five essential values woven throughout Hispanic literature: respect, trust, responsibility, caring, and sense of family. They then identified specific texts associated with each value. To explore their information further, go to http:almaproject.dpsk12.org/stories/storyReader$15.

Members of the Lakota Sioux tribe used oral narratives to pass on their culture's four major virtues: respect (for self, others, nature and the environment), generosity (sharing of one's time and material goods), wisdom (ability to accept guidance and make good judgments), and courage or fortitude (perseverance under hardship and patience). You can find more information by exploring the Native American Traditions Link Web site at http:id-archserve.ucsb.edu/natlink/old_natlink/1HomePage.html.

To understand your own values better, read one of these articles and compare the values it discusses with your personal and family values and experiences. For example, how does filial piety compare or contrast with your view of the role of parents? What values are woven into your favorite literary texts? What values would you most want to share with your classmates? How might your classmates respond to literature that praises an alternative value system?

Consider exploring values from another culture. For example, not every cultural group emphasizes change or science and rationality, personal ambition or democracy. The feature Performing Culture: Diversity in Cultural Values illustrates three alternative value emphases. Choosing a text from another cultural tradition allows you to examine life from a different perspective.

Uniqueness

Look for literature that is written in a distinctive style and uses creative and vivid language. A good example is Lincoln's Gettysburg Address. Lincoln could have said, "This country was founded on the principle of equality eighty-seven years ago." Instead, he chose the words, "Fourscore and seven years ago, our forefathers brought forth upon this continent a new nation, conceived in liberty, and dedicated to the proposition that all men are created equal. . . ." Obviously, his version was more vivid and memorable, and it has been a model of creative language usage for well over a century.

I recently asked an English professor to point out a contrasting example of a text noteworthy for its questionable language choices. He guided me to Henry Wadsworth Longfellow's "A Psalm of Life,"[5] a popular poem emphasizing the value of diligence. Although generations of schoolchildren have memorized it and it appears in many "best-loved" anthologies, my professor friend found it to be full of trite and confused images despite its noble sentiments. Read through these representative stanzas and see if you agree:

Art is long, and Time is fleeting,
    And our hearts, though stout and brave,
Still, like muffled drums, are beating
    Funeral marches to the grave.

In the world's broad field of battle,
    In the bivouac of Life,
Be not like dumb, driven cattle!
    Be a hero in the strife! . . .

Lives of great men all remind us
    We can make our lives sublime,
And, departing, leave behind us
    Footprints on the sands of time.

Footprints, that perhaps another,
    Sailing o'er life's solemn main,
A forlorn and shipwrecked brother,
    Seeing, shall take heart again.

Did you notice the mixed metaphor in the second stanza? Longfellow started with a battle image but inserted a metaphor of a cattle drive. Look for additional images that are confusing or muddled. Then discuss with your classmates the poem's imagery, as well as the themes and sentiments that explain its enduring popularity.

In addition to vivid, interesting language, look for a piece that develops a theme in a somewhat unexpected way. Search, also, for characters that will intrigue your listeners and for predicaments that will hold their interest. For example, the same general theme of "underdog surmounts difficulties to emerge triumphantly" is found in works as disparate as President Clinton's autobiography, Laura Hillebrand's narrative of the racehorse Seabiscuit, Tolkein's *The Lord of the Rings* fantasy trilogy, and the classic fairy tale "Cinderella." In each story the main characters confront a variety of challenges, and they overcome each daunting obstacle through a combination of luck, personal traits, and outside help from friends, trainers, wise wizards, and fairy godmothers.

STOP AND CHECK: Look at Uniqueness

*Read aloud the following poems, both
on the topic of trees. Then analyze
each for vivid and unique expressions:*

Trees[6]

I think that I shall never see
A poem lovely as a tree.
A tree whose hungry mouth is prest
Against the earth's sweet flowing
    breast;
A tree that looks at God all day,
And lifts her leafy arms to pray;
A tree that may in Summer wear
A nest of robins in her hair;
Upon whose bosom snow has lain;
Who intimately lives with rain.
Poems are made by fools like me,
But only God can make a tree.

JOYCE KILMER

The Trees[7]

The trees inside are moving out
    into the forest,
the forest that was empty all these
    days
where no bird could sit
no insect hide
no sun bury its feet in shadow
the forest that was empty all these
    nights
will be full of trees by morning.

All night the roots work
to disengage themselves from the
    cracks
in the veranda floor.
The leaves strain toward the glass
small twigs stiff with exertion

long-cramped boughs shuffling
    under the roof
like newly discharged patients
half-dazed, moving
to the clinic doors.

I sit inside, doors open to the
    veranda
writing long letters
in which I scarcely mention the
    departure
of the forest from the house.
The night is fresh, the whole moon
    shines
in a sky still open
the smell of leaves and lichen
still reaches like a voice into the
    rooms.
My head is full of whispers
which tomorrow will be silent.

Listen. The glass is breaking.
The trees are stumbling forward
into the night. Winds rush to meet
    them.
The moon is broken like a mirror,
its pieces flash now in the crown
of the tallest oak.

ADRIENNE RICH

Identify the vivid images in each
poem. Then identify any trite or
commonplace images. Come to class
prepared to discuss the following
questions with your classmates: Which
poet creates the most surprising or
unique images? Which sounds best
when read aloud? Which better meets
the criteria for uniqueness?

Significance

To perform well, you must spend large amounts of time with a text, which you
eventually invite your audience to experience. Your choice of material should
be worthy both of your time and of theirs. If you are choosing between two
pieces, one with a trivial theme and the second more consequential, choose
the latter. In his essay "The Rhetorical Situation," Lloyd Bitzer[8] argues that
rhetoric should address a social or personal need or **exigence.** This means that

specific historical or social situations invite specific rhetorical responses—speeches or performances that provide information and inspiration about these topics.

Many social topics beg to be addressed. For example, James McBride's memoir *The Color of Water* deals with racial issues, a significant subject in the United States. Bharati Mukherjee's novel *Desirable Daughters* addresses immigration and identity issues of foreign-born women in the United States. Lucy Grealy's *Autobiography of a Face* charts the journey of one woman whose face was deformed as a result of a serious childhood cancer and her response to cultural notions of feminine beauty. And the terrorist attacks of September 11, 2001, provided an unexpected and unwelcome need for speeches and performances related to religious zealotry, to war, to courage in the face of sure death, to the need for unity and community.

And the social often becomes the personal, which similarly provides rich performance possibilities. Relationships, betrayal, rejection, and courage are all subject matter for numerous literary texts. For example, Kirsten wrote about her own experience when interpreting a cutting from *The Color of Water:*

> McBride tells the story of his life as an African American man with a white mother. I look Caucasian, but my mother is African American. I know the struggle of what society tries to tell us to be, the unseen lines between colors. I have struggled and I continue to struggle with this concept.

She found that the author gave voice to her identity struggles. By interpreting his piece, she was able to share her bicultural background with a predominantly white audience.

Finally, topic significance varies across audiences. Think, for example, of film subjects. Movies for middle-schoolers explore different topics than do films aimed at baby boomers. Stereotypical "chick flicks" contrast in substance and style with "macho" themes. Regardless of topic or theme, the key with any performance is to show your listeners how and why the topic relates to them. (Chapter 6 describes how to create an introduction that relates a specific text to a specific audience.) For example, Christy chose prose by Alexie Sherman, a major contemporary Native American author. She later doubted her choice:

> I realized that I was the wrong person to perform such a story and I am not sure it was an appropriate piece for the audience. At a university with few Native Americans, this was a story about a hopeless elderly Indian who feels he has nothing to live for. I don't think many people could relate to it and understand what was going on in his head; even I had a hard time.

However, Christy underestimated the power of Sherman's story and of her performance. His poignant characters invited listeners to enter a world that they might not otherwise experience. And his protagonist's troubles—old age, lack of resources, despair, alcoholism—are significant themes that can relate on several levels to young people from middle-class backgrounds. Furthermore, Christy connected emotionally with her character, and this came through in her performance.

Emotionally Evocative Literature

Literature is often emotionally powerful. However, authors can provoke cheap tears or shock for the sake of shocking, whether by theme or by language. Skilled authors present emotions honestly and with integrity; less skillful writers manipulate emotions and use clichéd phrases. Allowing listeners to come into their own realizations or conclusions rather than manufacturing emotions generally results in a greater overall impact.[9]

It's easy to parody overblown emotions. Here, Mark Twain spoofs 19th century writers who created elaborate eulogies, especially about children who died young; his poem memorializes the unfortunate Stephen Dowling Bots, who fell down a well and was "drownded":[10]

Ode to Stephen Dowling Bots, [Deceased]

And did young Stephen sicken,
   And did young Stephen die?
And did the sad hearts thicken,
   And did the mourners cry?

No, such was not the fate of
   Young Stephen Dowling Bots,
Though sad hearts round him thickened,
   'Twas not from sickness' shots.

No whooping-cough did rack his frame,
   No measles drear, with spots:
Not these impaired the sacred name
   Of Stephen Dowling Bots. . . .

O no. Then list with tearful eye,
   Whilst I his fate do tell.
His soul did from this cold world fly
   By falling down a well.

They got him out and emptied him,
   Alas, it was too late;
His spirit was gone for to sport aloft
   In the realms of the good and the great.

In contrast, literature that suggests and stimulates further thought brings memories, moods, or images to mind for a more indirect influence.[11] Texts that meet this criterion contain layers of meaning, and each subsequent reading results in new insights. Classics provide a good example. In his book *Why Read the Classics?*,[12] Italo Calvino explains, "A classic is a book that has never finished saying what it has to say." He adds:

Classics influence, both by refusing to be eradicated from the mind and by concealing themselves in the folds of memory, camouflaging themselves as the collective or individual unconscious.

J. R. R. Tolkein's trilogy *The Lord of the Rings* is a 20th-century classic. In it, the ring is a potent symbol that can be interpreted several ways. Readers commonly link it with possessiveness and the seduction of pride, power, or domination over others. Some have suggested that the ring represents the buildup of nuclear weapons. Author Tom Shippley argues that it symbolizes addictions; they often make life seem better at first, but they ultimately destroy the addict's will and destiny.[13] As you can see, the symbolism is rich enough to stimulate a variety of creative associations.

In summary, discriminate among texts by looking for emotionally evocative works that convey universal values and themes and address significant topics. Search also for pieces that develop the themes in unique ways, using vivid, interesting language.

CONSIDER YOUR INTERESTS AND SKILLS

Because thousands of pieces meet the criteria described above, you must make additional decisions as you narrow down your choices. Let's face it: If you expect to perform well, you must invest time in each selection. Choose a piece of literature that interests you, that resonates with you in some way. Many pieces will fail to connect with your experiences or concerns, which will be apparent in your performance. However, when you find something you enjoy, your personal connection with the text can motivate you to share it with others, and your enthusiasm about it will be contagious.

It is also important to choose literature that you can perform with integrity. Look for texts that support your personal beliefs and values—or do the opposite and choose a text that highlights a perspective you do not share but are willing to examine with an open mind. You might eliminate a piece that offends you politically or morally, or you might choose the same piece *because* it offends you and you want to know more about both yourself and the perspective the text represents. In either case, your honesty or your openmindedness demonstrates your integrity.

Finally, find material that challenges you but is within your capabilities as a performer. Eliminate texts with too many characters to convey adequately as a solo performer; you would also be wise to eliminate works that call for emotional portrayals beyond your skill level. Other texts will not match your personality very well; for instance, you might avoid highly extroverted characters if you are shy. On the other hand, you might stretch yourself and portray a character who is very dissimilar. Courtney explains:

> I like comedy pieces filled with sarcasm and quick wit. I tried other forms, more serious and emotional pieces, but I felt my abilities were better aimed toward humorous pieces. *The Bean Trees* [by Barbara Kingsolver] was the easiest and most enjoyable piece, because by nature I am sarcastic, which

allowed me to portray Taylor pretty well; she had a similar personality. Yet I realized that this type of character became too easy and I needed to challenge myself with something that wasn't quite as close to home.

CONSIDER THE TIME ALLOTMENT

A major aspect of any performance situation is the time set aside for it. Generally, classroom performances run from three to ten minutes in length, including the introduction. If you are trying to decide between two equally desirable pieces, this factor can help you make your final choice. Read aloud each text you're considering, timing its length; if a work takes 35 minutes to read through, that means you'll have to eliminate 25 minutes of text—more than 70% of the total! In the end, you will be working with less than 30% of the original text. Setting that piece aside in favor of a shorter one would be a sensible decision. (You will find several guidelines for adapting your selections later in this chapter and in Chapter 7.)

ETHICAL CONSIDERATIONS

What role, if any, does ethics play in your selection and cutting, or editing, of texts? At first glance, this question may seem irrelevant. However, your performance takes place in public, in an educational setting where you have a captive audience. This means that listeners who want to complete the course are obligated to listen to your piece. In contrast, when listeners are in a private setting, they are free to choose what they want to hear.[14] Does this mean that you bear a responsibility to your listeners, or that you have some sort of obligation to them that carries with it an ethical dimension? Some professors and performers would agree. They have identified three areas that potentially have ethical implications: choosing texts, cutting and adapting them, and observing copyright laws.

Ethics and Text Choices

According to Professor Vern Jensen,[15] communication ethics require us to balance our rights against our responsibilities. He calls this "**rights–abilities.**" In other words, you have the rights to free speech and free expression, but you have responsibilities to yourself, your listeners, the creators of texts, and the situation. Here are just a few illustrations:

- Let's say your class is full of people who have highly negative attitudes toward another religious or ethnic group. In what circumstances might it be appropriate to select an honest text that presents the dark side of the group? When would it be better to select a text that challenges their prejudices?

STOP AND CHECK: Choosing Materials from the Internet

Thirty years ago, students searched for materials in college libraries, their personal bookshelves, and literature textbooks. These are all reputable sources because published works go through several screenings before appearing in texts. An author submits a manuscript to a literary journal or anthology, where an editor rejects it on the spot or gives it to reviewers to evaluate for both style and content. Editors then publish materials that pass their tests for literary merit, and they reject those that fail. Consequently, you can be confident that the poems, short stories, and plays that appear in anthologies and literary journals have passed some level of scrutiny. Many literary journals are affiliated with universities or with literary societies. In addition, magazines such as the *New Yorker*, the *Atlantic Monthly*, and *Harper's* have a long-standing reputation for high literary standards.

Today's students often find it easier to sit down at a computer, log onto the Internet, and browse through the millions of texts at their fingertips. Chances are, you will use the Internet to find at least one of your pieces. If so, here are some guidelines and sites that will help you search the Web more effectively:

- Look for sites with .org or .edu in the URL; usually, the materials there have been at least somewhat screened. (Some .com sites provide acceptable literature, but they often require more careful scrutiny on your part.)
- Check out sites sponsored by recognized groups such as the American Academy of Poets (www.poets .org). From there you can link to "find a poet" or "listening booth" to find thousands of usable texts.
- Many magazines such as the *Atlantic Monthly* have their own sites. Check out http:www.theatlantic .com/. From there, link to "fiction/poetry," and browse through the works you find.
- For famous writers such as Shakespeare or Wordsworth, use a search engine such as www.google.com and look up the writer by name. You can find the complete works of an author whose texts are in the public domain. For example, see www.jollyroger.com/shakespeare.
- An amazing number of public domain works are available online. Some of the best sites for texts of all kinds are:
  www.gutenberg.net
  www.bartleby.com
  www.bibliomania.com
  http:digital.library.upenn. edu
  www.literature.org

Go to the Internet and look at each site mentioned here. Then search for some of the authors or texts on the list you made for Chapter 1. Come to class prepared to discuss the benefits and drawbacks of Internet searches with your classmates.

- Perhaps you have a burning concern about a social issue such as abortion, environmental protection, or homosexual rights. You know that your listeners are more or less hostile to your perspective. What rights and responsibilities might you factor into your decision about choosing a selection that deals with the topic?

- How sensitive should you be when you know that the language would offend many of your listeners? (For example, the author may use racist terms or other slurs in your piece.)

STOP AND CHECK: Evaluate a Case Study

Emotionally powerful literature often deals with dramatic subjects such as rape, incest, violence, and war, and performers often explore darker elements of the human condition. At speech tournaments, each interpretation round, which is made up of six competitors, may feature as many as two or three texts with fairly graphic and sometimes violent sexual content. The rules for good sportsmanship require each competitor to listen politely to every other competitor in the round.

At one tournament, an interpreter who was a rape survivor found the graphic details in another competitor's story so upsetting that she quietly left the room and sought out a private space to regain control of her emotions. She later apologized to the performer, who berated her for leaving and told her she had a problem she needed to deal with. Fortunately, she was already seeing a counselor, but the performance and her competitor's reaction caught her off guard at an emotionally fragile stage of recovery.

Discussion Questions:
1. *Should the uncomfortable competitor have left the round? Why or why not? What does she owe to the performer? To the text? To herself?*
2. *How should the competitor have handled her apology? Why?*
3. *If the statistics are accurate, the chances are good that in any given classroom a number of students have gone through traumatic experiences (incest, rape, other abuse) that are often described in literature. How should a performer take into account their interests and needs when selecting and performing graphic texts on these topics?*

- How should ethics guide your decision to interpret a graphically violent piece?

The dialogical theory of communication, introduced in Chapter 1, envisions communication as a dialogue in which both the performer and the listeners cooperate to cocreate meaning. Although you as a performer have the right to present a variety of texts, your listeners also have the right to respond and react to them. Ideally, you and your listeners will work together toward the goal of better understanding life and its complexities.

Ethical Cutting and Adaptation

Because many pieces are too long for classroom performances, you must often eliminate sizable portions of the text. The basic rule for ethical cutting is to maintain the author's intent; consequently, every change or adaptation you make should keep intact the integrity of the piece. The following policies for the "Ethical Use of Literature" are generally agreed upon:[16]

- Don't rewrite the text so that your version differs from the original.
- Don't add or reassign scenes or lines. (However, you may have to add an explanatory line, especially if you eliminate a character.)

> ### STOP AND CHECK: Choosing Pieces to Perform
>
> Return to the lists you started in Chapter 1. Select several texts that meet the tests of universality, uniqueness, significance, and emotional evocativeness. Choose some that you can perform and that are appropriate to the situation. Assess the ethical dimension of your choices by considering your audience's needs, your purpose, the adaptations you would have to make, and applicable copyright laws.

- Don't change the ending.
- Don't change the gender or person of a character.

Here's an example: Parents complained when one elementary school teacher changed "Christmas" to "winter" in a text that her pupils performed publicly. In their eyes, this violated the original intent of the piece; they reasoned that she should not have chosen a text she could not accept "as is."

When you cut a piece, you can ethically eliminate characters that do not advance the plot, but you should not change them in any substantive way. For example, don't change a character's age, gender, relationships with another character, and so on. And don't alter any character's language or put your own words into his or her mouth.

Some texts contain vocabulary you may consider inappropriate, either personally or for a particular audience or a specific situation. If these words are so offensive you hesitate to perform them, select another piece rather than cutting out single words or softening their impact by substituting less offensive terms. Keep in mind that authors choose specific language for specific reasons. Don't rewrite the text to fit your taste, your audience's sensibilities, or the situation. However, if an offensive sentence is irrelevant to the piece as a whole, you can appropriately eliminate it.

Copyrights and Ethics

If you've followed the debate about using your personal computer to download music, you have heard a lot about copyright violations. The basic argument runs as follows. Not everyone is a talented artist or musician; those who are should be able to make their living off their creative and intellectual property. Consequently, downloading music and songs to your own computer without paying for them is actually stealing, because it deprives the creators of royalty income they would otherwise receive.

The same copyright laws apply to poets, novelists, playwrights, and other writers. The **Fair Use Provision** of the copyright laws allows you to use a piece freely for a one-time class performance, but if you perform the same piece for a paid public performance, you are ethically and legally obligated to pay a royalty fee. Fortunately, older texts are in the **public domain;** no one owns them, and you can use them freely.

SUMMARY

Because a performance requires your time as well as your listeners', select materials that are worth your efforts. Look for works with literary merit and for emotionally evocative texts that convey universal values and themes and address significant topics. Then go further and find pieces that feature unique and creative language.

In addition, consider personal and situational factors. Choose pieces you like and those that challenge you but still lie within your performance abilities. Then consider the time factor and select a piece that can fit into the constraints imposed by the situation.

Finally, consider the ethical implications of the materials you choose. What responsibilities do you have to your audience? To yourself? Remember that your classroom performances are public and are meant to be educational. Remember also that your audience is a captive one; they have little choice but to participate in your performance. You are cooperating with them and the text to cocreate meaning. Next, consider your ethical responsibilities to the text itself. Don't cut or alter the work in a way that changes the author's intent. Don't change characters or omit language you don't like. Finally, feel free to use works that are in the public domain or under the Fair Use Provision of the copyright law, but pay royalty fees if you take your performance into public arenas.

KEY TERMS

text	values	Fair Use Provision
literature	exigence	public domain
universal	rights–abilities	

QUESTIONS AND EXERCISES

1. Aesop's fables have passed the "test of time," which is one way to think about literary quality. Art students at the University of Massachusetts have illustrated the fables for contemporary audiences. Go to http:www.umass.edu/aesop/ or to www.aesopfables.com/ and link to several fables. Identify ways each tale illustrates the cultural value that is the moral.

2. Read classic literature from at least two other cultures. To find good texts, search your school's library or go to www.google.com and search for "classic literature." You can make your search even more specific; for example, "classic Scandinavian literature," "classic Jewish literature," or "classic Chinese literature" will give more focused results. Identify some of the

values in the literature. Then tell ways you could relate the texts to your specific classroom audience.

3. Classic literature passes tests for literary merit. Italo Calvino has identified 14 elements of classic literature. Search online for Calvino by name or by the title of his book, *Why Read the Classics*? Find information about as many of the 14 elements as you can, and take notes. Bring your notes to class, and discuss the elements with your classmates.

4. The Internet contains millions of texts, varying in literary quality. For example, compare www.poets.com with www.poets.org. The .com (commercial) source links to poets who copyright their own works; the .org (organization) source includes only poets who publish through reputable publishers. Read through a couple of poems on each site and compare and contrast them for literary merit.

5. Log onto the Internet and read James W. Pratt's paper "Something Should Be Done" at www.phirhopi.org/prp/spkrpts5.2/pratt.htm. Identify his basic argument, and come to class prepared to discuss with your classmates the ethical implications of his claim.

4

Analyzing Texts

This chapter will help you:

- Identify several ways that literary modes—lyric, dramatic, and epic—influence your performance

- Use the pentad (agent, act, scene, agency, purpose) to analyze a work

- Use the theory of transtextuality to consider intertextual, paratextual, metatextual, hypo- or hypertextual, and architextual aspects of a text

- Analyze a text through performance by playing, testing, choosing, repeating, and presenting

Students sometimes ask, "If this is a performance class, not a literature course, why do I have to analyze my text in such detail?" They are correct in that this is not a "literature class" and that the overall purpose of this course is not to study the finer points of literary theories and methods of analysis. However, because your goal should be to interpret a variety of texts with integrity, you must thoroughly understand each text before you can perform it. Given this fact, there are three good reasons to analyze each literary selection carefully:

- As you study the text, you will better understand what you are performing.

- Consequently, your analysis will help you make well-reasoned performance choices.

- Finally, analysis benefits your audience; your performance allows your listeners to discover and experience the insights you have gleaned through careful analysis of your text.[1]

No single analytic method is right for every text; the text itself will suggest the most effective methods for interpreting it, as this chapter discusses. Thus, you will be at an advantage if you have a number of analytic tools at your disposal.[2] Although there are many ways to approach a piece of literature, this chapter focuses on four particularly useful analytical methods: modal, dramatistic, transtextual analysis, and analysis through performance.

MODAL ANALYSIS

A **modal analysis** identifies who is speaking and who is being addressed in the literary text. Authors use various speakers or **personae** to express their ideas; these personae, in turn, address their remarks to a particular audience. As you read through the following excerpts, first think about the persona who is speaking, and then identify the audience to whom the words are directed.

To a Little Invisible Being Who Is Expected Soon to Become Visible[3]

ANNA LAETITIA BARBAULD

1 Germ of new life, whose powers expanding slow
2 For many a moon their full perfection wait,—
3 Haste, precious pledge of happy love, to go
4 Auspicious borne through life's mysterious gate.

5 What powers lie folded in thy curious frame,—
6 Senses from objects locked, and mind from thought!
7 How little canst thou guess thy lofty claim
8 To grasp at all the worlds the Almighty wrought!

On Digital Extremities[4]

GELETT BURGESS

I'd Rather have Fingers than Toes;
I'd Rather have Ears than a Nose;
   And As for my Hair,
   I'm Glad it's All There;
I'll be Awfully Sad, when it Goes!

From "Hasan's Wives"[5]

WADIDA WASSEF

. . . The lighter chores were of course the privilege of the spoiled and pampered favourite, very aptly called Sayyida, which in Arabic means "lady." The meaning of her name, from long association seems to have rubbed off on her person, the way she conducted herself. She would come tripping up the kitchen steps with the hem of her long gown caught between her teeth, ostensibly to keep her from stumbling but in reality to gratify the male staff with a glimpse of her ankles.

From the moment she appeared there would be as much traffic in the kitchen as in a public square. Abduh who goes upstairs suddenly remembers he has forgotten the duster and comes down to fetch it taking all day about it. Uthman who goes downstairs decides it is time for the master's coffee and takes forever making the water boil on a very low flame. The gardener who never brings the flowers unless he is repeatedly reminded, barges in with an armful and wiggling his eyebrows, throws voluble good mornings right and left, to Abduh and Uthman and "the lovely ones." Sayyida who was fully aware of what she was doing would keep her eyes bashfully averted while the devil looked out from beneath her drooping eyelids, heavily lined with kohl.

Who is speaking (**speaker mode**) and to whom (**audience mode**)? The title of the first poem is a dead giveaway: The persona is speaking to a coming child, who in the first line is addressed as "germ of new life." However, because this child cannot yet comprehend words, the secondary audience is probably the parents or other adults who will take the responsibility for raising the child. The speaker is **uncharacterized.** It may be a parent, most likely a mother, but it could also be a father, grandparent, pastor, or other adult interested in the upcoming birth. The text is not explicit.

The second poem is aimed at just about anyone The speaker is older, with a sense of the ridiculous, and is probably male, because more men than women go bald. He, too, is uncharacterized.

In the third excerpt, the text has previously revealed the unnamed speaker as a neighbor girl who watches with fascination the interactions among an old Egyptian man, his four wives, their various children, and their servants. The story is written in English, and the author explains many Arab words and customs; this indicates that her intended audience is probably English-speaking adults, minimally aware of Middle Eastern traditions.

As these examples show, authors adopt personae to present their ideas. (*Persona* is Latin and means the masks that the actors wore in classical theater.) Creators may have much in common with their persona, but they also differ in major and minor ways. Your interpretative task is to perform the personae inhabiting the text so that listeners feel sufficiently involved to respond to their thoughts and their predicaments.

We now turn to a discussion of the lyric, dramatic, and epic modes by answering two basic questions: Who is speaking in this text? To whom?

Lyric Mode

In the **lyric mode,** the persona is a single, undefined, and uncharacterized speaker. As the excerpts above demonstrate, lyric personae have no distinct personality, and they speak in monologues, not conversations. They are self-reflective; in other words, they muse about the ideas, people, objects, and events in their lives. They confide personal thoughts and emotions, and the audience eavesdrops on their private musings.

Some lyric speakers talk to themselves; others speak to an object or thing; some address another presence; still others want a general audience to know their thoughts. Following are examples of these audiences:

The personae address themselves. The first excerpt, from a diary written during World War II, is meant to be seen only by the writer himself. Writing a diary or journal allows him to sort out his thoughts. The second text records someone's responses to a dried, sloughed-off snakeskin she comes across during a walk. This text, too, seems meant only for her private contemplation, but we are allowed to overhear her musings.

Diary Entry[6]

O. NANSEN

January 13, 1944. Today it's two years since I was arrested [by the Nazis]. Two everlasting, senseless years. What's become of them? I daren't look back on them. My optimism is paling, too—in spite of good news from the east. When on earth are the *decisive* events coming?

Signal[7]

LUCI SHAW

I'd rather be a live snake,
    sinuous, sinister, dust
    dry but silver quick,
    the signature of an old
    sin, venomous, a target
    of boys' pebbles
than this empty lace of skin,
    this fine froth of scales,

this coiled shadow
of the real, this death wish
left, paralyzed, in the crack
of a hot rock.

Addressing an object or thing. Older lyric poetry is filled with literary personae who muse rapturously or solemnly about objects such as Grecian urns or nightingales. Here are two interesting intended audiences: a tiger and a book. In Blake's poem, the speaker stands in awe of a magnificent tiger; in Bradstreet's, the speaker is embarrassed by her book. Bradstreet's persona is quite close to her real-life situation. She wrote a book that she set aside, but well-meaning friends took it to the printer and had it published without her knowledge or permission. She speaks of it as her child and fears that critics will find its many flaws, which she cannot now correct.

The Tyger[8]

WILLIAM BLAKE

Tyger! Tyger! burning bright
In the forests of the night,
What immortal hand or eye
Could frame thy fearful symmetry?

In what distant deeps of skies
Burnt the fire of thine eyes?
On what wings dare he aspire?
What the hand dare seize the fire? . . .

The Author to Her Book[9]

ANNE BRADSTREET

Thou ill-form'd offspring of my feeble brain,
Who after birth did'st by my side remain,
Till snatcht from thence by friends, less wise than true,
Who thee abroad expos'd to public view.
Made thee in rags, halting to th' press to trudge,
Where errors were not lessened (all may judge).
At thy return my blushing was not small,
My rambling brat (in print) should mother call. . . .

Addressing a particular presence. Thousands of lyric works have been addressed to specific people, both dead and alive; thousands more call out to God, the gods, or other supernatural entities. Here are two examples:

Psalm 19:14[10]

KING JAMES BIBLE

Let the words of my mouth, and the meditation of my heart,
    be acceptable in Thy sight, O LORD, my strength, and
    my redeemer.

Terence, This is Stupid Stuff[11]

    A. E. HOUSMAN

Terence, this is stupid stuff;
You eat your victuals fast enough;
There can't be much amiss, 'tis clear,
To see the rate you drink your beer.

Addressing a general audience. A general audience could be just about anyone—a single uncharacterized individual or a larger unspecified group. The first poem below, by Marianne Moore, is a word-picture describing Mt. Rainier in Washington State. The second poem narrates the final few minutes of a man who is condemned to hang at 8:00 a.m. Neither piece addresses a specific listener.

An Octopus[12]

of ice. Deceptively reserved and flat,
it lies "in grandeur and in mass"
beneath a sea of shifting show-dunes;
dots of cyclamen-red and maroon on its clearly defined
                                  pseudo-podia
made of glass that will bend—a much needed invention—
comprising twenty-eight ice-fields from fifty to five hundred
                                    feet thick,
of unimagined delicacy. . . .

Eight O'Clock[13]

    A. E. HOUSMAN

He stood, and heard the steeple
   Sprinkle the quarters on the morning town.
One, two, three, four, to market-place and people
   It tossed them down.

Strapped, noosed, nighing his hour,
   He stood and counted them and cursed his luck;
And then the clock collected in the tower
   Its strength, and struck.

Knowing the persona and the intended audience will help you decide how to use your body as you perform your text and where to look as you speak. Imagine, for example, how a persona would actually address a coming child or a book. Where would a speaker look to describe a mountain or narrate the goings-on of the family next door? Your answers to questions such as these will help you make the most appropriate performance choices.

Performance Analysis: A Real-Life Challenge to Death When asked for his last words, convicted Oklahoma City bomber Timothy McVeigh presented a reporter with a lyric poem that he had written on a piece of notebook paper. Because McVeigh had omitted the title and author, the reporter initially announced that the bomber was the poet. Outside the prison where McVeigh was executed, the reporter carefully unfolded the paper, looked directly into the camera, and intoned the following poem, "Invictus" by William Ernest Henley:[14]

1 Out of the night that covers me
2 Black as the Pit from pole to pole,
3 I thank whatever gods may be
4 For my unconquerable soul.
5 In the fell clutch of circumstance
6 I have not winced nor cried aloud.
7 Under the bludgeonings of chance
8 My head is bloody, but unbowed.
9 Beyond this place of wrath and tears
10 Looms but the Horror of the shade,
11 And yet the menace of the years
12 Finds, and shall find, me unafraid.
13 It matters not how strait the gate,
14 How charged with punishments the scroll,
15 I am the master of my fate:
16 I am the captain of my soul.

Proud and defiant: These two words summarize the persona's stance. Although the poet addressed a general audience, McVeigh borrowed his voice to defy a specific audience: the government he had wanted to destroy and the justice system that ultimately decided his earthly fate.

This was possible because the persona is **uncharacterized;** he (or she) is unnamed; nothing is revealed about his age, height, weight, marital status, or other information you learn about a **characterized** persona. He is not conversing with another character; he appears to be thinking aloud. Or perhaps he's standing atop a stump in a lonely meadow, shouting these words defiantly into the wind. The text doesn't say. However, McVeigh craftily orchestrated a final performance. He knew that he could not actually perform "Invictus," but that one of the cadre of reporters at his death scene would perform it for him. And he was correct.

Although the persona in "Invictus" does not directly address a particular audience, we readers or listeners are let in on his inner thoughts, and his words exist in the **timeless present;** therefore, they could convey someone's personal and emotional state in 1875, and they seem just as fresh when McVeigh offered them to his executioners in 2001.

If Timothy McVeigh had probed the poet's background to see how closely the persona in "Invictus" reflected Henley's life, he might have chosen different last words. Unlike McVeigh's situation, which was a result of his own actions, William Ernest Henley endured hardship and suffering brought about by uncontrollable circumstances. At age 12, he was diagnosed with tubercular arthritis, which forced him to drop out of school. At 16, doctors amputated his leg just below his knee, and thereafter he walked on a wooden leg. Later, the disease recurred in his right leg, and Henley feared he would lose it, too. In fact, he entered surgery expecting an amputation, but he came out of chloroform and happily discovered that his foot was still there. He wrote "Invictus" during this 20-month hospitalization period. Some critics believe that the "night that covered [him]" and the "black pit" referred to anesthesia.[15]

Henley went through the night, the Pit, and the Horror of the shade; McVeigh consigned these to the people he killed and wounded and to their families. In short, although the speaker in this poem is defiant, his defiance is not comparable to Timothy McVeigh's unrepentant stance in response to his self-inflicted predicament. Consequently, McVeigh's final performance was ultimately misguided.

Dramatic Mode

In the **dramatic mode,** the characters are **defined,** meaning that we recognize them as males or females of a specific age, ethnicity, educational level, and so on. These characters interact in the present tense with other characters, most commonly in conflict situations. Each has distinctive physical characteristics and a recognizable speaking style. We witness their conversations and interactions, but we never interact with them. Some entire texts, such as plays and screenplays, are dramatic. In contrast, sometimes only parts or sections of a work are written in the dramatic mode.

Here is an example from "The Blue Devils of Blue River Avenue," a short story by Poe Ballantine about two boys whose neighbor is on trial for criminal abuse of a child. The "I" in the story is a newcomer in an older working-class neighborhood in San Diego. He has already made one friend, but he watches with awe as a newcomer, Homer Ashmont, becomes instantly popular. One day, on a walk to school, Homer appears alongside him:[16]

"I'm Homer," he said.

"Hi," I said, shaking his hand. "I know."

"How come you walk to school by yourself all the time?"

"I don't know."

"My mom said you weren't allowed to go over to the Sambeaux house."

"That's right."

"I can't go over there anymore either. Did you hear about what happened?"

"Yeah."

"I never heard of nothing like that before. Hey, do you like beef stroganoff?"

"I guess."

"We're having it tonight. Do you want to come over to my house for dinner?" . . .

"O.K."

Remember how your elementary school teachers read stories such as this that include dialogue between characters? They created vocal characteristics that distinguished each persona. Similarly, when you perform dramatic scenes, you will create distinctive physical and vocal characteristics for each persona, using skills described in Chapter 5.

The following example of the dramatic mode was excerpted, or cut, from Nilo Cruz's Pulitzer Prize–winning play *Anna in the Tropics,* which is about a lector in a Cuban cigar factory.[17] Juan Julian, the lector, has been reading Leo Tolstoy's classic novel *Anna Karenina,* which chronicles the adventures of an unfaithful wife in tsarist Russia. This excerpt features a conversation between two cigar rollers, a husband and wife, as she reveals her knowledge of his extra-marital affair. As you read, think about these questions:

- Who initiates the conversation?

- What are the questions? Who asks them? When? Why?

- How does Conchita control the direction of the conversation?

- Where are the breaks and pauses? What do they reveal about each speaker's emotions?

- How does Palomo try to keep the topics impersonal?

- Notice the characters' use of the pronoun "you." (Read through this excerpt aloud, emphasizing every "you" that you find.) How does Conchita use "you" to reveal her attitude toward Palomo? How does Palomo use the pronoun?

Conchita: And how do you like the novel that Juan Julian is reading . . .?

Palomo: I like it very much.

Conchita: Doesn't it make you uncomfortable?

Palomo: Why would it make me uncomfortable?

Conchita: The part about the lover.

Palomo: It seems like in every novel there's always a love affair.

Conchita: And do you ever think about everything that's happening between Anna Karenina and her husband?

Palomo: I do . . . But I . . .

Conchita: So what goes through your mind when you listen to the story?

Palomo: I think of all the money those people have.

Conchita: You would say something like that.

Palomo: Why? Because I like money?

Conchita: I'm talking about literature and you talk about money.

Palomo: And what do you want me to say?

Conchita: I want you to talk about the story, the characters . . . You don't care about anything, do you? Juan Julian could be reading a book by Jose Marti or Shakespeare and everything goes in one ear and out the other.

Palomo: I pay attention to what he reads. I just don't take everything to heart the way you do.

Conchita: Well, you should. Do you remember that part of the book in which Anna Karenina's husband is suspicious of her having an affair with Vronsky? . . .

Palomo: I know what you're getting at.

Conchita: I just want to have a civilized conversation. The same way the characters speak to each other in the novel. I've learned many things from this book.

Palomo: Such as?

Conchita: Jealousy. For Anna's husband jealousy is base and almost animalistic. And he's right. He would never want Anna to think that he's capable of such vile and shameful emotions.

Palomo: But you can't help being jealous. It's part of your nature.

Conchita: Not anymore.

Palomo: Well, that's a change.

Conchita: Oh, I could see the husband so clear in the novel. How the thoughts would take shape in his mind, as they have in my own mind. I mean, not the same . . . because he's an educated man, surrounded by culture and wealth, and I'm just a cigar roller in a factory. He is well-bred and sophisticated. I barely get by in life. But with this book I'm seeing everything through new eyes. What has been happening in the novel has been happening to us. No. Don't look at me that way. You might not want to admit it, but Anna and her husband remind me of us. Except I'm more like the husband.

Palomo: So what does that make me then, Anna Karenina?

Conchita: You are the one who has the secret love, not me.

Palomo: Oh, come on. It's late. Let's go home. I can't work like this.

Conchita: That's exactly what Anna said when the husband confronted her about the lover: "It's late. Let's go to sleep."

Palomo: I think you are taking this a little too far.

Conchita: Am I?

To better understand Conchita and Palomo, jot down how Cruz characterizes them. Identify as much as you can about each character's demographic, psychological, and emotional characteristics, using the categories in Chapter 2. Picture what they look like, how they'd react to specific situations, what kind of dispositions they have, and so on.

Knowing that this is an excerpt from a play will help you understand the performance decisions you must make. You know you will interpret more than one persona, and you must decide ways to express their vocal and physical characteristics. How you answered the analysis questions and the characteristics you listed about Conchita and Palomo will guide your decisions about how much emotion to display and which emotions to display through vocal variations and bodily movements.

Epic Mode

The **epic mode** combines the lyric and dramatic modes. The lyric sections are distinguished by the presence of a narrator or a storyteller whose role is to reveal the other characters' thoughts and motivations, to present their actions, and to summarize the past or explain what is happening in the present. Many narrators are uncharacterized; we know little about them, although we can often surmise their attitudes toward the people and events they describe. Other narrators are actual characters within the story—sometimes major, sometimes minor. They report what happens and confide their responses to what is taking place around them. (Chapter 7 provides more information about narrators.)

Epic mode is fairly easy to identify because it intersperses narrative sections with lines of dialogue. This example from Junot Diaz's short story "Drown"[18] has a first-person narrator, a drug dealer who lives with his mother. Beto is his brother, who is gay. Diaz omits quotation marks around the lines of dialogue, but the format of his writing provides the clues you need to determine who is speaking:

> She's never understood why [Beto and I] don't speak anymore. I've tried to explain, all wise-like, that everything changes, but she thinks that sort of saying is only around so you can prove it wrong.
>
> >> He asked me what you were doing.
> >> What did you say?
> >> I told him you were fine.
> >> You should have told him I moved.
> >> And what if he ran into you?
> >> I'm not allowed to visit my mother?
> >
> > She notices the tightening of my arms.
> >> You should be more like me and your father.
> >> Can't you see I'm watching television?
> >> I was angry at him, wasn't I? But now we can talk to each other.
> >> Am I watching television here or what?

At the outset, identify the lines of narration (the lyric lines) and the lines of dialogue (the dramatic lines). Then analyze the intended audience for each persona and direct your focus toward the intended audience. For example, because the narrator addresses a general audience, you should similarly look out at various people in the audience when speaking the lines of narration. This changes for the lines of dialogue. The persona is addressing a specific character in a specific place. You should do the same. Place each character in a different location, and address the words toward that imaginary place. (Chapter 5 describes character placement in detail.)

The following excerpt is taken from James McBride's book *The Color of Water*.[19]

> [One] Saturday afternoon, [Mommy] announced she was going to drive my stepfather's car.
>
> She sat behind the wheel, tapping it nervously and muttering while I settled in the front seat . . . We didn't bother with seat belts. She stuck the key in the ignition. The engine roared to life. "What do you do now?" she asked.
>
> "Put it in gear," I said.
>
> "Oh, I know that," she said. She slammed the car into drive and pulled off in a cloud of burning rubber and smoke, swerving down the street, screaming hysterically— "Woooooooooooo!"
>
> "Slow down, Ma!" I said.
>
> She ignored me. "I don't have a license!" she shrieked as the car veered from side to side. "If I get stopped I'm going to jail!" She went about four blocks, ran a stop sign without pausing, then at the next intersection whipped a wide, arcing left turn, stabbing the accelerator pedal and sending the big sedan reeling down the wrong side of the street as oncoming traffic swerved to avoid us.
>
> "Watch it! What are you doing? Ma! Stop the car!" I hollered.
>
> "I need to go to the A&P! I need to go to the A&P," she shrieked. "This is what I'm driving for, right?" We jerked along for a few blocks, no cops anywhere, and miraculously arrived at the A&P. . . .

Epic texts often contain tag lines such as "I said" or "she responded." You can almost always cut at least some during your performance. For example, you would probably say:

"What do you do now?" ~~she asked~~.

"Put it in gear," ~~I said~~.

"Oh, I know that," ~~she said~~.

James McBride is telling his own story, so he is both the narrator and a major character through whose eyes the other characters come to life. Since he is addressing a general audience, you can speak directly to your listeners during the narration. During the conversation, act as if you actually were in the driver's seat when you say the mother's lines, and then speak from the passenger seat when you read the son's lines. The following excerpt includes analysis and performance notes in brackets.

> [lyric section: directly address the audience] She stuck the key in the ignition. The engine roared to life.
>
> [dramatic section: assume "Mommy's" character] "What do you do now?"
>
> [dramatic: assume the son's character and look at Mommy] "Put it in gear."
>
> [dramatic: Mommy's character again] "Oh, I know that."

STOP AND CHECK: Do a Modal Analysis

Return to the list of possible pieces to perform that you started in Chapter 1. Select three texts, and do a modal analysis on each one. Then identify several ways that different modes would alter your performance strategies.

[lyric section: narrator explains to the audience] She slammed the car into drive and pulled off in a cloud of burning rubber and smoke, swerving down the street, screaming hysterically—

[dramatic section: assume Mommy's character] "Wooooooooooooo!"

[dramatic section: assume the son's character] "Slow down, Ma!"

[dramatic: assume Mommy's character] "I don't have a license! If I get stopped I'm going to jail!"

[lyric section: narrator talks to the audience] She went about four blocks, ran a stop sign without pausing . . .

In summary, analyzing the speaker mode and the audience mode will help you to identify the lyric, dramatic, and epic elements of a text. Understanding the various personae and their intended audiences will help you to know what role to take as you perform the texts.

DRAMATISTIC ANALYSIS

Although modal analysis is helpful for analyzing who speaks and who is being addressed, you need other analytical tools to understand additional elements of your text. One of the most prolific scholars of the 20th century, Kenneth Burke, proposed a model called the **pentad**[20] as a way to consider a specific communication text. According to Burke, an imaginative work is a creator's answer to the questions posed by a particular situation.[21] Consequently, each communication event is somewhat like a drama. It involves five elements: the act, the agent, the scene, the purpose, and the agency. (Figure 4.1 shows a diagram of this pentad.) When doing a dramatistic analysis, think of yourself as a journalist probing for answers to the following questions: Who? What? When? Where? How? Why?

Agent—Who?

When you identify the **agent** or agents, you are answering the question, "Who is acting in this situation?" The agents are the characters. They sometimes act individually; at other times they combine to form groups of **co-agents** who join in combat against villains or **counteragents.** Some are human or superhuman; others are objects or animals. Object and animal agents may or may

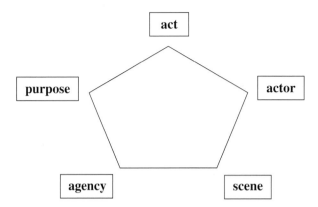

FIGURE 4.1 The Pentad

not be personified. For example, the black stallion in the novel by that name is never anything but a horse, but the donkey in the *Shrek* movies has distinctly human characteristics. Inanimate forces such as hailstones or earthquakes can also be agents. Think of movies such as *Twister,* in which a major agent is a powerful storm.

Begin your analysis by finding out everything you can about each agent. Probe the piece, looking for information about their likes and their looks, their desires and their motivations, their demographic characteristics and their psychological makeup. (See Chapter 2.) As you probe, jot down specific ideas you can use to perform that character.

Act—What?

In a lyric text, the persona's words and thoughts are the **act.** However, in epics or in dramatic texts, the **act** refers to the events or plot—what the agents are doing. Look carefully at what each agent thinks, says, and does. In short, when you analyze the act, you answer the question, "What is happening?"

Scene—Where? When? In What Circumstances?

Explore the **scene** to answer the questions, "Where is this happening?" "When did it take place?" and "What are the surrounding circumstances?" Elements of scene include not only the date and geographical location of the act but also its cultural or social context. According to Burke, certain scenes invite a specific kind of act and a certain type of agent. [22] Given the cigar factory lector's reading of *Anna Karenina*, for example, we can conclude that Conchita will confront Palomo regarding his infidelities.

Agency—How?

When you analyze the **agency,** you scrutinize the text for answers to the question "How did the agent accomplish the act?" Agency includes tools such as knives or poison, methods such as flattery or direct confrontation, and means such as e-mail or face-to-face messages.[23] It also involves the language and structure of the text itself.

Look especially closely at the language. Consider distinctions that range from formality to informality, complexity to simplicity, abstraction to concreteness. Take note of vivid words and phrases, including similes, metaphors, alliteration, hyperbole or overstatement, and other figures of speech, which are described in Chapter 9. For example, return to the dialogue between Conchita and Palomo on pages 59–60. The questions there ask you to probe the agency of language. Notice how each character uses the word "you" and what their use of that pronoun reveals; notice also that Conchita controls the topic by initiating the questions and by returning to the painful subject of infidelity after Palomo tries to neutralize the conversation.

Nonverbal communication, such as tone of voice and facial expressions, is an element of agency. In *The Color of Water* excerpt on pages 62–63, Mommy screams hysterically and her son hollers back. Mommy slams the car into gear and burns rubber as she pulls out into the street. Her uncoordinated, aggressive movements combine with the screams and the hollering as part of the overall act—the terrifying drive to the supermarket.

Look at the form or arrangement of words and sentences the author selects. Notice the length of the sentences, the overall structure of the work, and the rhyme and rhythm patterns, if any. For example, Conchita's sentences are typically longer than Palomo's. When she finally confronts him, he uses very simple sentences that show how anxious he is to cut off the conversation: "Oh, come on. It's late. Let's go home. I can't work like this."

Finally, examine the overall arrangement of ideas. Does the text have an introduction and conclusion? Does the story follow a chronological pattern, or does the author use another organizational method? (Alternate organizational strategies include problem-solution, cause-effect or effect-cause, and pro-con patterns.) All these verbal, nonverbal, and organizational strategies are the agencies the creator uses to accomplish the act.

Purpose—Why?

Examine **purpose** on two levels: the creator's general purpose, and the personae's purposes for their utterances. In many texts the two seem quite close. For instance, both Henley and the persona in "Invictus" proudly defy their circumstances, and both poet and persona in the limerick "Extremities" aim to entertain. In contrast, personae in a satirical text might pompously take their words and actions very seriously, but the author's purpose is to poke fun at a person, idea, or institution.

Probe, also, for the **subtext,** which is anything a character thinks or feels but cannot or will not put into words. Think of the text as what the agents say and the subtext as what they really think or mean. For instance, James McBride hollers, "Watch it! What are you doing? Ma! Stop the car!" (text) He probably is thinking, "You idiot!" (subtext), but he does not say this directly. In Cruz's play, Palomo does not directly admit his infidelity, but by his silence he concedes that he has indeed been unfaithful to his wife. Characters communicate the subtext nonverbally, so searching for inconsistencies between their words and their behaviors will help you discern the characters' underlying feelings and motivations.[24]

When you identify the purpose, you have the answer to *why* the act happens, since you know the agent's goal or reason for performing it. Conchita had a specific purpose for confronting Palomo about his infidelity, and Nilo Cruz, the playwright, uses their situation to point out the relevance of literary themes to the lives of ordinary people.

In summary, the pentad is a five-element model that is useful for analyzing the who, what, when, where, how, and why of a literary work. Understanding the characters who are acting in scenes for various purposes by using the agency or means at their disposal—which in the case of literature is usually language—enables you to better portray the subtleties in each text.

A Sample Dramatistic Analysis

The poem "In the Orchard," by Muriel Stuart, lends itself well to a dramatistic analysis. It is unusual for a poem because it is written entirely in the dramatic mode: two distinct characters are deeply involved in a conversation.

In the Orchard[25]

MURIEL STUART

1 "I thought you loved me." "No, it was only fun."
2 "When we stood there, closer than all?" "Well, the harvest moon
3 Was shining and queer in your hair, and it turned my head."
4 "That made you?" "Yes." "Just the moon and the light it made
5 Under the tree?" "Well, your mouth, too." "Yes, my mouth?"
6 "And the quiet there that sang like the drum in the booth.
7 You shouldn't have danced like that." "Like what?" "So close,
8 With your head turned up, and the flower in your hair, a rose
9 That smelt all warm." "I loved you. I thought you knew
10 I wouldn't have danced like that with any but you."
11 "I didn't know. I thought you knew it was fun."
12 "I thought it was love you meant." "Well, it's done." "Yes, it's done.
13 I've seen boys stone a blackbird, and watched them drown
14 A kitten . . . it clawed at the reeds, and they pushed it down
15 Into the pool while it screamed. Is that fun, too?"
16 "Well, boys are like that . . . Your brothers . . ." "Yes, I know.
17 But you, so lovely and strong! Not you! Not you!"
18 "They don't understand it's cruel. It's only a game."
19 "And are girls fun, too?" "No, still in a way it's the same.
20 It's queer and lovely to have a girl . . ." "Go on."

21 "It makes you mad for a bit to feel she's your own,

22 And you laugh and kiss her, and maybe you give her a ring,

23 But it's only in fun." "But I gave you everything."

24 "Well, you shouldn't have done it. You know what a fellow thinks

25 When a girl does that." "Yes, he talks of her over his drinks

26 And calls her a—" "Stop that now. I thought you knew."

27 "But it wasn't with anyone else. It was only you."

28 "How did I know? I thought you wanted it too.

29 I thought you were like the rest. Well, what's to be done?"

30 "To be done?" "Is it all right?" "Yes." "Sure?" "Yes, but why?"

31 "I don't know. I thought you were going to cry.

32 You said you had something to tell me." "Yes, I know.

33 It wasn't anything really . . . I think I'll go."

34 "Yes, it's late. There's thunder about, a drop of rain

35 Fell on my hand in the dark. I'll see you again

36 At the dance next week. You're sure that everything's right?"

37 "Yes." "Well, I'll be going." "Kiss me . . ." "Good night." . . . "Good night."

Agents. (Note: Line numbers are in parentheses.) This poem presents a young woman who speaks first and last, and a young man who defensively and sometimes flippantly answers her questions. They have been sexually intimate; their dialogue reveals that it was her first experience (24) but not his (29). She says she thought he loved her (12), but he makes it clear that he was not serious (1, 11, 18, 23) and thought she knew this (11, 24, 26).

They are probably working class or lower middle class, from a farming community or small town in which "loose" girls in the 1920s would get bad reputations. We learn that he drinks, they both like to dance, and he knows her brothers. She's probably attractive, but not beautiful. She seems to have pretty hair and enjoys dressing up. He seems more self-confident of the two; he is clearly less emotionally involved in the conversation.

Act. She has initiated the meeting to tell him something important (32). There is no real introduction; instead, the poem abruptly opens with her words, " 'I thought you loved me,' " to which he responds, " 'No, it was only fun.' " His explanations are shallow, and he blames her for tempting him: " 'you shouldn't have danced that way' " (7). She protests against his accusatory tone (8, 12). Then they both admit "it's done" (12).

The tension rises when she gives examples of boyish cruelty (13–15), which he lamely defends (16). But she rejects his explanation; she wants him to be different: " 'Not you! Not you!' " (17). His defensiveness continues as he explains it away—"they" are playing "a game" (18).

She matches his impersonal tone to ask the loaded question, " 'And are girls fun, too?' " (19). Like a fool, he starts to explain "what it's like to have a girl" but, realizing the potential for misunderstanding, he falters until she demands, "'Go on'" (20). Tension builds as he describes sexual conquests that were "only in fun" (23).

This triggers the climax. She reveals her vulnerability: "'But I gave you everything'" (23). And he blames her again: "'you shouldn't have.'" Tension peaks (24–26) when they discuss "'what a fellow thinks/When a girl does that.' 'Yes, he talks of her over his drinks/And calls her a—' 'Stop that now.'" At this, her hopes are dashed, although she once again protests (27). The final blow comes when he lumps her in with "the rest" of his conquests (29).

After that, the dialogue winds down: "Well, what's to be done?" (29) This question must hit her hard; it is clear she means nothing to him, and she withdraws. There are parting questions, "'Is it all right?' 'Yes.' 'Sure?'" (30) and one final "'why?'" (30). Before leaving, he says, "'You said you had something to tell me'" (32). But it's too late; she refuses to share her secret with him. (Their past history and her refusal to confide in him after this exchange imply that she is pregnant, but this is not explicitly stated.) Sure, there's a polite "'I'll see you again at the dance next week'" (35–36), but she knows it's a pleasantry; she has been grouped with "the rest." They part with a final, perfunctory kiss.

Scene. The title reveals that they meet in an orchard, probably in a small, rural community where a weekly dance is a popular activity. The trees provide privacy and suggest that her news is important. As they talk, it turns dark, and it is starting to rain (34–35). They're discussing a tryst that took place after a late summer or early autumn dance—he refers to the "harvest moon" (2). We can't tell how much time has elapsed, but she has initiated the meeting to tell him something (36). If she is pregnant, this meeting probably takes place about six or eight weeks later.

The language indicates that this poem is set early in the 20th century. For example, he uses the word "fellow" (24), which is less common today, and uses "queer" to describe the moonlight in her hair (3). They both refer to young adults as "boys" and "girls." It's now more acceptable for both sexes to be sexually active; the stigma she faces reflects earlier norms.

Agency. The poem is organized chronologically, with events unfolding in time. Because it's entirely made up of conversation (and is thus in the dramatic mode), the language is the most important aspect of agency. The poet doesn't separate the speakers by giving each a new line, as is common in drama; instead, their words follow on the same line. Only the quotation marks show where one speaker begins and the other ends.

The sentences and phrases are short, which is typical of informal conversations. At significant points the boy's words trail off, making him appear reluctant and unsure of what to say. Her flow breaks twice, once during the story of the kitten's drowning (14) and again when she decides to leave and dismisses what she wanted to tell him (33).

The questions are interesting. She asks seven questions in the first 19 lines (four come in the first five lines) to get him to talk. She is trying to reassure herself and calm her fears. Only after the climax (24–27) does he ask his first

---

STOP AND CHECK: Do a Dramatistic Analysis

Do a dramatistic analysis of one of your texts. Write a three- to five-page paper analyzing the act, actor, scene, purpose, and agency. Then read Chapter 5 and identify specific performance strategies that your analysis suggests.

---

question. The tables have turned; he must now keep the conversation going and is now the one who needs reassurance. Is it significant that, instead of asking "Everything's <u>all</u> right?" (36), he only asks, "Everything's right"? (Does he perhaps suspect a pregnancy?)

He interrupts once, stopping her before she says what girls are called who do "that" (27). Throughout the poem, they use the word "it" for what they've done. In fact, she has a hard time being direct; she doesn't say "I love you;" instead, she uses the past tense, "I loved you" (9).

Purpose. The woman's purpose or desire is to be loved and respected by her first lover and to tell him something significant. Although she'd like to deny that he felt "it was only fun" (1), the subtext of his side of the conversation quickly reveals his lack of romantic feelings. Each shallow reason he presents, each repetition of "fun" makes her realize he does not care for her. But she hopes for his respect and affection, so she repeats one variation or another of the theme, "You're the only one" (10, 12, 27). This illusion, too, is shattered when he categorizes her with "the rest" (29). Given this rejection, she refuses to divulge her secret.

The boy, on the other hand, is uncomfortable with being called out. He tries to blame her (7–9, 24–25) or excuse his behavior (2–3, 5–6). He may not have meant to hurt her, but he certainly doesn't love her, and he wants her to know that.

Stuart wrote this poem in the 1920s, perhaps to protest the sexual "double standard." Men could be sexually active and have their exploits dismissed as "sowing their wild oats" or "boys will be boys." Women, in contrast, were disgraced and ostracized for being sexually available. And woe to the unmarried woman who found herself pregnant!

A thorough dramatistic analysis such as this helps you identify where to pause, where to read more softly, and where to increase your volume. You could have the girl drop her gaze (12) and fix him with a cold stare (20). You could speak lines 13–15 with intensity and lines 25–26 in cold fury through clenched teeth. "Not you! Not you!" (17) would be louder and "Yes, I know./It wasn't anything really . . . I think I'll go" (32–33) would be calmer and softer.

In short, the pentad is an analytic method that you can apply to a wide variety of texts, including prose, poetry, and drama. It is especially useful for examining narratives or stories that feature characters acting in specific situations.

TRANSTEXTUAL ANALYSIS

During the 20th century, several literary critics shifted focus from the texts' creators, goals, and intentions to the texts themselves, examining the interrelationships of a text with the other texts that exist within an overarching cultural framework.[26] Put another way, a text (defined broadly) is part of a larger discourse or set of conversations within a culture; discovering those relationships is at least as valuable as looking at the who, what, when, where, why, and how of modal and dramatistic analysis.

Gerard Gennett, a contemporary French theorist and scholar, proposed the **theory of transtextuality.** This theory is useful for analyzing "everything that brings a text into relation (manifest or hidden) with other texts."[27] Gennett identifies five elements of transtextual analysis: intertextuality, paratexts, metatexts, hypo- or hypertexts, and architextual relations. A thorough transtextual analysis lends light on the culture and discourse in which the text emerged and where it exists.

Intertextuality

Intertextuality is a term coined by the French philosopher Julia Kristeva. The prefix *inter* literally means *between* or *among.* Kristeva used *intertextuality* to refer to structural relations between and among texts, in other words, to the presence of other texts within a text itself. You can think of intertextuality as a dialogue between an interwoven mosaic of texts that sometimes blend, sometimes clash. These interwoven texts can be literary, cultural, or personal. Closely examine your literary selection for intertextuality, such as references to other literary works, visual arts like paintings or films, and cultural memories, traditions, and events.[28] Be aware of direct quotations, paraphrases, even plagiarism, which is a type of intertextuality. In addition, consider the stories and activities—the texts—within your personal experiences that are interwoven with the work you have chosen.

The play *Anna in the Tropics* is rich in intertextual elements. In even the brief cutting on pages 59 and 60, Cruz alludes to at least two texts: Jose Marti's revolutionary works and Shakespeare's plays. In addition, the play's title refers to the literary character Anna Karenina, and the entire drama is crafted around Leo Tolstoy's novel of the same name. In the play itself, the lector reads eight sections directly from the novel. Consequently, the fictional Anna, her husband, and her lover become vivid in Conchita's and Palomo's minds, and the adventures of Tolstoy's characters influence Conchita to confront her husband about his infidelity.

Finally, consider the personal texts you bring to the play. Each individual has potential personal connections to Cruz's drama. One audience member might follow news reports about Cuba; another might deplore the Cuban boycott; still another might subscribe to the magazine *Cigar Aficionado.* Other demographic categories can also be salient. A Latina, a working-class listener, an Idahoan, and a divorced man will all bring distinctive perspectives to the piece of literature.

Paratexts

The second element, **paratexts** (*para* means *beside*), are all the devices and conventions that stand alongside the actual poem, story, or play and function to mediate the text to the reader. They include materials such as titles, subtitles, captions, and prefaces, as well as stage directions, footnotes and endnotes. Author notes on each scene are additional paratexts that invite study, as are abstracts and key words, which summarize the work's major themes. The author's name may also be a paratext that stands alongside the text. For instance, just the name "Shakespeare" or "Toni Morrison" can suggest what type of text it is or what the overall subject might be.

Both Cruz and the play's editors provide paratextual information for *Anna in the Tropics*, including a history of its productions, notes on the characters (Conchita is the 32-year-old daughter of a cigar factory owner; Palomo is her 41-year-old husband), notes on the play's time and place (Tampa, Florida, 1929), the setting (an old warehouse), and the costumes (clean, well-pressed, and starched white linen clothes). In addition, Cruz provides a "Playwright's Note" that informs the reader that lectors and cigar rollers were removed from factories after 1931 and replaced by cigar-rolling machines. The title *Anna in the Tropics* alerts you to the play's setting and highlights its major theme: the life-changing potential of literature.

Cruz dedicates the play to Janice Paran, whose advice helped him restructure Act II. The back cover provides a short summary of the play and an introduction to the playwright. Although he may never be world famous, Nilo Cruz is establishing a name for himself as one of the best up-and-coming Latino playwrights. You can read about some of his accomplishments in notes found at the end of the play itself and on the back cover.

Metatexts

Metatexts (*meta* means *after*) are materials in a third category. They include comments and opinions composed by someone other than the author after the text is written. Literary or theater critics produce metatexts when they review a novel, play, screenplay, or book of poetry by putting each work into context and commenting on its merit or lack thereof. Both professional and lay critics summarize the contents, identify themes, compare the work to others like it, and state their opinions. Remember that a review is just one person's opinion; the very same text that brings raves from one critic may be panned by others.

A text often provides excerpts from positive reviews. You can find additional reviews and commentaries online or in magazines, newspapers, or literary journals. For example, Karren Alenier illuminates some aspects of *Anna* in an online review:[29]

The lector, who often dressed elegantly and was seated like royalty on an elevated chair in the middle of the factory, was not only the factory workers' escape from boredom, but also their teacher about the world. In today's terms, the lector was like a rock star who could influence not only what listeners knew about getting along with people, especially the opposite sex, but also their political views.

The play's back cover includes an excerpt from a *Miami Herald* review with phrases such as "shimmeringly beautiful." To find your own reviews, search on Google for the exact phrase "Anna in the Tropics."

Hypotexts and Hypertexts

In Gennett's terminology, **hypotexts** are the foundational or preceding texts that a second work, the **hypertext,** elaborates on or transforms. (*Hypo* means *under* and *hyper* means *over*.) For instance, J. R. R. Tolkein's *The Hobbit* precedes his **sequel**, *The Lord of the Rings*; Mary Shelley's *Frankenstein* is the hypotext for the **spoof** *Young Frankenstein;* and a **translation** of Victor Hugo's *Les Miserables* is the English hypertext of the original.

Cruz builds on Tolstoy's *Anna Karenina* as his hypotext. Tolstoy's plot, detailing an affair within the Russian nobility and its consequences, is echoed among Cruz's working-class Cuban characters in a south Florida cigar factory. Knowing about the tragedy that befalls Anna because of her relationship to the two men in her life provides us with clues about the infidelities that develop throughout this play. Both Anna's and Conchita's stories build on universal human narratives of betrayal and disaster.

Architexts

Architexts (*archi* means *earlier* or *primitive*) are links between the text and the various types of discourse to which it belongs. Literary genres include prose, poetry, and drama. Those broad categories are further subdivided into fictional and nonfictional prose; lyric, narrative, or epic poetry; and dramatic tragedies, comedies, or blends of the two. These categories can also be subdivided. For examples, there are romantic comedies, dark comedies, satiric comedies, and so on.

Characters can be categorized as **stock figures,** character types that commonly appear in specific genres. In medieval romantic sagas, beautiful damsels in distress were rescued by knights in shining armor who galloped to their rescue. In contemporary war dramas, courageous soldiers become brothers as a result of their foxhole experiences; a pretty nurse often hovers at the bedside of a fallen hero. Science fiction features mad scientists and intrepid time travelers. Westerns feature hired guns, kindly madams, outlaws, and incorruptible sheriffs.

Archetypes are more fundamental than stock figures. They are the symbols, themes, or characters that appear and reappear in myths, dreams, rituals, and folklore across the globe. They probably derive from early explanations of natural processes such as birth, death, seasonal changes, and weather. For instance, the

---

STOP AND CHECK: Do a Transtextual Analysis

Do a transtextual analysis of one of the texts you have chosen to perform. Write a three- to five-page paper analyzing elements of intertextuality, paratexts, metatexts, hypo- or hypertexts, and architextual relations. Then identify specific performance strategies that your analysis suggests.

---

color green signifies life and red symbolizes passion across many cultural groups. Jealous older men married to beautiful young women are archetypal characters, as are kings, warriors, magicians, wicked stepmothers, and wise women.

Anna in the Tropics is in the drama genre: It is a tragedy, not a comedy; its themes include infidelity, the transformative power of literature, and the end of a way of life. Arguably, Conchita and Palomo are archetypes of the wandering husband and the wronged wife.

In summary, you can use Gerard Gennett's theory of transtextuality as a method of textual analysis. Explore your text's relationship to other texts, both personal and private (intertextuality); gain information from within the text itself (paratexts); learn what others say about it (metatexts); search for foundational texts (hypor- or hypertexts); and understand the discourse genre it belongs to as well as its type of characters (architexts).

ANALYSIS THROUGH PERFORMANCE

Ronald Pelias, a professor at Southern Illinois University, suggests that you explore the characters and situations within your text through performance, through "letting others live through [your] own voice and body."[31] For example, invite first Conchita and then Palermo into your mind. Make their thoughts and emotions yours; move the way they move, and speak as they speak. To accomplish this challenge, use Pelias's five-step process for exploring each persona: playing, testing, choosing, repeating, and presenting.

Playing

Approach your piece with a playful attitude. This means being flexible and creative, willing to try a range of possible vocal and bodily behaviors. Let's say you decide to perform "In the Orchard." Start by letting the girl come to life through your body and voice. Do things she that would do—try everyday movements such as walking across a room, brushing her hair, or dancing. Get to know her posture and her vocal characteristics. Try out different vocal variations for her; give her an accent or make her pensive, then flirty, thoughtful, or perky. Act as she would act around her brothers and around the boy. After you are comfortable with your knowledge of her characteristics, give the boy the same treatment. Have him walk, dance, laugh with his friends. Stand him

---

PERFORMING CULTURE: Alternative Ways to Analyze Literature

The analysis strategies this chapter presents are all common in Western cultural settings. However, these are only a few methods of analysis. A Marxist critic would examine the power relations inherent in the text. In Cruz's play, for example, the factory owners arguably keep their workers willing to work in unjust working conditions by providing a lector, whose fictional stories lull them into ignoring harsh economic realities. They are trapped by the profit motives of capitalism, an oppressive system. Womanist critics analyze texts from the perspective of feminists of color.[30] Go to www.press.uchicago.edu/cgi-bin/hfs.cgi/00/12952.ctl and read a review of Nigerian author Chikwenye Okonjo Ogunyemi's book, *African Wo/Man Palava: The Nigerian Novel by Women*. Identify some characteristics of African womanist thought listed there. How might a womanist critic approach a text such as "In the Orchard" or *The Color of Water*?

---

up and sit him down. Try out vocal variations, gestures, and facial expressions that he might use.

Playing is a lot like brainstorming. During this stage, release your inhibitions and try out your intuitions. Don't automatically reject ideas that may seem silly or outrageous at first. Wonder, "What if?"

Testing

After you are thoroughly familiar with both characters, try out performance ideas that came to you during your literary analysis. It is in the testing stage that you decide how to use your voice and body to speak specific lines effectively. For example, how exactly should the girl look at the boy as she talks about the blackbird and kitten? Would a slight sideways glance work best? Or would it be more effective to gaze steadily and directly at him? Should he be cocky and direct? Should he dart glances at her or become visibly concerned when she withdraws at the end? Now is the time to test whether or not talking through clenched teeth accompanied by a cold stare would really work for lines 25–26. Try out your ideas for both characters as they progress through the gamut of emotions.

Experiment with a number of ways to perform the same character. For instance, portray the young woman as submissive and helpless and the young man as unwilling to let her cling to him. In a second reading, perform her as a spunky girl with a problem but a lot of inner strength, and portray the boy as a real cad who seduces her and leaves her. One student portrayed her as a maniacal girl who could barely conceal her outrage; she seemed capable of committing either murder or suicide. He, in contrast, was played as a fairly naïve, rather klutzy guy who happened to seduce someone who was very unstable. By the poem's end, he was portrayed as terrified by what she might do to express her rage.

Test small sections at a time; for example, just have the girl tell the story of the blackbird and the kitten (13–15). Nothing else. Try out several performance possibilities for just that segment of the poem. Then move on to another few lines, and develop interpretation of the dialogue in that small section. Finally, put a few sections together and consider the overall effect of various interpretations.

Choosing

You have played with characterizations and tested ways to perform specific lines. Now, decide which ideas you've tested seem most appropriate, given the text, your audience, and your skills. Commit yourself to a particular interpretation, but make choices that you can perform consistently. (For example, do not give a character an Irish brogue if you cannot consistently maintain that accent for three minutes, let alone ten!) The physical and vocal characteristics you choose regarding one character will affect your choices for other characters. For instance, if you portray the girl in the orchard as maniacal, you will almost inevitably portray the boy as cautious and fearful of what she might do to him.

This is the turning point in analysis through performance. After you make your choices, develop those choices throughout your entire performance. Consistency is vital if your characters and personae are to be believable.

Repeating

This is another way of saying: Rehearse, rehearse, rehearse. Go over your piece—one section at a time and as a whole—and incorporate the vocal and bodily decisions you have made. Use familiarization techniques, explained in Chapter 6. Of course, you can always refine and hone your performance, making a pause just a bit longer, adding a short intake of breath to indicate fear, using a little more nasality in an older character's voice and slightly more breathiness in a younger voice, and so on. This stage is vital because the more you repeat, the better you will know the text, the more consistently you will perform your characters, and the more confident you will be.

Presenting

The final step is to perform your choices before an audience. In the classroom, this will include feedback both during and after you perform. Your classmates will tell you whether they accept and validate your interpretation. You will be able to discern whether your choices did what you intended—your comical character was comical (or not), your depressed person actually sounded depressed (or not). Your characters should be understandable and believable from beginning to end. Your portrayal of emotion should make sense, given the characters and the situation.

Your interpretive decisions should be obvious to the audience, whose responses may vary from wild applause to polite boredom. If listeners seem bored or confused, you will know you got something wrong. Perhaps they

---

STOP AND CHECK: Analyze a Videotaped Performance

Watch a videotaped performance of a literary text. How consistently did the performer convey the author's intent? How believable was the performance?

Did it engage you? Stretch your imagination? If so, how? Why? How would you perform the same piece?

---

were unable to identify with the characters or the situation, or maybe your introduction failed to explain important background details. Perhaps you overestimated your personal performance skills and were unable to perform as you intended. Or you may have failed to interpret what you discerned in the piece. If they listened intently, seemed engaged with the ideas in the text, and said positive things about your choice of a text and your portrayal of the emotions and ideas in the text, you can be assured that you made some right decisions. Whatever the reasons for success or failure, performance is a method of analysis that helps you better understand a literary text.

SUMMARY

This chapter discussed four major ways to analyze your text in order to interpret it effectively. A modal analysis explores the literature in terms of who is doing the speaking and to whom the ideas are addressed. In lyric mode, the persona is single, undefined, and uncharacterized. Lyric personae are self-reflective; they may address themselves, an object or thing, a specific other, or a general audience. Speaking in the timeless present, they convey thoughts that seem as fresh now as when they were created. In the dramatic mode, the characters directly address other characters using the present tense, generally in a conflict situation. The plot and action unfold through the lines of dialogue. The epic mode is a combination of the lyric and the dramatic modes. A narrator fills in details about the setting and the characters (lyric mode), but the characters break into dialogue throughout the text (dramatic mode). Modal analysis is particularly helpful for determining appropriate places to focus during your performance.

Dramatistic analysis explores five elements of the text in depth. You probe for information about the agent or agents who perform the action (who), the act or happenings in the plot (what), the scene or setting (where and when), the agency or means to accomplish the act (how), and the purpose of the piece (why). Dramatistic analysis will help you better understand the characters and their motivations, and your interpretation will be richer as a result.

Transtextual analysis explores the relationship between your text and other texts. Intertextuality traces the structural relationships between texts by identifying the presence of other texts within the text. Authors provide paratexts, or author-composed materials such as titles, prefaces, and stage directions that help you better understand the work. Metatexts are what others say about the texts; they are the opinions and commentaries expressed by readers and listeners, both professional and lay critics. Hypotexts are foundational texts that underlie a derivative hypertext. Architexts are the links to the types and genres, or the themes, stock figures, and other literary forms to which the text belongs.

By testing performance possibilities, you can probe additional ways to present your text. Experiment with potential characterizations, test a variety of interpretive possibilities, and choose the ones that best convey the meanings you have uncovered in other types of analysis. Repeat these steps through rehearsal, and then present your interpretation to an audience. Use audience feedback to determine whether your analysis was believable and your performance had integrity.

KEY TERMS

modal analysis	epic mode	theory of transtextuality
personae	pentad	intertextuality
speaker mode	agent	paratexts
audience mode	co-agent	metatexts
uncharacterized	counteragent	hypotexts
lyric mode	act	hypertexts
timeless present	scene	architexts
dramatic mode	purpose	
defined characters	subtext	

QUESTIONS AND EXERCISES

1. Select one of the sample texts provided at the end of Chapters 7 to 9, and analyze it by using modal or dramatistic techniques.

2. Choose a text from the "Pieces I Like" list you started in Chapter 1. Do a modal, dramatistic, or transtextual analysis that will prepare you to perform the piece in class.

3. Analyze a popular movie that was based on a play, using transtextual analysis. How true is the movie to the play? What has the filmmaker left out or changed? What "credits" help you understand it better? What did film critics say about it? To which movie genre does it belong? Which characters, if any, are stock characters?

4. Log onto InfoTrac College Edition and search for article A92049116 by Margarete Landwehr (Summer 2002, *College Literature*). It's a technical article about the concept of intertextuality. Read the definition of intertextuality, as well as the section on its origins. According to Landwehr, dialogue takes place among various texts, writers, addressees (or characters), the contemporary context, and earlier cultural contexts. How does this concept compare and contrast with the types of analysis described in this chapter?

5. Choose a simple but familiar children's book. Go through the first three steps described in "Analysis through Performance": playing, testing, and choosing. Try out a number of possible performance strategies.

5

Using Your Voice
and Body

This chapter will help you:

- Describe a number of vocal variations

- Practice using vocal variations to create characters and to highlight varied moods and meanings

- Divide a text into meaningful phrases

- Describe several aspects of facial expressions and bodily movements

- Practice using facial expressions and bodily movements to portray emotions

- Practice integrating physical and vocal variety in interpretations

- Define terms related to focus: onstage focus, offstage focus, inner-closed focus, semi-closed focus, character placement, and closed focus

- Practice various types of focus and character placement

"Would you like some wine too, sir?" I asked, glancing up.

He was leaning against the cupboard that surrounded the bed . . . He looked back and forth between Catharina and me. On his face was his painter's look.

"Silly girl, you've spilled wine on me!" Catharina pushed away from the table and brushed at her belly with her hand. A few drops of red had splashed there.

"I'm sorry, madam. I'll get a damp cloth to sponge it."

"Oh, never mind. I can't bear to have you fussing about me. Just go."

I stole a look at him as I picked up the tray. His eyes were fixed on his wife's pearl earring. As she turned her head to brush more powder on her face the earring swung back and forth, caught in the light from the front windows. It made us all look at her face . . .[1]

The characters in this book, *Girl with a Pearl Earring,* glance up, lean backwards, look back and forth, push away, and brush on face powder. Similarly, your characters will move, interact, and react to one another, revealing their thoughts and emotions through their eyes, their facial expressions, their posture and gestures. Consider, for example, how different this scene would be if the girl glanced at the floor instead of glancing up or if she stared at the man instead of stealing a look. Characters also convey their meanings by a repertoire of vocal possibilities, such as raising their voices, whispering, pausing, moaning, or shrieking.

This chapter discusses many vocal and physical elements that you can use to make your performances more realistic and convincing. Although these elements are presented separately here, in reality you will constantly integrate vocal variations and bodily movements to bring your texts to life.

VOCAL EXPRESSIVENESS

Test your skill at creating the following characters. Say the phrase "I need you to help me" five times, each time speaking as the character would:

- A Mafia godfather
- That annoying used car salesperson on television
- A celebrity of your choice
- A nagging child
- Someone who has a really bad cold

To create each character, you adjusted your rate of speech, volume, pitch, and so on. In this section, we will examine several important vocal variables that suggest personality traits, express emotion, and help you create more effective oral performances.

Rate and Volume

Your **rate** is the speed at which you talk. A normal rate, the one used by readers of books on tape or by video narrators, is about 150–160 words per minute.[2] However, some people naturally speak more rapidly, and others speak more slowly. Age, mental attitude, emotional state, and region of origin are all factors that influence a speaker's rate. Some situations lend themselves to a slower rate; others call for faster speech. In this example of speedy speaking from the children's book *The Wind in the Willows,*[3] Rat approaches Mole while carrying a wicker basket and rattling off a list of its contents:

"What's inside it?" asked the Mole, wriggling with curiosity.

"There's cold chicken inside it," replied the Rat briefly; "coldtonguecold-hamcoldbeefpickledgherkinssaladfrenchrollscresssandwichespottedmeatgin-gerbeerlemonadesodawater—"

"O stop, stop," cried the Mole . . . "This is too much!"

In your characterizations, pay attention to **speech flow,** which is the rate plus the number and duration of **pauses,** or temporary breaks of varying length. Some characters speak haltingly; their word flow is punctuated with starts, stops, and stuttering.[4] Others' words flow fluently and smoothly. A character's state of mind often influences his or her speech flow; halts and stammering suggest uncertainty, whereas fluency is associated with self-confidence. Here's an example from Susan Glaspell's play *Suppressed Desires,* which pokes fun at Freudian psychology. Henrietta, a disciple of psychoanalysis, sees her husband Stephen just after he's visited her psychiatrist. Pair up with a partner in class and read the excerpt aloud, and then discuss how the pauses reflect each character's state of mind:[5]

Henrietta: And what did he say?

Steve: He said—I—I was a little surprised by what he said, Henrietta.

Henrietta: [*Breathlessly.*] Of course—one can so seldom anticipate. But tell me—your dream, Stephen? It means—?

Steve: It means—I was considerably surprised by what it means.

Henrietta: *Don't* be so exasperating!

Steve: It means—you really want to know, Henrietta?

Henrietta: Stephen, you'll drive me mad!

Steve: He said—of course he may be wrong in what he said.

Henrietta: He *isn't* wrong. *Tell* me.

Steve: He said my dream of the walls receding and leaving me alone in a forest indicates a suppressed desire—

Henrietta: Yes—yes!

Steve: To be freed from—

Henrietta: Yes—freed from—?

Steve: Marriage.

Henrietta: [*Crumples. Stares.*] Marriage!

Steve: He—he may be mistaken, you know.

Henrietta: *May* be mistaken?

Steve: I—well, of course, I hadn't taken any stock in it myself. It was only your great confidence— . . .

Henrietta: Did he know who you were?

Steve: Yes.

Henrietta: That you were married to me?

Steve: Yes, he knew that.

Henrietta: And he told you to leave me?

Steve: It seems he must be wrong, Henrietta.

Volume, loudness or softness, ranges from shouting to whispering. Our moods and the situations we're in lead us to turn up or tone down our volume.[6] For example, a man who yells angrily at an umpire's bad call will speak softly during a romantic dinner with his love interest. If you need to whisper, use a **stage whisper,** which is loud enough to be heard.

The following excerpt from the novel *Bel Canto*[7] is set at a party in a South American country. Mr. Hosokawa, a wealthy Japanese businessman, and Gen, his interpreter, have just been entertained by a famous opera singer. The lights suddenly go out, and the partygoers are taken hostage by terrorists. Read through the excerpt aloud, and discuss how to vary your rate and volume interpretation with a small group of your classmates.

"There will be a request for ransom," Mr. Hosokawa told Gen. They were both watching Roxane and her accompanist now, thinking at several points that the accompanist was dead, but then he would shift or sigh. "It is Nansei's policy to pay ransom, any ransom. They'll pay it for both of us." He could speak in his smallest voice, a sound too minimal to ever be called a whisper, and still Gen understood him perfectly. "They will pay it for her as well. It would only be fitting. She is here on my account." . . . Mr. Hosokawa sighed. Actually, in some sense, everyone in the room was here on his account and he wondered what such a ransom could add up to. "I feel that I have brought this on us."

"You are not holding a gun," Gen said. The sound of their own Japanese spoken so softly it could not have been heard twelve centimeters away, comforted them. "It was the President they meant to take last night."

"I wish they had him," Mr. Hosokawa said.

Pitch Variation

Pitch is your tone, the high or low sound of your voice. **Pitch variation,** sometimes called **inflection,** involves using rising or falling tones. Using no pitch variation results in a **monotone.** A loud monotone conveys anger, and a soft monotone communicates boredom or illness.

A rising intonation at the end of a sentence signals a question (I'm going, too?); a falling intonation indicates a declarative sentence (I'm going, too.). However, some people consistently end their sentences with a rising intonation, even when they are not asking a question. This phenomenon is called **uptalk** or **High Rise Terminals (HRTs)**.[8] Here's what Sabrina sounded like when she called me one day: "Dr. Jaffe? I'm Sabrina? I'm in your 9:00 class? I have a question?" Uptalk made her seem tentative and uncertain. Compare that to the impression I'd had if she had said, "Dr. Jaffe? I'm Sabrina. I'm in your 9:00 class, and I have a question."

Range includes all the tones your voice can make, from the highest pitches to the lowest rumbling tones. Although men have lower voices and women higher, male and female voices overlap in the middle pitch ranges. You almost instinctively use different parts of your range to portray adult men (low), adult women (higher), and children (high).

The opening paragraph of the following story, "Orientation,"[9] shows one character explaining office procedures to a new employee. As the story progresses, the new hire realizes that she has joined a completely dysfunctional group and that her guide is not exactly normal. Try a variety of vocal variations to portray the guide. For instance, speak softly and use a monotone pitched in your lower range; another time, speak rapidly and use a lot of inflection in a higher pitched voice. Or try speaking very rapidly, but pause after each sentence.

> Those are the offices and these are the cubicles. That's my cubicle there, and this is your cubicle. This is your phone. Never answer your phone. Let the Voicemail System answer it. This is your Voicemail System Manual. There are no personal phone calls allowed. We do, however, allow for emergencies. If you must make an emergency phone call, ask your supervisor first. If you can't find your supervisor, ask Phillip Spiers, who sits over there. He'll check with Clarissa Nicks, who sits over there. If you make an emergency phone call without asking, you may be let go.

Duration

Duration, or **extent,** is how long sounds, syllables, or words are held. Extended sounds result in a **drawl,** which is typical of speech in parts of the American South. In contrast, **clipping,** or **fast pitch drops,** are sharply cut off sounds at the end of words. In the United States, clipped tones typically indicate anger and irritation. For example, remember when you were little and you'd ignore your mom's request until she said:

"I | said | come | inside |"

She spoke very precisely, with the end of each word cut off sharply. You knew then that she was really serious, and you'd better head in—the sooner the better! In the following scene from *The Secret Life of Bees,* Sue Monk Kidd indicates angry, clipped tones by her punctuation. Read the scene aloud, clipping the words, "Leave. Her. Alone.":[10]

> I saw her running across the room. Running at him, yelling, "Leave. Her. Alone." . . . I saw him take her by the shoulders and shake her, her head

bouncing back and forth. I saw the whiteness of his lip. And then—though everything starts to blur now in my mind—she lunged away from him into the closet, away from his grabbing hands, scrambling for something high on a shelf. When I saw the gun in her hand, I ran toward her, clumsy and falling, wanting to save her, to save us all.

Clipped speech generally evokes a negative or defensive response in the recipient, and fast drops in pitch can signal an escalating argument. However, if one character in your text is angry but another wants to defuse or deescalate the argument, try using clipped tones for the first character and slower speech for the second.

Stress

Volume, rate, pitch, and duration are linked to **stress,** or emphasis. Stress occurs when some words or parts of words are spoken louder, slower, or at a different pitch than others. It is an important indication of your interpretation of a literary passage. For example, the poem *Warning* by Jenny Joseph[11] opens with the lines, "When I am an old woman I shall wear purple/With a red hat which doesn't go, and doesn't suit me." Examine how different stress patterns suggest different aspects of the speaker's personality:

> When *I* am an old woman *I* shall wear purple
> With a red hat which doesn't go, and doesn't suit me.

Emphasizing *I* suggests that she is comparing herself to women whom she considers too sedate and too proper.

> When I am an *old* woman I shall wear purple
> With a red hat which doesn't go, and doesn't suit me.

In this interpretation, the speaker focuses on her age. She doesn't yet consider herself old, but we don't know her age; she could be anywhere from 30 to 70. We do know that she is planning a defiant response to the aging process.

> When I am an old woman I shall wear *purple*
> With a *red* hat which doesn't go, and doesn't suit me.

By having the speaker emphasize the colors, you portray her resistance to conventions. Older, more "mature" women commonly wear subdued pastels in harmonious shades; she is defying this expectation. (This poem provided the impetus for the Red Hat Society, described in the Performing Culture feature.)

Authors often italicize or capitalize words to indicate stress. Exclamation points are another cue. Here's an example from Cristina Garcia's novel *Dreaming in Cuban.*[13] Read it aloud, using the cues Garcia provides:

> Mom has decided she wants me to paint a mural for her second Yankee Doodle Bakery.
>
> "I want a big painting like the Mexicans do, but pro-American," she specifies.

PERFORMING CULTURE: The Red Hat Society

Literature can contribute to changes within individuals and in society. Older Americans are often ignored or rendered invisible; American culture values youth over age. However, thousands of baby boomers enter the "over 50" category every day. Poets, prose writers, diarists, and dramatists consistently grapple with the theme of aging, and their insights help others better enact this process.

Sue Ellen Cooper of Fullerton, California, and some of her close friends read Jenny Joseph's "Warning" and, on a whim, went out to tea wearing red hats and purple dresses. They enjoyed themselves so much that they invited more friends and called themselves the Red Hat Society. A friend in Florida learned of their gatherings and started her own group. Their story was picked up by a magazine, which resulted in more societies being formed. Now, all across the United States are chapters of this "disorganization," whose major purpose is for women over 50 to have fun as they defy conventions and counter stereotypes by aging with humor and fun.[12]

You can read more about the Red Hat Society by logging onto the Internet and accessing www.redhatsociety. com. To read the entire poem, go to http://www.ladyjayes.com/oldwoman. html.

"You want to commission *me* to paint something for *you?*"

"*Si,* Pilar. You're a painter, no? So paint!"

"You've got to be kidding."

"Painting is painting, no?"

"Look, Mom, I don't think you understand. I don't *do* bakeries."

"You're embarrassed?" My bakery is not good enough for you?"

"It's not that."

"This bakery paid for your painting classes."

"It has nothing to do with that, either."

"If Michelangelo were alive today, he wouldn't be so proud."

"Mom, believe me, Michelangelo would definitely *not* be painting bakeries."

"Don't be so sure. Most artists are starving. They don't have all the advantages like you. They take heroin to forget."

Diction

Pronunciation is how individual sounds and whole words are said. Whenever you have a question about pronunciation, consult your dictionary for standard as well as variant, but acceptable, ways to say the word. For example, the word *data* is acceptably pronounced as "DAY-tuh" or "DATT-uh." However, "DAY-tuh" is listed first in most American dictionaries, indicating that it is the preferred pronunciation.

Articulation is how the sounds are actually said. The human voice can articulate hundreds of sounds, and each language or dialect uses a somewhat different set. An accent results when a speaker of one language learns a new language but keeps some of the sounds of his or her native speech. For example, many languages do not use the *th* sound. That's why you'll hear foreign speakers say *dis* for *this* or *ze* for *the*. Other variations, like the vowel sound in *thoity* for *thirty,* characterize a regional accent, such as Brooklynese. Children sometimes **lisp** or substitute *th* for *s* (*thmile* for *smile*); they may substitute *w* for *r* or *l* (*wadio* for *radio; wike* for *like*).

A **dialect** is a distinctive form of pronunciation, language structure, and vocabulary that is identified with a geographical area or a social class.[14] The British pronounce some sounds differently than the Irish, and they both use different pronunciations than Australians (for example, *I say* may sound like more like *Oy sigh* in one dialect). In some dialects, speakers reverse sounds; saying *aks* for *ask* is common. If your character speaks a dialect of English, try to incorporate the dialect's characteristic patterns into your interpretation.

Another aspect of articulation is precision and clarity in speaking. You can clearly enunciate every sound of the following sentence: *What are you doing?* Or you can slur some of the sounds together: *Whuhchuh doon?* In all English-speaking countries, women tend to pronounce more precisely (*going*) than men (*goin'*).[15] Formal situations call for more precise enunciation: The president giving the State of the Union address, a doctor holding a press conference, or a teenager doing a workshop on peer counseling all generally enunciate carefully. In contrast, the same person in informal, personal situations is less precise. Teens catching up on gossip, the doctor talking to herself, or the president speaking to his children may slur or drop sounds.

Practice diction with this excerpt from Murray Schisgal's play *Extensions:*[16]

Betsy: . . . We used to know thousands of people, literally and actually thousands of people.

[*They pronounce each name with great deliberation and enjoyment.*]

Bob: Do you remember Mr. and Mrs. Francoise De Pre Labouchere?

Betsy: Of course I remember them. They owned a rooming house in Charleston, South Carolina. We used to play badminton with them every afternoon. Do you remember Josiah Burbank Skeffington?

Bob: The juggler with the Canadian circus. He taught me how to catch red snappers in that lake near Toronto. Josiah Burbank Skeffington.

Betsy: There was a Mr. and Mrs. Raymondo Archibald Orlioffski from Mapleville, Indiana.

Bob: Mrs. Heather Courtney Berlinvasser. . . .

Betsy: Daniel Montenegro.

Bob: Muhamed Abdul Razak Fayed.

Betsy: We knew thousands of people, thousands of them. We were so popular . . .

STOP AND CHECK: Practice with Dialects

In this selection from Mark Twain's Huckleberry Finn,[17] Huck describes a small town with its "loafers" who sat around "chawing tobacco, and gaping and yawning and stretching—a mighty ornery lot." Practice using vocal variation to create the characters of Huck, Bill, Hank, Jack, and Lafe.

. . . they called one another Bill, and Buck, and Hank, and Joe, and Andy, and talked lazy and drawly, and used considerable many cuss words. . . . What a body was hearing amongst them all the time was:

"Gimme a chaw 'v tobacker, Hank."

"Cain't; I hain't got but one chaw left. Ask Bill."

Maybe Bill he gives him a chaw; maybe he lies and says he ain't got none. Some of them kinds of loafers never has a cent in the world, nor a chaw of tobacco of their own. They get all their chawing by borrowing; they say to a fellow, "I wisht you'd len' me a chaw, Jack, I jist this minute give Ben Thompson the last chaw I had" —which is a lie pretty much everytime; it don't fool nobody but a stranger; but Jack ain't no stranger, so he says:

"*You* give him a chaw, did you? So did your sister's cat's grandmother. You pay me back the chaws you've awready borry'd off'n me, Lafe Buckner, then I'll loan you one or two ton of it, and won't charge you no back intrust, nuther."

"Well, I *did* pay you back some of it wunst."

For a map of U.S. dialects, see http:www.geocities.com/Broadway/1906/dialects.html. Find an area of the country that interests you, and read about the distinctive pronunciation and grammatical patterns that make up that region's dialect. Then go to the University of Kansas's Web site, the International Dialects of English Archive, at www.ukans.edu/~idea/index2.html to hear speakers of various dialects read the same text.

Bob: I couldn't walk down the street without bumping into somebody I knew.

Betsy: I couldn't stick my head out the window without someone yelling . . . [*Imitates.*] "Hey, Betsy, how you doin' honey?"

Bob: [*Imitates.*] "Hey, how's it goin' there, Bobby? How are tricks?" They used to yell at me from their cars, from their stoops . . .

Betsy: "Yoo-hoo, Betsy, remember me from the Players Club in Philadelphia?"

Bob: "How about a drink with us after the show, Bob-old-boy?" . . .

Betsy: It was amazing.

Another element of pronunciation is syllabic stress. The word *police* is pronounced "POE-leese" in some speech communities. People say "pot-PORE-ee" (*potpourri;* standard pronunciation is "poe-per-EE"), and "com-PARE-uh-bul" (*comparable;* standard pronunciation is "COMM-purr-uh-bul"). If you are unclear about syllable stress, consult your dictionary.

Vocal Quality and Vocalizations

Quality refers to vocal attributes or features that create perceptions in the listeners. Memorable vocal qualities often distinguish memorable characters. For instance, the character Fran on the sitcom *The Nanny* spoke with an annoying **nasal** quality; she sent the sounds through her nasal passages. A **denasal** quality occurs when nasal passages are *not* used to project the sound. It's the "stuffed-up" way your voice sounds when you have a really bad head cold. **Hoarseness** is a raspy or strained quality of voice that's typical of heavy smokers or an overused voice, such as President Clinton's. **Orotund** voices sound resonant, clear, full, or rounded, usually with a slower rate and louder volume, such as James Earl Jones's. **Breathy** sounds result when a lot of air is expelled while speaking. Breathiness, plus slower, softer, lower tones, is typical of sexual come-ons.

Although some voices consistently have a specific quality, typically we modify our vocal qualities for various situations. For example, we often use nasal qualities for whining or nagging, and breathiness shows our excitement. Here are some snippets from texts that call for variation in vocal qualities:

From the short story "Brownies" by ZZ Packer:[18]

> "Girls, girls," said our parent helper, Mrs. Hedy. . . . She wagged her index finger perfunctorily, like a windshield wiper. "Stop it now. Be good." She said this loudly enough to be heard, but lazily, nasally, bereft of any feeling or indication that she meant to be obeyed, as though she would say these words again at the exact same pitch if a button somewhere on her were pressed.

From a monologue by Claudia Shear:[19]

> "C'mon, give me a painting." (I was always whining.)
>
> "Give you a painting? Give you a *painting*? Do you know how important a good painting is? Do you know how much a good painting is *worth*?"
>
> "Well, give me a bad one, then."
>
> "No. I can't do that."
>
> "Why not?"
>
> "Because the bad ones are my *enemies*!"

From the short story "Honored Guest" by Joy Williams:[20]

> Helen felt sick but she would drag herself to school. Her throat was sore. She heated up honey in a pan and sipped it with a spoon.
>
> "I'm going to just stay put today," Lenore said.
>
> "That's good Mom, just take it easy. You've been doing too much." Helen's forehead shone with sweat. She buttoned up her sweater with trembling fingers.
>
> "Do you have a cold?" her mother said. "Where did you get a cold? Stay home. . . . You've probably got a fever."
>
> "I have a test today, Mom," Helen said. . . .

"What if I die today?" Lenore said suddenly. "I want you to be with me. My God, I don't want to be alone!"

"All this week there are tests," Helen said.

"Why don't I wait then," Lenore said. . . .

Vocalizations are sounds such as screams or moans that wordlessly carry meanings. Characters laugh, cry, sigh, or yawn. They say *ah-h-h-h, br-r-r-r, m-m-m-m,* and *uh-huh.* Animal sounds such as *moo-o-o-o-o, me-e-e-ow,* and *ruff-ruff* are other vocalizations. In a cutting from a play, be sure to perform the vocalization. However, when you perform prose or poetry, it's usually more appropriate to suggest the vocalization than to actually do it. Here are some examples to experiment with:

From Sandra Cisneros' short story "Bien *Pretty*": [21]

Flavio laughed. I laughed too. We both laughed. We laughed and then we laughed some more. And when we were through with our laughing, he packed up his ant traps, spray tank, steel wool, clicked and latched and locked trays, toolboxes, slammed van doors shut. Laughed and drove away.

From "Socrates Wounded" by Alfred Levinson: [22]

Xanthippe: Any word from *your* husband?

Hera: (*Grunts*): Uh-uh. He's still out there, whatever it's called—I can't keep up with the names. Probably the last one demobilized. And he's a slow walker. Can't see *him* hurrying to get back—if he's alive.

Phrasing

Phrases are small groups of words that form the basic unit of sentence construction. Divide the sentences in your text into meaningful phrases and, as you rehearse and perform, proceed phrase by phrase through the passage. Pause briefly between phrases, or occasionally use a longer pause for emphasis. It's easy to rush pauses, especially for beginners, so experiment as you rehearse. When appropriate, put in a l-o-n-g break for effect. You may think you're pausing interminably, but in the adrenaline-rushed present of a performance, what seemed long in rehearsal will probably be just about right.

To identify phrases, first look at the punctuation. Commas, semicolons, colons, and end punctuation provide clues to phrasing and make some phrases easy to spot. Other phrases take more time to identify; as you prepare your manuscript, use slash marks to insert pauses.

Read through the following cutting from a short story by Ray Bradbury. On their ninth wedding anniversary, a woman tells her husband she's a "new" woman, not the person he married, because she once heard that every nine years the human body totally renews itself: [23]

I could feel it happening all year. Lying in bed, I felt my skin prickle, my pores open like ten thousand tiny mouths, my perspiration run like faucets, my heart race, my pulse sound in the oddest places, under my chin, my wrists, the back of my knees, my ankles. I felt like a huge wax statue, melting. After midnight I was afraid to turn on the bathroom light and find a stranger gone mad in the mirror. Every hour of every night and then all day, I could feel it as if I were out in a storm being struck by hot August rain that washed away the old to find a brand-new me.

This passage has many short, easily spotted phrases that the punctuation marks make clear. Only the final sentence is somewhat more complex. As you prepare your manuscript, choose a format that works for you. Use slash marks to divide the phrases, or add extra spaces where you'd draw out the words or pause slightly. Double-space between lines for the longest pauses. Here's one way to write out this passage:

I could feel it happening all year.

Lying in bed,   I felt my skin prickle,

my pores open   like ten thousand   tiny   mouths,

my perspiration run like faucets,   my heart race,

my pulse sound   in the oddest places,

under my chin,   my wrists,   the back of my knees,   my ankles.
[sped up]—

I felt like a huge   wax statue,

melting.

After midnight   I was afraid to turn on the bathroom light

and find a stranger gone mad   in the mirror.

Every hour of every night and then all day,

I could feel it

as if I were out in a storm being struck by hot August rain

that washed away the old

to find a brand-new me.

In longer phrases ("my perspiration run like faucets"), try raising your pitch early in the phrase and lowering it on the final syllables.[24] Experiment with speeding up in some lines ("as if I were out in a storm being struck by hot August rain") and slow down others, drawing out each word ("to find a brand-new me.")

BODILY EXPRESSIVENESS

Literary characters move from head to toe. Their face and eyes, their posture and gestures make tiny, almost imperceptible twitches, as well as large, sweeping moves. Movements can substitute for words (nodding or waving), add to words (pointing out a direction), display emotional states (drooping shoulders or wide grins), or

STOP AND CHECK: Put It All Together

Try marking the phrases in this excerpt from Chilean author Isabel Allende's book Paula.[25] *She describes her experiences in Belgium in a study program where she was grouped with 30 men from the Congo. She eventually became so frustrated that she decided to withdraw from the classes.*

The director asked me to explain my sudden departure to the class, and I had no choice but to face that united front and in my lamentable French tell them that in my country men did not enter the women's bathroom unzipping their fly, did not shove women aside to go through a door first, did not knock each other down for a place at the table or to get on a bus, and that I felt badly mistreated and was leaving because I was not used to such foul behavior. A glacial silence greeted my peroration. After a long pause, one of them spoke to say that in his country no decent woman publicly exhibited her need to go to the bathroom, nor did she try to go through a door before the men but in fact walked several steps behind, and that his mother and his sisters never sat at the table with him, they ate what the men left. He added that they felt permanently insulted by me, that they had never seen a person with such bad manners, and, as I was a minority in the group, I would just have to make the most of it. "It is true that I am a minority in this course, but you are a minority in this country," I replied. "I am willing to make concessions, but you must do that, too, if you want to avoid problems here in Europe." It was a solution worthy of Solomon; we agreed upon certain basic rules, and I stayed on. They never wanted to sit with me at the table or on the bus, but they stopped bursting into the bathroom and physically shoving me. During that year, my feminism got lost in the shuffle. I walked a modest two meters behind my companions, never looked up or raised my voice, and was the last one through the door.

- Use marks to indicate pauses.
- Underline words or phrases you'd stress.
- Use arrows to indicate rising or falling intonation.
- Make decisions regarding volume and rate.

Share your work with a small group of classmates.

betray nervousness (nail biting or fidgeting with jewelry).[26] The following excerpts indicate movements, from highly visible to almost too slight to notice.

From "The Open Meeting" by A. R. Gurney:[27]

Verna: [*Covering her ears.*] I will not listen to this! . . . [*Pounding the table with her fists.*] No, no, no, NO! I want the subject changed, do you hear me? CHANGED! Nobody's interested in these personal remarks! Now stop it! . . .

From a science-fiction short story by Cherry Wilder:[28]

"I will be returning to Russia with the Ostrov family," she said.

"Your last visit, *chere Rosaline*?"

:-) :-(;-) >-l :-D

FIGURE 5.1 Emoticons

A twitch of the fine drooping hair around the mouth.

"No, not quite," she smiled and lied with perfect composure. "I will be here tomorrow morning."

Lots of little mannerisms give away our mental state. We can often tell when someone is frustrated, delighted, grieving, or disgusted by reading their body language. How we use our bodies can also suggest personal traits such as introversion or extroversion, self-confidence and self-consciousness. This section explores aspects of facial expressions, posture, and gestures. It concludes by discussing various ways to focus your eyes during a performance.

Facial Expressions

Many people regularly use emoticons, those little faces we add to e-mail messages. (See Figure 5.1.) Their popularity illustrates how much we rely on facial expressions as cues for interpretation: We read faces for emotional messages (she's sad; he's not really sorry), and we study facial expressions to understand someone else's thoughts (Mom's frowning—that means, "Stop that THIS MINUTE!"; Uncle Joe's wink says "just kidding"). Expressions around the eyes and mouth are especially important when communicating.

We employ various eye movements to play out our roles as friend, student, son or daughter, romantic partner, employee, and so on. We show surprise (wide-open eyes), fight sleepiness (long, slow blinks), or send a threat (squinting and half-open lids). We give one another the "once over," an up-and-down, whole-body gaze. And we drop our eyes in embarrassment or roll them heavenward in disgust. Even our eyebrows show emotions such as displeasure, surprise, and confusion.

Duration is the length of a look. Looks range from very short glances to more sustained gazes to prolonged stares. Use varied duration to portray characters as they look at objects and people in the stories you present. Here are a few eye behaviors that you can add to your interpretations to make your characterizations more vivid.

- **Glances** are short in duration. We often dart glances at others, especially at more powerful, intimidating persons. Or glances may be dismissive, indicating that the other person is unworthy of a more prolonged gaze. Sidewise glances are brief looks out of the corner of the eyes. Use them when your characters are sitting side-by-side or at angles from one another.

- **Gazes** are more sustained, direct looks. We typically gaze at pleasant things or people we like. Couples in love frequently gaze into each other's eyes.

- **Staring**, holding a steady, unblinking gaze, is typical of angry or dominating people. Small children also stare, especially at deformities or unusual situations. A wide stare indicates fear.

- **Gaze avoidance**, refusing to look at something or make eye contact with someone, can signal emotions such as disgust, anger, or embarrassment. Or it may indicate a desire to avoid interaction.

The lower half of the face is also expressive. How could we show happiness, tenderness, or scorn without using our lips, our teeth, and our jaws? Smiles range from a "barely there" smile to a wide, toothy grin. We flash brief smiles and hold frozen grins. Genuine smiles include crinkled eyes, but fake grins do not involve the eyes. We may show our teeth or intentionally hide them.

When we're frustrated or lost in thought, we sometimes purse our lips briefly before speaking. When we're disgusted, we wrinkle our noses and raise our upper lip. A threatening snarl comes with teeth bared. Speaking through barely open lips signals a sick or depressed character. We bite our lower lip or clench and unclench our jaw under tension. Experiment with these and other facial expressions to create believable characterizations.

Other Bodily Movements

Facial expressions combine with posture and gestures to express personal traits and moods. Some characters have distinctive bodily movements. For instance, one person characteristically tilts her head when she talks; another walks with a swagger. Confident people tend to use sweeping gestures, which contrast with the awkward, abrupt movements of the socially inept. Some people are smooth and coordinated; others are not.

When your text calls for it, experiment with erect or slumped posture, swaying or leaning. Extend your arms expansively, or hold them protectively to your side. Clench and unclench your fists. Tilt your head to one side (to suggest inquisitiveness or submissiveness); hold your nose in the air (pride or superiority), or bow your head (reverence or shame). Thrust out your chin (power or stubbornness), or tuck it toward your chest (modesty or shyness) as you portray your characters and their moods.

Read through this cutting from *The Girl with the Pearl Earring*[29] and experiment with ways to depict the movements in it. The story is set in the Netherlands during the era of the bubonic plague. Because of their father's career-ending injuries, both Griet (the narrator) and Frans must work six days a week while their younger sister Agnes remains at home:

> One Sunday I decided to visit my brother. . . . I left the house early and walked to his factory, which was outside the city walls not far from the Rotterdam Gate. Frans was still asleep when I arrived. The woman who answered at the gate laughed when I asked for him. "He'll be asleep for hours yet," she said. "They sleep all day on Sundays, the apprentices. It's their day off."
>
> I did not like her tone, nor what she said. "Please wake him and tell him his sister is here," I demanded. . . .

The woman raised her eyebrows. "I didn't know Frans came from a family so high on their throne you can see up their noses." She disappeared and I wondered if she would bother to wake Frans. I sat on a low wall to wait. . . .

Frans appeared at last, rubbing sleep from his face. "Oh Griet," he said. "I didn't know if it would be you or Agnes. I suppose Agnes wouldn't come so far on her own."

He didn't know. I couldn't keep it from him, not even to tell him gently.

"Agnes has been struck by the plague," I blurted out. "God help her and our parents."

Frans stopped rubbing his face. His eyes were red.

"Agnes?" he repeated in confusion. "How do you know this?"

"Someone found out for me."

"You haven't seen them?"

"There's a quarantine."

"A quarantine? How long has there been one?"

"Ten days so far."

Frans shook his head angrily. "I heard nothing of this! Stuck in this factory day after day, nothing but white tiles as far as I can see. I think I may go mad."

"It's Agnes you should be thinking of now."

Frans hung his head unhappily. . . .

"Frans, have you been going to church?"

He shrugged. I could not bring myself to question him further.

"I'm going now to pray for them all," I said instead. "Will you come with me?"

- Where could you substitute a movement for the words? (Example: "He shrugged.")

- Identify places you could eliminate explanatory words and use vocal variation to convey the meaning. (Example: " 'Agnes has been struck by the plague,' I blurted out." Instead of reading "I blurted out," you could omit the words and blurt out the news.)

- Where would you use a modified movement to accentuate the words? (Example: "Franz shook his head angrily.")

We express emotions by combining vocal, facial, and bodily movements. And our expression varies depending on the character's personality and the situation. For example, anger is sometimes seething (with clenched jaw, arms folded across the chest, refusal to make eye contact, low monotone voice); at other times, it boils over (clenched fists, hands on hips, direct stare, loud tone). Emotions are often mixed: joy commonly accompanies surprise, anger partners

STOP AND CHECK: Practice Eye and Body Movements

These excerpts from short stories give you an opportunity to suggest the characters' personalities and their actions.

From Deborah Galyan's story "The Incredible Appearing Man":[31]

"Plumber," he says.

His Panama hat is an odd touch, shadowing dark glasses. A blue work shirt and jeans. Cowboy boots, very tooled. But the grin is center stage.

"I didn't call a plumber."

He takes a notebook out of his shirt pocket and looks in it.

"Plumber," he says, "nonetheless." . . .

. . . When he reaches the truck, he looks back at me. One, two, three, I count and shut the door. Three is as long as I can look without looking too long. My hands are shaking. Nothing happened, I tell myself. But my hands are shaking, and there's no denying it. . . .

. . . He takes my chin in his palm and moves my face from side to side. It's an odd feeling, as if his fingers are wired to some internal circuitry in my brain. I slide my eyes across the street to see if my retired neighbor Caroline is out in her yard and watching . . .

From "Past My Future" by David Huddle. The characters are in a restaurant. Robert is a married family friend who molested the narrator when she was a teenager:[32]

The four of us sat at our table gawking at the people around us.

"Is that Robert? Isn't that Robert and Suzanne?" my mother asked my father. She was sitting up straight in her chair and squinting across the room. . . . Then, because she was sitting beside me and I wasn't looking the right way, my mother actually pulled my chin to turn my head in the proper direction. . . .

I became aware that I had half risen from my chair and my parents and my boyfriend were staring at me. Easing back down into my seat, I turned to them and found three frozen faces. Allen had even paused in chewing his food. Our lives depended on what I was going to do next, I knew that. It took all my strength to smile at Allen and resume eating.

with disgust, and fear and loathing can occur simultaneously. You might portray a character who tries to mask one emotion (fear, for instance) with another (such as confidence). Portraying emotions without underplaying or overdoing them is an important skill.

Experiment with ways Connie might express her mounting terror in this cutting from a short story by Joyce Carol Oates. She is home alone when two strange men drive up in a car. One comes to the door and asks her to go for a ride with them:[30]

"Where are we going?" . . .

"Just for a ride, Connie sweetheart."

"I never said my name was Connie," she said.

"But I know what it is. I know your name and all about you lots of things." Arnold Friend said. He had not moved yet but stood still leaning back against the side of his jalopy. "I took a special interest in you, such a pretty girl, and found out all about you like I know your parents and sister are gone somewheres and I know where and how long they're going to be gone . . . Honey—? Listen, here's how it is. . . . I ain't coming in that house after you."

"You better not! I'm going to call the police if you—if you don't—"

"Honey," he said, talking right through her voice, "honey, I'm not coming in there but you are coming out here. You know why?"

She was panting. The kitchen looked like a place she had never seen before, some room she had run inside but which wasn't good enough, wasn't going to help her. . . .

"You listening, honey? Hey?"

"—going to call the police—"

"Soon as you touch the phone I don't need to keep my promise and can come inside. You won't want that."

She rushed forward and tried to lock the door. Her fingers were shaking.

"But why lock it," Arnold Friend said gently, talking right into her face. "It's just a screen door. It's just nothing." . . .

"What do you want?" she whispered.

"I want you," he said.

. . . "You're crazy," she whispered. . . . "What do you. . . . You're crazy, you . . ."

"Huh? What're you saying, honey?"

Her eyes darted everywhere in the kitchen. She could not remember what it was, this room. . . .

Focus

After you've chosen your text, analyzed it, and practiced various ways of presenting it vocally and physically, you're almost ready to perform. But where should you look during the performance itself? Directly at the audience? Over their heads somewhere? It seems weird to think of performing these lines from "In the Orchard" (found in Chapter 4) while looking in the direction noted in brackets:

"I thought you loved me . . ." [*looking at one audience member*]

"No, it was just in fun . . ." [*focusing on another individual*]

If you were performing in an actual theater, the stage would bound your interactions, and you'd use an **onstage focus,** meaning you would look directly at the other actors and the objects that were actually located on the stage. You might occasionally cross the **fourth wall,** the invisible barrier between the actors and audience, and interact with the audience; for example, Shakespeare's characters often say an aside to the audience, and playwrights in ancient Greece used a chorus to narrate. But, in general, you'd look at actors and props you could really see. You'd sit beside a real person, actually pick up a real book, or look into a real mirror as the script required.

In an unstaged solo performance, however, there's no stage, no other actors, no props, no set or backdrop, no fourth wall. You use an **offstage focus,** which means you place the scene out in the audience instead of on the stage.

Literary characters often face one another, stand side by side, or sit in a circle. Some are shorter than others; some sit while others stand. Onstage, you'd play your character in relationship to another actor. However, in a solo performance, where you focus your eyes indicates the relationship that the characters have with the audience and with one another. There are four ways to focus: open, inner-closed, semi-closed, and closed. Character placement is another aspect of focus.

- **Open focus** means you make eye contact with audience members and talk directly to them.
- **Inner-closed focus** means you don't focus on a particular person or object; you talk to yourself and let the audience overhear as you look from place to place in a slightly unfocused manner.
- **Semi-closed focus** occurs when you address God or an imaginary or absent person or object. "Place" the addressee, and then focus on that location.
- **Closed focus** means you focus out front, over the audience's head.
- **Character placement** means you "place" or locate each character and significant object somewhere; when you interact with each, you look at that particular place.

Focus can be a difficult concept to grasp, so let's work through each type one by one, beginning with open focus.

Open Focus In open focus, you make eye contact with individual audience members and talk directly to them. Use open focus for narration and instruction: when the characters are aware of the audience, when they narrate a scene or address a group (such as a jury, a congregation, or loyal subjects), when they give an aside or recite a soliloquy. Figure 5.2 illustrates open focus.

Read through this speech known as "Tribute to the Dog,"[33] delivered in 1869 by Missouri Senator George Vest, as if you were speaking directly to a jury. Vest represented a man who took his neighbor to court for killing his dog. The neighbor pled guilty but balked at paying $150 for a "mere animal." After this speech, the jury awarded the plaintiff $500 in damages! Look at three places in your audience: in the middle, off to the right, and off to the left.

> Gentlemen of the jury: the best friend a man has in the world may turn against him and become his worst enemy. His son or daughter that he has reared with loving care may prove ungrateful. . . . The money that man has, he may lose. . . . The people who are prone to fall on their knees to do us honor when success is with us may be the first to throw the stone of malice when failure settles its cloud upon our heads.

the audience

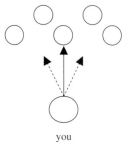

you

FIGURE 5.2 Open Focus

The one absolutely unselfish friend that a man can have in this selfish world, the one that never deserts him and the one that never proves ungrateful or treacherous . . . is his dog. . . . [A] man's dog stands by him in prosperity and in poverty, in health and in sickness. . . . He will kiss the hand that has no food to offer . . . He guards the sleep of his pauper master as if he were a prince. When all other friends desert he remains. . . . If fortune drives the master forth an outcast in the world . . . the faithful dog asks no higher privilege than that of accompanying him to guard against danger, to fight against his enemies, and when the last scene of all comes, and death takes the master . . . no matter if all other friends pursue their way, there by his graveside will the noble dog be found, his head between his paws, his eyes sad but open in alert watchfulness, faithful and true even to death.

Inner-Closed Focus Use inner-closed focus when your characters are thinking, brooding, dreaming, musing, or talking to themselves. Try talking to yourself about something important, and notice that you look out the window, off into space, or down at the floor. Review the material on modal analysis from Chapter 4; inner-closed focus is often useful for texts in the lyric mode.

Experiment with this excerpt from a Civil War diary written by Mary Boykin Chestnut, a Southerner. She's musing, not talking to anyone in particular, but we are allowed to overhear her thoughts. Read the text aloud as if you were in the quiet of your own room, contemplating the great tragedy engulfing your society. Put in pauses, and change your focus between ideas.

July 26. Columbia, South Carolina.[34]

. . . When I remember all the true-hearted, the . . . gallant boys who have come laughing and singing and dancing across my way in the three years past! I have looked into their brave young eyes, and helped them as I could, and then seen them no more forever. They lie stark and cold, dead upon the battlefield or mouldering away in hospitals or prisons. I think if I dared consider the long array of those bright youths and loyal men who have gone to their death almost before my very eyes, my heart might break too. Is anything worth it? This fearful sacrifice, this awful penalty we pay for war? . . .

September 2.

Atlanta is gone. Well that agony is over. . . . There is no hope, but we will try to have no fear. . . .

Semi-Closed Focus Use semi-closed focus when the persona is praying or talking to an absent person or object. Like inner-closed focus, this focus is typically used with texts in the lyric mode. You mentally "place" the addressee in a specific location, and then consistently focus on that place. Try it on these literary cuttings:

From "Remembering Lobo" by Pat Mora.[35] When you speak the aunt's words, address the gravestone, which you've placed on the floor about six feet in front of you.

   [*open focus*] One time I heard my aunt scolding her dead husband. She'd sweep his gravestone and say [*semi-closed*] "*Porque?* Why did you do this, you thoughtless man? Why did you go and leave me like this? You know I don't like to be alone. Why did you stop living?" [*open focus*] Such a sight to see my aunt with her proper black hat and her fine dress and her carefully polished shoes muttering away for all to hear. . . .

From Psalm 51. First turn so that the speaker is not directly facing the audience; then have him focus slightly above a normal human's height to address God.

Have mercy on me, O God,
   according to your unfailing love;
according to your great compassion
   blot out my transgressions.

Character Placement and Closed Focus As a solo performer, you must portray all the characters, which is no easy task. Mastering the art of **character placement** will help you perform complex scenes. Character placement is an integral part of closed focus: You place each character (and object) in an imaginary scene, and then direct your focus and interactions toward each one as if you were *really* seeing them. Use closed focus for texts in the dramatic mode.

For example, in David Smilow's short play *Brights*,[36] the characters are in a car that is being tailgated. Stage directions indicate that Fred is driving and Karen is beside him in the passenger's seat. Both Fred and Karen rely on additional stage directions to tell them where to look.

"Place" yourself as Fred in the driver's seat. (Figure 5.3 illustrates Fred's placement and focus.) When you're not looking in the rearview mirror, which is up and to your right, focus on the road ahead. Occasionally glance over at

when you perform Fred

the road ahead

the rearview mirror

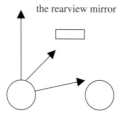

Fred   Karen   Figure 5.3 Character Placement and
                                 Closed Focus

Karen on your right. (You could hold the manuscript in the "ten-two" position that Fred might use to drive.)

After you feel comfortable with Fred's placement, switch to Karen's perspective in the passenger seat. Look out at the road or over at Fred, who sits to
your left. Occasionally, turn your head slightly to look out the back window.
Now, work through these lines from the play, using character placement and
appropriate focus:

> **Fred:** Jerk. (*He squints up at the rearview mirror.*) This guy's tailgating me.
> With his high beams on.
>
> (*KAREN glances out the rear window.*)
>
> **Karen:** No, honey. It's just the two headlights.
>
> **Fred:** They're those high-low kind. They've got to be. Look how bright
> they are. Ass. . . . Why do people do this?
>
> (*KAREN looks out the rear window again.*)
>
> **Karen:** Wow. He is pretty close. . . . Sweetie, don't let it bother you.
>
> **Fred:** . . . [H]ere's Route Eight, so . . . (*He turns the wheel. A second later, the
> interior's flooded with light again.*) Oh, terrific. . . .
>
> **Karen:** Sweetie, don't let it bother you.
>
> (*FRED's gripping the wheel tighter and stares at the rearview mirror.*)
>
> **Fred:** What does this idiot want? . . .
>
> (*KAREN looks at him as if for the first time.*)
>
> . . .
>
> (*FRED meets her gaze.*)

The key is consistency. Always look at the mirror, the road, and Karen from Fred's perspective when you read his lines, and always think of yourself in Karen's place when you read her lines. To perform *Brights* successfully, you must suggest that you really are in a car and that the imaginary road Fred and Karen are on winds off into the distance somewhere over your listeners' heads.

Switching Focus You will have to switch focus with texts in the epic mode, moving from open focus during the narration to closed focus and character placement during dialogue sections and to semi-closed or inner-closed focus to portray characters' inner thoughts. The following text by Denise Simard is a good example. The author sometimes addresses the audience directly, sometimes thinks, and sometimes talks to another character. Read through it and practice different focal points. (Italicized directions are added in brackets.)[37]

[*Open focus.*] You've searched and searched but have yet to stumble across an ad that calls out to you by name, one you're truly qualified for. Your degree is in English but it might as well be in sales because nobody out there cares about "The Psychological Burdens of Secret Knowledge in *The Scarlet Letter.*" The bottom line is always, Can you think on your feet and talk your way out of a paper bag?

Lately you feel as if the bag is plastic and you're suffocating, but you go on the interviews anyway and sit through the chitchat and the company profile and the obligatory questions concerning your schooling, your past experience. You sit through Office Manager Jill, whose sentences end on an up note that her chin follows. [*Closed focus; in Jill's voice, talk to the interviewee, placed directly across from you.*] "What would you say are your three biggest *accomplishments?*"

[*Open focus*] YOU THINK: [*Inner-closed focus.*] I learned how to drive a stick on the Connecticut Turnpike one night en route from New York City to Boston after smoking hash in the bathroom of a Roy Rogers. I can peel an apple in one piece. I've befriended my student-loan collector.

[*Open focus*] YOU SAY: [*Closed focus, speaking as interviewee to Jill.*]

"While at the law firm, I reorganized their billing schedule, allowing their computer to generate bills on a rotating weekly basis. This past year for Thanksgiving, I cooked and distributed thirty-six turkey dinners to the homeless. In college, I taught myself sign language to enable better communication with my boyfriend's mother."

[*Open focus*] YOU KNOW: While at the law firm, you walked four blocks to Office Max and bought the latest upgrade of Timeslips, the billing software. An accomplished meal for you is macaroni and cheese from the box with a sprinkle of cheddar baked on top. The only phrase you know in sign language is *I love you,* and you learned that from the cards the deaf and homeless distribute. On the way to this interview, you bought one for thirty-three cents and some pocket lint.

You don't get that job. But, hey, you didn't really want it, anyway.

STOP AND CHECK: Practice Focus Skills

Read through this text, and then discuss with your classmates how you would focus if you were to perform it. First, separate the narration from the conversation and plan to use open focus for those sections; next, identify the addressees, decide where to place them; then use closed focus to address them in that place. Decide if inner-closed or semi-closed focus is called for in the excerpt.

From "Call If You Need Me," a short story by Raymond Carver. The woman is the narrator's wife; Richard is their child; they have decided to separate. Susan is his lover.[38]

The next afternoon, after her arrangements were made and her suitcases packed, I drove her to the little airport where she would catch a flight to Portland and then transfer to another airline that would put her in Pasco late that night.

"Tell your mother I said hello. Give Richard a hug for me and tell him I miss him," I said. "Tell him I send love."

"He loves you too," she said. "You know that. In any case, you'll see him in the fall, I'm sure."

I nodded.

"Good-bye," she said, and reached for me. We held each other. "I'm glad for last night," she said. "Those horses. Our talk. Everything. It helps. We won't forget that," she said. She began to cry.

"Write me, will you?" I said. "I didn't think it would happen to us," I said. "All those years. I never thought so for a minute. Not us."

"I'll write," she said. "Some big letters. The biggest you've ever seen since I used to send you letters in high school."

"I'll be looking for them," I said.

Then she looked at me again and touched my face. She turned and moved across the tarmac toward the plane.

Go, dearest one, and God be with you.

She boarded the plane and I stayed around until its jet engines started . . .

I drove back . . . Then I went into the house and, without even taking off my coat, went to the telephone and dialed Susan's number.

SUMMARY

Your voice is a wonderful instrument that allows you to suggest an elderly man or a child, a depressed individual or an excited human being. You can portray moods and express emotions by using a range of vocal variations. You can create different impressions by varying your rate, volume, pitch, and duration. Your pronunciation and articulation of specific sounds can suggest dialects. Adding vocal qualities such as breathiness or nasality allows you to create additional characters. Finally, skillful usage of phrasing adds further polish to your performance.

Our bodies also have a language of their own. Facial expressions, especially how we use our eyes and mouths, reveal personality characteristics as well as display emotions and moods. Duration, how long a look lasts, ranges from short glances to long unblinking stares; gaze avoidance also conveys meaning. Finally, the entire body from head to toe expresses our fleeting moods as well as our more permanent personality traits. Portraying emotions without underplaying or overdoing them is one mark of a good performer.

In contrast to the onstage focus of theater, interpreters use offstage focus and look at or over the audience. In open focus, you talk *to* the audience; in inner-closed focus, you think or talk to yourself. In semi-closed focus, you direct your gaze at an imaginary character, an absent person, or a supernatural character. In closed focus, you give each character a "place" somewhere over the heads of your listeners and always address each character in that place.

KEY TERMS

rate	clipping/fast pitch drops	phrases
speech flow	stress	duration
pauses	quality	glances
volume	nasal quality	gazes
stage whisper	denasal quality	staring
pitch	hoarseness	gaze avoidance
pitch variation	orotund quality	onstage focus
inflection	breathy quality	fourth wall
monotone	vocalizations	offstage focus
uptalk/high rise terminals	pronunciation	inner-closed focus
range	articulation	semi-closed focus
duration/extent	lisp	character placement
drawl	dialect	closed focus

QUESTIONS AND EXERCISES

1. Choose a children's picture book with just a few sentences per page, and record yourself reading it and incorporating the vocalic elements listed in this chapter. Record until you are satisfied with your interpretation, and then bring the tape to class and play it for a small group of your classmates. Hold up the book and show the pictures while the tape plays.

2. Go to InfoTrac College Edition and search for the article "'EawrFolk': Language, Class and English Identity in Victorian Dialect Poetry." Read the poems aloud to hear the characteristics of their dialects.

3. Do you use uptalk, or HRT? Go online to http:www.guardian.co.uk/g2/story/0,3604, 555379,00.html and read more about this vocal phenomenon.

Identify the type of characters or situations you could interpret by using uptalk.

4. What vocalizations do you make for the following: excitement, fear, sorrow, pain, outrage, shocked surprise, a blow to the stomach? How might you work those into an interpretation?

5. What stereotypes do you have about differences in the way that men and women vocally express emotions? Log onto InfoTrac College Edition and skim the article "Gender Stereotypes in the Expression and Perception of Vocal Affect" in *Sex Roles: A Journal of Research*. How similar were the results to your stereotypes? What new or surprising information did you discover?

6. Irony, or saying something but meaning something else, is accomplished mainly by tone of voice. Read the following selection from the *Manual of Conduct In School and Out* by the Deans of Girls in Chicago High Schools (1921),[39] but use vocal variations that signal listeners not to take your words literally:

If you are well brought up, girls, you will not loiter on the street to talk to one another; much less to boys. Street visiting is taboo.

Boys, a gentleman does not detain on street corners a girl or woman friend. If he meets one with whom he wishes to speak more than a moment, he asks permission to walk a little way with her. During the moment that he does detain her, a gentleman talks with his hat in his hand.

7. The art of elocution, or using one's voice to communicate meaning, has a long history. For historical advice, go online to http:www.artsci.gmcc.ab.ca/people/einarssonb/VocalReading Handout.htm and read the excerpts by Alfred Ayers (1897) and Thomas Sheridan (1787). What similarities and differences do you find between this chapter and those works?

8. Read the following classifieds, using the suggested vocal qualities:

[Nasal] Thirteen-piece cherrywood dining set, large table with leaves, chairs, beveled glass hutch and buffet, heirloom quality. Cost $8400, sacrifice for $2750. Will separate.

[Denasal] 21-inch men's 10-speed hybrid bike. Looks and rides like new. Zero miles since complete pro overhaul. Includes new helmet. $115.

[Breathy] Three horses for sale: one pinto mare, four years old; one Tennessee Walker, 21 years old; one quarter horse mare, 15 years old. All broke to ride and pack.

[Hoarse] Cage. Custom-made oak and glass for snake or lizard. Complete with lights and fixtures. $150.

[Orotund] Enjoy those lazy days of summer . . . Let us do the work! We specialize in Total Landscape Maintenance, clean-up, and bark dusting. Free quotes. Bonded and insured.

9. Comedians Jim Carrey and Lucille Ball are masterful at

expressing extravagant emotions. Watch some *I Love Lucy* reruns or a Jim Carrey movie with the sound turned off, and identify specific ways they combine eye movements, facial expressions, and bodily gestures to create comedic performances.

10. Watch a dramatic movie that features emotions such as fear, sadness, wariness, or hope. Analyze the combinations of nonverbal elements that make the performances compelling. (Examples: *Seabiscuit*, *A Beautiful Mind*, or *The Hours*)

11. Paul Ekman is the foremost expert on facial expressions. Log onto the Internet and read the excerpt of his 2003 book, *Emotions Revealed*, at http:www .henryholt.com/holt/ emotionsrevealedexcerpt.htm.

12. Use InfoTrac College Edition to read the article, "It's Not What You Say; It's How You Say It" by James P. T. Fatt. It's in the June-July 1999 issue of *Communication World*. What additional gestures does the author describe that you could incorporate into your performances?

13. Choose a text from the list you made in Chapter 1, and underline all the words that indicate the characters' bodily actions. Then read the text aloud, creating focal points and suggesting the actions.

14. Choose a text with at least two characters. Create focal points by placing each character in an imaginary location, using offstage focus. Practice performing the text. Be consistent in your character placement and focus.

6

Preparing for Performance

This chapter will help you:

- Craft an introduction for a specific audience

- Familiarize yourself with the text

- Use a manuscript effectively

In her end-of-the-semester self-evaluation, Suzanne emphasized the importance of planning her performance and rehearsing it in advance:

> In addition to my analysis and the initial responses I make to the text, I know that I have to memorize or at least super-familiarize myself with the piece. I know that once I do this I have to plan out each page turn, each focus change, each vocal inflection, etc. Overall, I am more aware of what it takes to have the basic skills for a good performance.

After you have chosen and analyzed your text, there are a few additional details to consider before you actually perform. This chapter tells how to create an introduction and familiarize yourself with the text through rehearsing. It concludes with suggestions for using a manuscript and a podium effectively.

CREATING AN INTRODUCTION

Listeners typically ask themselves a number of questions about any performance: What's this text about? Why should I listen? Will this be interesting? To answer those questions about your performance, create an introduction that draws attention to the theme, shows the relevance of the piece to their lives, provides necessary background material, and identifies the title and author.[1]

This section illustrates how to create an introduction for a prose cutting from the book *Bird by Bird: Some Instructions on Writing and Life* by Anne Lamott.[2] Lamott is a writing teacher and professional writer, and *Bird by Bird* is a humorous book about how to write.

Draw Attention to the Text

Begin by drawing the audience into the text. Often, starting with a **teaser,** a short excerpt from the piece, gains listeners' attention and draws them in. Teasers are brief, only thirty seconds to a minute long, and they precede the formal introduction. Either select the opening lines or choose some dramatic lines from within the body of the text. The first chapter of *Bird by Bird* begins: "I grew up around a father and a mother who read every chance they got, who took us to the library every Thursday night to load up on books for the coming week. . . . [O]ur house was very quiet after dinner—unless, that is, some of my father's writer friends were over." Not bad . . . but the following scene, four pages into the text, would be a more dramatic teaser:

> The first poem I wrote that got any attention was about John Glenn. The first stanza went, "Colonel John Glenn went up to heaven / in his space-ship, *Friendship Seven*." There were many, many verses. . . . The teacher read the John Glenn poem to my second-grade class. It was a great moment; the other children looked at me as though I had learned to drive. It turned out that the teacher had submitted the poem to a California state schools

competition, and it had won some sort of award. It appeared in a mimeographed collection. I understood immediately the thrill of seeing oneself in print. It provides some sort of primal verification; you are in print; therefore you exist.

Instead of using a teaser, you could use a rhetorical question, a vivid description, a definition, a startling statistic, a series of short examples, or a reference to a current event—something that will focus listeners' attention directly on the theme you will be developing. Consider exaggerating or using humor when appropriate. Here are three possibilities for *Bird by Bird:*

> Papers. I figure by the time I graduate from George Fox University that I'll have written 147 of them—counting the short ones!

> Do you ever get writer's block? You're sitting at your desk, it's two o'clock in the morning, a paper is due in six hours, and you have neither the inspiration nor the energy to finish the thing.

> According to *Webster's New Collegiate Dictionary, write* means (1) to form (e.g., letters) on a surface with a tool, as a pen or pencil; (2) to compose and set down; (3) to express; (4) to communicate, as by correspondence.

> A *writer* is one who writes.

> *Writer's block* is a usually temporary psychological inability to begin or continue work on a piece of writing.

Show Relevance

Next, give your listeners a reason to listen. Link the theme to their interests, experiences, and needs; explain how it connects to their lives. The link might be general, dealing with a social issue that your listeners may not experience personally, or it might be specific and address common experiences.

For an audience of college students, you could easily link Lamott's piece to the here-and-now writing experiences of typical students. For an audience of residents at a nearby retirement home, you should be more general, since most retirees write letters, not term papers or articles or books. However, many retirees enjoy reading. Explore ways to link your performance to their interest in books. Here are ideas for linking the text to two different audiences:

> If you've ever found yourself staring at a blank computer screen waiting for inspiration to hit so that you can crank out another term paper, you will relate to the theme of this piece: writer's block. The dictionary says it's a usually temporary condition, but at two o'clock in the morning, it may seem terminal.

> You may have never written anything for publication, but think of all the reading you do—books, newspapers, magazines—and think of all the writers, poets, and playwrights whose work you love. For every book you've ever read, for every play you've enjoyed, there's probably a frustrated author who's somehow overcome writer's block to create that special work.

Provide Background Information

It is sometimes vital to include background information; in other situations, this it less important. However, background information often helps your audience better understand your text. Here are a few ideas:

- Provide necessary background information on the characters, the setting, or the situation. If your selection is part of a longer text, tell what precedes and what follows your excerpt. When you perform literature from another culture, explain relevant customs. Facts such as these are called **internal information** because they refer to material within the literature itself.

- Provide **external information,** or information that is extraneous to the story line, such as facts about the author. What awards has she won? What experience does she have with the topic? Answering these types of questions can help your listeners better appreciate the piece.

- Share insights you've gained from the piece, or explain the perspective you'll take in your interpretation. You might create a program of prose and poetry about women's roles and inform your listeners that you're presenting material from a feminist perspective; and then briefly explain what that means. Or perhaps you gained new understandings about racial issues as a result of reading *The Color of Water;* you could briefly explain the insights that your chosen excerpts illustrate.

The bottom line is to supply background material that will improve your audience's understanding of and appreciation for your selection.

Identify the Text and Author

Because listeners need to know what you are performing, identify the text's title and author. You can work in this information at various points during your introduction, such as after you gain attention but before you relate to the audience, when you give background information about the author, and so on. It is common to state the title and author just before launching into the text.

Put It All Together

The above elements all need to be included, but their order is flexible. In fact, you may gain attention and relate to the audience at the same time. It's also possible to make links to the audience as you present background information. Here's an example of a complete introduction for *Bird by Bird* for a university audience in the middle of the semester:

> If you've ever found yourself staring at a blank computer screen waiting for the inspiration to crank out another term paper, you will relate to the theme of this prose: writer's block. The dictionary says it's usually a temporary condition, but at two o'clock in the morning, it seems terminal!
>
> Anne Lamott, author of *Bird by Bird*, knows how depressing writer's block is. In fact, the title of her hilarious book comes from an incident

---

STOP AND CHECK: Create an Introduction

Create an interesting introduction for one of the texts you will perform. Use the questions below to help you.

What is the theme of your text?

How will you draw listeners' attention to it?

Identify a few ways the theme might relate to their lives, and then choose the one that best suits the specific audience and occasion.

What internal information do they need to understand the text?

What external information must they have?

Who is the author? What's the title of the text? Where and how will you work this into your introduction?

Write out the major points you'll include in your introduction.

---

involving her brother. When he was ten, he'd had three months to write a report on birds, but he'd put it off so long that the night before it was due he just sat—completely blocked at the daunting prospect ahead. His dad sat down beside him, put his arm around his shoulder and said, "Bird by bird, buddy. Just take it bird by bird."

This semester, my assignments include writing six very l-o-n-g research papers. "No way!" I think. "How will I ever get this done?!" Then writer's block sets in. Paper by paper, buddy, paper by paper—but it still seems overwhelming.

Perhaps that's why I enjoyed Lamott's book so much. Lamott taught writing for many years, and her basic approach is quite simple: "Lighten up. Write. Get something—anything—down on paper. You're going to have to revise anyway. One paper at a time, buddy."

Are you in a similar boat? It's midterm and you have several papers yet to write. Ah, you need Lamott's tips for dealing with writer's block. So to get you through the rest of the semester, here's advice from *Bird by Bird*, by Anne Lamott.

Deliver the introduction **extemporaneously.** This means that you carefully prepare in advance what you'll say, but you don't memorize or read your introduction. Instead, you choose the exact wording as you speak it.

FAMILIARIZING YOURSELF
WITH THE TEXT

Familiarization means you know your selection well enough to look up from it most of the time, but you keep the text in hand and refer to it occasionally. (Some instructors ask you to look up at least 80% of the time.) In her final self-analysis, Heather affirmed the importance of familiarization:

More familiarization would have made an enormous difference in where the pauses fell. Pauses should be for dramatic effect, not because the performer is confused!

What are the best strategies for familiarization? The answer, of course, depends on you and on your text. Think about the ways a choir learns music. The singers initially **sight read,** meaning they go through an unfamiliar piece, looking down at every word and note. (You did this when you first selected the text.) Sometimes the singers **memorize** every word and note, learning each detail by heart and performing without sheet music. In other performances, they keep their sheet music in hand, but they know the words and music well enough to look at the director most of the time, glancing at the score only now and then. This is familiarization—the kind you use in interpretation. You are not sight reading, and you don't need to memorize every single word. Instead, you should become so familiar with the selection that you can perform with just a few glances at your script.

Don't try to learn the text from beginning to end; instead, learn one section at a time, as a choir typically does. The singers first go over the piece from beginning to end, and the director identifies troublesome parts for the group to rehearse. Choirs typically work over a few difficult measures and then move to larger sections before finally rehearsing the entire song—but they stop whenever a problem arises and rework the problem measures. Borrow some of their techniques. Read your piece in its entirety, noting the sections that cause you problems. Then go through each section individually, working out the rough spots. Finally, string together several difficult sections before you return to the text as a whole.

You have already done quite a bit of preliminary work on familiarization. You have analyzed your selection (Chapter 4) and planned ways to present it vocally and physically (Chapter 5). So you come to the final rehearsal period aware of the big picture and some of the details. Now pull everything together and commit it to memory. Here are some specific ideas to help you.

To learn the **logical content**, or the words and the flow of ideas, copy or type the text yourself; this forces you to encounter each word individually.[3] Then put spaces between phrases, indicate pauses with slashes, underline stressed ideas, and so on, as described in Chapter 4. It may help to break up the text into smaller, more easily learned units. The example on page 112 from *The Ladies Auxiliary* (a longer excerpt is included at the end of Chapter 7) illustrates how to divide a single paragraph into smaller thought units. A group of women are watching Batsheva, a newcomer to their community, as she tows a giant Hanukkah menorah into her yard:[4]

We assembled at our windows, blinds pulled up, curtains pushed aside, waiting to see what was going to happen.

Not content with the view from inside, our children gathered at the edge of her lawn. We didn't have the heart to stop them, and even if we had, we doubted they would listen.

FIGURE 6.1 Visualize the Text's Imagery

If you are a visual learner, familiarize yourself with the text by creating drawings that illustrate the text.

The trees inside are moving out into the forest

the forest that was empty all these days
where no bird could sit  
no insect hide
no sun bury its feet in shadow . . .

We felt a small itching to let everything be all right again between Bat-sheva and us. We remembered how nice Sukkot had been when we were all gathered in her yard. But we reminded ourselves that this time we hadn't been invited to join and we stayed in our homes.

After you write out the cutting, memorize the overall flow of ideas. For example, if you were performing "The Trees" from Chapter 3 (page 41), you would commit to memory the trees' progress as they move from the inside to the outside of the house:

- Stanza 1: an empty, but soon-to-be filled forest
- Stanza 2: the trees' roots and leaves begin to disengage from the house
- Stanza 3: the speaker sits inside, writing letters in the moonlight as the trees begin to depart
- Stanza 4: the glass shatters and the moon breaks like a mirror as the trees complete their escape

Once you can recite the general flow of ideas from memory, you are ready to learn the order of details within specific stanzas, paragraphs, or sentences. The first stanza in "The Trees" (see Figure 6.1) lists specific items that the empty forest lacks: birds, insects, sun. Here are some suggestions for learning these items in order:

- Create an abbreviation from the first letter of each word. Thinking "B.I.S." can help you remember "bird, insect, sun."
- Visualize the images. Imagine a lone bird sitting on a branch, an insect crawling into view, and the sun strolling into the scene.
- Consider sketching out the images, as shown in Figure 6.1.

In addition to the text's logical content, learn its **emotional content**, the flow of passions and emotions that is found in the combination of single thoughts and whole images. For example, the emotions move from wistfulness to stubbornness in this paragraph from *The Ladies Auxiliary*:

We assembled at our windows, blinds pulled up, curtains pushed aside, waiting to see what was going to happen [*curiosity*]. Not content with the view from inside, our children gathered at the edge of her lawn [*excite-*

ment]. We didn't have the heart to stop them [*indulgence*], and even if we had, we doubted they would listen [*annoyance*].

Write marginal notations to indicate performance cues that convey emotion. For instance, "raise eyebrows slightly" could indicate curiosity and "frown" could accompany annoyance.

As you can see, learning the logical and emotional content of your selection requires time and effort, but the energy spent in rehearsal will pay off when you finally stand in front of a live audience.

USING A MANUSCRIPT

The presence of a written text is common in oral interpretations of literature. It reminds the audience and the performers that they are jointly participating in an interpretation of the words and ideas of an absent author. Consequently, knowing how to use a manuscript effectively is an important element of performance.

There is a difference between a script and a script book. The **script** consists of the words of the text, which can be photocopied, handwritten, typed, or read directly from the book. A **script book** is the folder or notebook that holds the script. Your instructor will provide details about his or her specific requirements. Most commonly, a script book is black, so it doesn't draw attention to itself. Sturdy folders or three-ring binders are the norm.

You probably won't perform directly from a book in class, unless, of course, one of your assignments is to interpret a children's picture book. Then you must do two things: (1) display the pictures while you (2) read upside down. If your career plans include teaching young children, you will hone these skills to perfection. A book is also used in formal places of worship, where a lector or reader stands behind a podium or **lectern** and reads from a scriptural text. If you are ever a lector in a religious service or wedding ceremony, for example, place the book fairly high on the lectern so you can more easily make eye contact with the listeners.

If you perform competitively on your university's speech team, an "unwritten rule"[5] requires the use of a small black notebook, and you are judged on the quality of your bookwork. (Appendix A gives guidelines for effective use of the manuscript in competitive performances.) Other performers, such as Readers Theatre ensembles, often keep their scripts in identical folders or notebooks and coordinate their page turns.

If you use a notebook or folder, hold it closed with both hands in front of you while you give your introduction. Then purposefully open it and begin your interpretation. If you start with a teaser, open your script book at the beginning, perform the teaser, and then close it while delivering your introduction. Reopen it to complete your performance. Hold the book with one hand, at an angle that prevents the audience from seeing the pages, and turn each page purposefully. When you finish, close the script book, pause a second or two, and return to your seat.

A book or script book is not essential; you can type or write out the text on note cards or plain paper. However, make sure the paper is sturdy enough to keep the pages from drooping or flopping. Consider mounting the script on black construction paper, which presents a more polished appearance. During your performance, hold the manuscript with one hand, leaving the other free for gestures. If you have several pages, stand in front of a mirror and practice moving the top page to the bottom of the stack until you are pleased with the overall result. The basic idea is to have the text present and to use in a manner that enhances and does not distract from the performance.

SUMMARY

It's important to craft an introduction that is adapted to your specific audience. Gain attention by beginning with a teaser, a short, intriguing piece of the text, or by using a rhetorical question, startling statistic, or other attention-grabbing strategy. In addition, show the relevance of the piece to the listeners, provide any background information that is necessary for an understanding of the text, and introduce the selection by title and author before you perform.

Familiarize yourself with the text by learning both its logical and emotional content. Start with the whole, then identify problem areas, and work out the bugs in each section before you again rehearse the whole piece. First learn the general flow of ideas; next, concentrate on specific details, using visualization, textual notations, and other strategies to reinforce your memory.

Finally, prepare and practice with your script. Whether you use a script book or manuscript mounted on sturdy paper, rehearse until the presence of the script enhances rather than detracts from your interpretation.

KEY TERMS

teaser	familiarization	emotional content
internal information	sight read	script
external information	memorize	script book
extemporaneously	logical content	lectern

QUESTIONS AND EXERCISES

1. Partner with a classmate and jointly work on your introductions. Give and accept advice from one another.

2. Select a literature sample from Chapters 7, 8, or 9 in this text. Jot down two or three ways you could relate that literature to

your classroom audience. Share your ideas with a small group of your classmates.

3. Make an audio recording of the text you have chosen to perform. Play back the recording as a way to familiarize yourself with the text.

4. Outline the logical content of your selection, and then jot notes about the emotional content in brackets in the margins. Familiarize yourself with your text's logical and emotional content.

5. List the advantages and disadvantages of performing a script from a book, a notebook or folder, or manuscript sheets. Which do you prefer? Why?

6. In front of a mirror, practice with your script until you are satisfied with your script skills.

7

Performing Prose

This chapter will help you:

- Perform nonfiction prose, including expository texts, essays, opinion pieces, journals, diaries, letters, speeches, biographies, and autobiographies

- Analyze the characters

- Explain elements of plot: setting, challenge, rising action, climax, denouement

- Understand the narrator's involvement, characteristics, and stance

- Analyze the intended audience

- Find and perform cultural stories: fables, tales, parables, myths, and legends

- Cut excerpts from short stories, novellas, and novels

- Do a performance analysis of the text

After lunch every day, my fifth-grade teacher, Mr. Learn (an appropriate name for a teacher!), would read aloud from one of the *Hardy Boys* mysteries, stopping just as the action reached a climax. We'd beg, "Don't stop, Mr. Learn! Keep reading!" And if our enthusiasm was great enough, he'd generally give in and read a while longer.

Stories have wide appeal. You probably have your own memories of teachers, librarians, parents, and other relatives reading to you. Very young children pore over the pictures as they listen. Older children and adults follow the plots in more complex tales. For example, Bethel College professors Scott Johnson and Alesha Seroczynski began reading the *Harry Potter* books to and with 12- to 15-year-old juvenile offenders, who soon became engrossed in the series.

The dictionary[1] defines **prose** as "the ordinary language people use in speaking or writing; a literary medium distinguished from poetry especially by its greater irregularity and variety of rhythm and its closer correspondence to the patterns of everyday speech." The words *commonplace* and *ordinary* are associated with the language of prose, which is the genre of literature most commonly performed. In addition to stories, performers read news broadcasts, formal speeches, radio ads, audiobooks, reports, and other forms of prose. This chapter discusses both nonfiction and fiction and provides guidelines for analyzing and performing prose texts.

NONFICTION PROSE

The two major divisions of prose are nonfiction and fiction. **Nonfiction prose,** which explains facts or presents information based on real happenings, can be lively and interesting when it presents descriptions and explanations creatively. This section describes several types of nonfiction that is suitable for performance.

Expository Prose

Exposition is writing or speech that describes or discusses theories, problems, or issues.[2] Consequently, **expository prose** explains, describes, and clarifies. News reports are an example of this genre, as are descriptions of processes or procedures, explanations of historical events, self-help manuals, scientific papers, and so on. Here's an excerpt of expository prose from the 12th century called "Celtic Music and Music in General," by Giraldus Cambrensis:[3]

> The sweet harmony of music not only affords us pleasures, but renders us important services. It greatly cheers the drooping spirit, clears the face from clouds, smooths the wrinkled brow, checks moroseness, promotes hilarity; of all the most pleasant things in the world, nothing more delights and enlivens the human heart. . . .
>
> Moreover, music soothes disease and pain; the sounds which strike the ear operating within, and either healing our maladies, or enabling us to bear them with greater patience. It is a comfort to all, and an effectual remedy

to many: for there are no sufferings which it will not mitigate, and there are some which it cures. . . .

When performing expository prose, first carefully analyze the structure of the overall work. Is it written in chronological order? Or is it organized in a problem-solution, cause–effect, or pro-con pattern? Once you know its general structure, examine the paragraphs, sentences, and words.

- Although the above excerpt is too short for you to determine the overall pattern of the text, Cambrensis uses a **spatial pattern,** ordering his points by region. He first discusses the music of Wales, and then he describes the music of Ireland.

- The first paragraph begins with a "not only . . . but . . ." pattern. The second opens with "moreover," which signals that the author is continuing the previous paragraph's argument.

- The second sentence in the first paragraph consists of a series of five phrases made of verb plus direct object ("cheers . . . the spirit"; "smooths . . . the brow"; "promotes hilarity"). He breaks what might become monotonous by using a semicolon and varying the final line and a half.

- The second paragraph includes two contrasts: "either . . . or" in the first sentence and "there are no . . . and there are some" in the last. Throughout, punctuation signals the end of phrases and provides cues for pauses.

- Identify unfamiliar or rarely used words, such as *moroseness* or *hilarity.* Look them up so you pronounce them correctly.

During the performance, use open focus and address the audience as a lecturer might. Emphasize the "not only . . . but" construction in the first sentence, and pause slightly before moving to the verb series. Speed up slightly for the series, and slow down after the semicolon. Emphasize the verbs throughout. Of course, enunciate clearly, especially the less familiar words. And pause slightly after commas, somewhat longer after semicolons, and even longer after periods.

Essays and Opinion Pieces

Essays are short pieces that analyze, describe, or interpret a subject from a personal perspective or viewpoint. They can be humorous and lighthearted or serious and somber. Well-written essays on interesting topics are often overlooked but are possible performance options. Here's an excerpt from an essay by Lavonne Adams about a child beauty pageant for three- to five-year-olds: [4]

> The four Tiny Miss contestants return to the stage. One is hiding behind the emcee; the rest are waiting expectantly, anxious smiles frozen on their faces.
>
> "And your new, 1991 Tiny Miss Holly is contestant number . . . three!"
>
> The audience cheers, screams, whistles. A crown is placed upon a small head.
>
> "When she grows up," the emcee tells the audience, "she wants to be a cheerleader." . . .

> **STOP AND CHECK: Perform Nonfiction Prose**
>
> Prepare a suitable piece of expository prose, such as a news report, an essay, or an opinion piece, to perform for a small group of your classmates.

There is a brief intermission. I see one of the defeated Tiny Miss contestants standing next to the stage. She's surrounded by friends and family. Her father is talking softly to her as she hangs her head dejectedly. I move closer, catch the funereal tones of the adult voices as her parents pat her shoulder consolingly. "You looked real pretty, honey"—"You did a good job"—"You'll be ready for them next year."

The punctuation strongly suggests where you'd pause, and in some instances, for how long. Packed into this short piece are several characters: the narrator, the emcee, the dejected loser, her parents. Each calls for distinctive vocal variations, facial expressions, and bodily posture and movements. Incorporate funereal tones where the author suggests them. Read the excerpt aloud a couple of times, experimenting with different performance ideas.

Opinion pieces are personal commentaries, such as newspaper editorials, syndicated columns, reviews, or letters to the editor, in which a writer makes a judgment about the merits of an issue or reflects upon a social happening. Some are suitable for classroom presentations. Browse through newspapers or magazines for columns, or go online and search for a columnist such as Dave Barry (humor), Chris Hewitt (movie reviews), Nicholas Kristof (social issues). In this excerpt from *Youth Outlook*, Shani Jackson reviews the San Francisco production of Def Poetry Jam:[5]

Poets have been using their words to unleash comedy, revolution and information into the Bay Area since June 21, when Russell Simmon's Def Poetry Jam premiered at Theater on the Square.... The nine poets ... for the most part, did not disappoint. The audience, on the other hand, didn't deserve their tickets. The audience, too cool to shout or laugh raucously, came close to killing the mood of the show with their signifyin' ways, but the poets were too good to let that happen.

When you perform an opinion piece, consider the author's bias or stance toward the topic. Is she sympathetic? Involved? Cynical? Lighthearted? Amused? Angry? Consider ways to incorporate the author's tone into your interpretation.

Journals, Diaries, and Letters

Because **journals** and **diaries** are personal records of everyday events, they often give insights into how individuals responded to social and cultural issues in specific eras. Thus, they can provide compelling performance materials. For example, Anne Frank's diary shows a young Jewish girl's response to the Holocaust. At the end of this chapter, you will find a cutting from Gideon

Welles's diary that provides a dramatic eyewitness account of Abraham Lincoln's deathbed scene. The following brief excerpt from Abigail Jane Scott's diary is an insider's account of her trip across the Oregon Trail, which began April 2, 1851, and ended October 1, six months later:[6]

June 12th

   Traveled 20 miles; At noon we for the first time hailed the rock known by the name of "Nebraska Court House." . . . It is on the South side of the river and rises up as if [to] mock the scenery around it with its bold and majestic front. . . . We passed five new made graves; we camped this evening on the river bank without buffalo chips and with no wood at all except a few small sticks of cedar which will answer for boiling water &c. but we made out a supper in the way of bread by eating sea-biscuits. A hard storm came up about six o'clock, and although but little rain fell yet the wind blew so hard that the wagons rocked to and froe; One of the tents got blown over and the many laughs and jests occasioned by the predicament of the inmates of the tent . . . made us all forget to regard the fury of the storm; We got everything straightened up again and all went off peacibly and well.

Letters can be formal and instructive, intended for a broad audience; for instance, newsletters and politicians' letters to their constituents are widely distributed. Letters can also be personal, intended only for one other person: a stranger, an acquaintance, a friend, relative, or romantic interest. *Galileo's Daughter,* a biography by Dava Sobel, includes several letters that the famous scientist received from his oldest child. (His letters to her were destroyed.)

Here's a letter from Mark Twain in answer to one from his neighbor, Jeannette Gilder:[7]

Hartford, May 14, 1887

My Dear Miss Gilder:

   We shall spend the summer at the same old place—the remote farm called "Rest-and-be-Thankful" on top of the hills three miles from Elmira, N. Y. Your other question is harder to answer. It is my habit to keep four or five books in process of erection all the time and every summer add a few courses of bricks to two or three of them, but I cannot forecast which of the two or three it is going to be. It takes seven years to complete a book by this method but still it is a good method: gives the public a rest. I have been accused of "rushing into print" prematurely, moved thereto by greediness for money, but in truth I have never done that. Do you care for trifles of information? Well, then, *Tom Sawyer* and *The Prince and the Pauper* were each on the stocks two or three years, and "Old Times on the Mississippi" eight. One of my unfinished books has been on the stocks sixteen years, another seventeen. This latter book could have been finished in a day, at any time during the past five years. But as in the first of these two narratives all the action takes place in Noah's ark, and as in the other the action takes place in heaven, there seemed to be no hurry and so I have not hurried.

Tales of stirring adventure in those localities do not need to be rushed to publication lest they get stale by waiting. In twenty-one years, with all my time at my free disposal, I have written and completed only eleven books, whereas with half the labor that a journalist does I could have written sixty in that time. I do not greatly mind being accused of a proclivity for rushing into print but at the same time I don't believe that the charge is really well founded. Suppose I did write eleven books, have you nothing to be grateful for? Go to—remember the forty-nine which I didn't write.

Truly Yours

S. L. Clemens

Letters and diaries are in the lyric mode, even though they are nonfiction. When you choose to perform one, incorporate the interpretation skills called for by that mode. Here's where knowledge about the author's personal characteristics can make your performance more meaningful: Abigail Scott had been on the Oregon Trail for several months; Galileo's eldest daughter was a nun, and Galileo himself was charged with heresy; Mark Twain was a crusty, slightly tongue-in-cheek writer who toured the country giving lectures, much like a stand-up comedian of today.

Speeches

Mark Twain commented on four speeches, saying that when he heard them, they made him "drunk with enthusiasm," but in print, "they don't seem the same." He concluded, "[T]here's nothing like the human organ to make words live and throb and lift the bearer to the full altitudes of their meaning."[8] Some speeches are so famous that they are still widely performed. Among these are Lincoln's Gettysburg Address and Martin Luther King, Jr.'s speech "I Have a Dream." While no one can duplicate Lincoln's or King's delivery, a good performance of their speeches can make their words echo from the era in which they were spoken, down to this day and time.

Biographies and Autobiographies

A **biography** tells facts about the life of another individual, either living or dead. An **autobiography** is a personal history, told by the actual person. Remember that authors' attitudes provide the lenses through which they present their subjects and that their perspectives are often less than objective.

Autobiographers generally present themselves positively by minimizing their negative qualities and highlighting or even exaggerating their accomplishments. Biographers include both admirers and detractors; both may have a specific point they want to get across. Here's an excerpt from Malcolm Muggeridge's glowing biography of Mother Teresa:[9]

> I never met anyone more memorable. . . . Once I had occasion to see her off, with one of the Sisters, at Calcutta railway station. It was the very early morning, and the streets were full of sleeping figures; sleeping with that strange, poignant abandon of India's homeless poor. We drove up to the station, absurdly enough in a large American limousine which happened to be at my disposal. The porters rushed expectantly forward, and then fell back disappointed when I got out followed by two nuns wearing the white saris of their order, made of the cheapest possible cloth, and carrying for luggage only a basket of provisions, most of which, I well knew, would be distributed along the way. I saw them to the train, and settled them in a third-class compartment. . . .
>
> When the train began to move, and I walked away, I felt as though I were leaving behind me all the beauty and all the joy in the universe. Something of God's universal love has rubbed off on Mother Teresa, giving her homely features a noticeable luminosity; a shining quality. . . . Outside the streets were beginning to stir; sleepers awakening, stretching and yawning; some raking over the piles of garbage in search of something edible. It was a scene of desolation, yet it, too, seemed somehow irradiated. This love, this Christian love, which shines down on the misery we make, and into our dark hearts that make it; irradiating all, uniting all, making of all one stupendous harmony. Momentarily I understood; then, leaning back in my American limousine, was carried off to breakfast, to pick over my own particular garbage-heap.

When interpreting a biography or autobiography, follow many of the guidelines for interpreting narratives in general, which will be discussed in the following section.

FICTIONAL PROSE

Fiction emerges from a creator's imagination, rather than from actual events. Fictional stories can be unrealistic or realistic. Unrealistic stories feature impossible characters or plots that break rules of nature. Animals talk; carpets fly; people do superhuman things; fairies and leprechauns inhabit the world. In contrast, realistic stories have a *might be* quality. Their characters are like actual people; the plots could happen. This section first describes elements of stories and then turns to types of stories.

Elements of Stories

Stories tell about actors who respond to some sort of conflict and change as a result. Here, we look at characters and the plots in which they are involved.

Characters   Characters, either real or fictional, human, animal, or personified object, are the agents in narratives. The characters' personal traits motivate and influence their decisions. Their beliefs and values, their energy level and temperament, and their past all affect what they say and do, how they react to others, and how others interact with them. Here is a memorable character: David Sedaris's father. Sedaris describes him and indicates how others react to him: [10]

> My father always struck me as the sort of man who, under the right circumstances, might have invented the microwave oven or the transistor radio. You wouldn't seek him out for advice on a personal problem, but he'd be the first one you'd call when the dishwasher broke or someone flushed a hairpiece down the toilet. As children, we placed a great deal of faith in his ability but learned to steer clear while he was working. The experience of watching was ruined, time and time again, by an interminable explanation of how things were put together.

The following description of Seabiscuit reveals some of the racehorse's most significant traits. Read it aloud, using your voice and body in ways that express the colt's personality: [11]

> The colt was practically sneering at him. Smith [the trainer] was standing by the track rail . . . when a weedy three-year-old bay stopped short in front of him, swung his head high, and eyed him with an arch expression completely unsuited to such a rough-hewn animal. "He looked right down his nose at me," Smith remembered later, "like he was saying, 'Who the devil are you?'"
>
> . . . The colt was a descendant of the mighty Man o' War . . . but his stunted build reflected none of the beauty and breadth of his forebears. The colt's body, built low to the ground, had all the properties of a cinder block. . . . He had a sad little tail barely long enough to brush his hocks. His stubby legs were a study in unsound construction, with squarish, asymmetrical "baseball glove" knees that didn't quite straighten all the way, leaving him in a permanent semicrouch. Thanks to his unfortunate assembly, his walk was an odd, straddle-legged motion that was often mistaken for lameness. . . . His gallop was so disorganized that he had a maddening tendency to whack himself in the front ankle with his own hind hoof. One observer compared his action to a duck waddle. . . .
>
> But somehow, after throwing a fit in the starting gate and being left flat-footed at the bell, the colt won his race that day. While being unsaddled, he leveled his wide-set, intelligent eyes on Smith again. Smith liked that look, and nodded at the horse. "Darned if the little rascal didn't nod

back at me," Smith said later, "kinda like he was paying me an honor to notice me." He was a horse whose quality, an admirer would write, "was mostly in his heart . . ."

We expect characters to behave in certain ways given their traits and backgrounds. Otherwise, we think they're acting *out of character.* That is, we expect a horse with "heart" to win despite obstacles; we expect children to respect but avoid an earnest father. When the characters act logically, we are more likely to accept the overall story as credible.

Plot The **plot** is what happens in the story. It's the action. Throughout the story, the characters' values, assumptions, and/or behaviors are challenged. Their responses and the resulting changes in their lives are the elements of plot. The plot usually develops in several stages, including the setting, the challenge, rising action, the climax, and the denouement.

The Setting The **setting** introduces the characters and locates them in a specific time and place. Scenes often open in an initial state of balance or **status quo,** in which the characters cope adequately with their situation.

The Challenge At this point, the **heroes** or **protagonists** (the **agents** or **co-agents** you want listeners to identify with), meet opposition (the **antagonists** or **counteragents**). Antagonists may be other characters: Indiana Jones (protagonist) searches for the lost Ark of the Covenant for positive reasons; Hitler's agents (antagonists) seek the Ark with evil motives. Sometimes antagonists are economic, physical, natural, or social forces: the Great Depression, AIDS, a devastating flood, or religious persecution. **Inciting incidents** trigger the conflicts and disrupt the status quo. See Figure 7.1.

Rising Action At this point, the problem intensifies. You must build suspense so that your audience wonders what the characters will do and how the story will turn out. Figure 7.2 shows the rising action.

The Climax The conflict escalates until something irrevocable happens. This is the **climax,** the turning point of the narrative, the point of no return. The choices made here determine the final outcome. At this point, the actor's true characteristics come to the foreground. Figure 7.3 illustrates the climax.

The Denouement In the **denouement,** the tension in the story relaxes and balance is restored. However, things are somehow different. Political alliances are altered, heroes become famous, individual characters gain insights into their own strengths or weaknesses. The diagram now looks like Figure 7.4.

setting (status quo)   inciting incident

FIGURE 7.1 The Inciting Incident

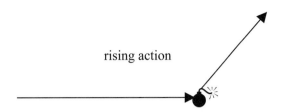

rising action

setting (status quo)   inciting incident

FIGURE 7.2 Rising Action

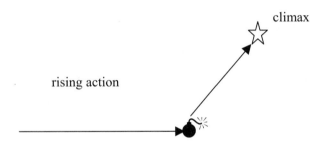

climax

rising action

setting (status quo)   inciting incident

FIGURE 7.3 Climax

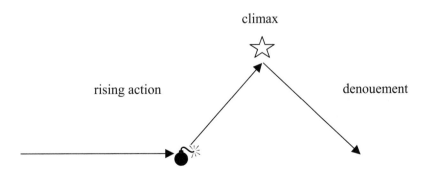

climax

rising action   denouement

status quo   inciting incident

FIGURE 7.4 The Denouement

Listeners decide whether or not the scenario seems reasonable and if the conflict seems realistic or possible. This does not mean that the story must be true in every detail. We accept myths, folktales, and unrealistic stories such as *The Little Engine That Could* as containing a form of truth when they examine important cultural beliefs or demonstrate appropriate ways to live.

Setting, challenge, rising action, climax, and denouement occur chronologically. Most stories follow this pattern, although some begin with the denouement and work back through the events.

Analyze the Narrator

Narrators tell the story. Consequently, an important step in preparing your prose performance is to analyze the narrator. All narrators take a **stance,** or an approach to the story or a point of view, that involves many elements. This section describes several ways to think about your narrator.

Determine the Narrator's Involvement Some narrators are involved in the story (**first person**); others stand outside and observe others' actions (**third person**). Occasionally, a narrator directly addresses the audience as "you" (**second person**). Some narrators are major characters in their stories; others are not. Some know the thoughts and feelings of one or more characters; others do not. Narrators can be subjective or detached.

First-Person Narrators First-person narrators can be major or minor characters. If **major characters,** they participate in the actions they're recounting. They reveal their personality characteristics by what they choose to tell, their style or language, their tone, and their attitude toward the events.

Here's an example from *A Dog's Life* by Peter Mayle of a narrator who's a major character and who reveals many things about himself in the course of his story. He's a dog whose owners have left for a long lunch. He goes to the forbidden upstairs bedroom and discovers the bed:[12]

> . . . And rather a fine bed at that—not too high, with an ample supply of pillows and an inviting expanse of what I later found out was an antique bedspread. It looked like the standard-issue white sheet to me, but antique linen isn't one of my interests. I incline more to the fur-rug school of interior decoration myself.
>
> Nevertheless, the bed had a definite appeal—as it would to you if you normally spent your nights in a basket on the floor—and so I hopped up.
>
> At first, I was a little disconcerted by the degree of softness underfoot, which reminded me of the times when I'd accidentally trodden on the Labrador. But once I adapted my movements, I found I could explore in short and rather exhilarating bounces, and I made my way up to the head of the bed, where the pillows were kept.
>
> They were poorly organized, in my view, laid out in a neat row, which may suit the reclining human figure but is not a convenient arrangement

for a dog. . . . I set to work, dragging the pillows to the middle of the bed, until they formed a kind of circular nest. And there I settled, in great comfort, and dozed off.

To perform a piece like this, you could assume a somewhat confessional but nonchalant and rather amused tone. After all, how else does one perform a dog that gets into trouble for soiling expensive bedding?

Narrators who are **minor characters** play minimal roles in their stories; they observe others who are acting around them. As a result, they work less on creating impressions of themselves than on creating impressions of other characters. In *Daisy Fay and the Miracle Man*,[13] the narrator, a young Southern girl, focuses on the adventures of her bingo-playing grandma:

[W]hen my Grandma Pettibone came in the door, the whole VFW hall got quiet. They were scared of her because she was on a winning streak and could play seventeen cards at once. She was wearing her lucky blue and white polka-dotted dress and her multicolored jeweled earrings.

She must have gone over to Bootie's Beauty Shop that day because her hair was bright purple. Her two friends Ollie Meeks and Pearl Tatum were with her. They are the three most feared bingo players in the state of Mississippi and even play penny bingo in the daytime just to keep sharp. . . . One of the reasons my Grandpa Pettibone left was because he said those old women used to scare his chickens to death yelling, "Bingo."

When Momma saw Grandma, she said, "Mother, you know I hate your hair purple!"

Grandma said, "It is not purple, it is bluish gray and I have the box top to prove it, miss," and pulled it out from her purse and gave it to Momma.

Momma didn't say anything else . . . but Grandma's hair was purple. She had two round circles of powdered rouge on her cheeks and a little dot of lipstick on her lips. . . . I don't think she looked like a Shriner clown, no matter what Momma said.

This narrator's tone is fond and amused when reporting her grandma's doings. Everything she reveals, down to the dots on the dress and the dots on the cheeks, portrays a flamboyant and proud senior citizen, who embarrasses her daughter and entertains her granddaughter. Even their names, "Grandma" and "Momma" instead of "Mother" and "Grandmother," add to the impression we get of the narrator and her relationship with the other characters.

Second-Person Narrators These narrators appear less frequently in prose than in poetry; however, because they address the reader directly, using "you," it's easier to feel personally involved in the story. For instance, the *Choose Your Own Adventure* books are written in second person and invite the reader to make choices that determine different outcomes. Here's another example from a story by Sandra Cisneros:[14]

What they don't understand about birthdays and what they never tell you is that when you're eleven, you're also ten, and nine, and eight, and seven, and six, and five, and four, and three, and two, and one. And when you wake up on your eleventh birthday you expect to feel eleven, but don't you open your eyes and everything's just like yesterday, only it's today. And you don't feel eleven at all. You feel like you're still ten. And you are—underneath the year that makes you eleven.

As you can see, second-person writing invites personal involvement differently than first- or third-person narration. The text often has an air of confidentiality.

Third-Person Narrators Third-person narrators can sometimes see into their characters' minds but not always. **Omniscient narrators** know their characters' motivations, emotions, and thoughts; narrators with **limited omniscience** have this information about one or a few characters, not all. **Objective narrators** don't reveal the character's feelings, motivations, or thoughts. **Subjective narrators** are emotionally involved in the story. They don't conceal their own biases, likes and dislikes, hopes and dreams. In contrast, **detached narrators** take a comparatively reportorial stance; they are less involved emotionally in the unfolding events.

Analyze the Narrator's Characteristics Find out all you can about your narrators. If possible, identify their gender and age. Look at their **style,** or language. Does the narrator use standard grammar, or nonstandard and colloquial forms? Is the language formal or conversational? Does it seem serious or lighthearted? Is it exaggerated or restrained? Jot down all the performance ideas that the language suggests.

Consider the narrator's attitudes and emotions toward the characters and the events in the story. This will help you discern the **tone** of the piece. Some narrators objectively report; others are disgusted by what they recount. Some are awestruck; others are amused. Narrators may feel superior to some characters and inferior to others. As a result, the text's tone may be sarcastic, amused, outraged, ironic, mournful, regretful, passionate, or condescending.

Some narrators have a strong need to control the narrative in a way that creates a specific impression of themselves and the other characters. They attempt this control through what they say, as well as what they omit. They are aware that their revelations convey impressions about themselves as well as the other characters. However, other narrators may reveal more about themselves than they intend. For instance, as the story unfolds, some may come across as compulsive or evil; just think of the narrators in such stories as Edgar Allen Poe's "The Tell-Tale Heart" or "The Cask of Amontillado."

All these factors influence your narrator's credibility. Some are trustworthy; others are not. Narrators can lie or conceal or slant the truth. You must assess their truthfulness.

Narrators' perspective is crucial to the meanings we take from stories. Their approval or disapproval of the characters' choices helps us identify the heroes and the villains. Their choices limit our viewpoint, because we only see and hear what they want us to. They invite us to share their perspective, privileging one viewpoint over another.

For example, when retelling the Biblical story of David and Goliath, the narrator could take a number of perspectives. The Biblical narrator casts David as the hero. Every day, Goliath, a giant from Philistia, challenges the trembling army of Israel. No one rises to the challenge until David arrives at the battlefield to visit his older brothers. Slingshot in hand, he topples the giant with a rock aimed directly at his forehead. Then, using Goliath's own sword, he severs the giant's head and presents it to the king.

In contrast, Frederick Buechner retells the story from Goliath's perspective:[15]

Goliath stood ten feet tall in his stocking feet, wore a size 20 collar, a 9½-inch hat, and a 52-inch belt. When he put his full armor on, he not only looked like a Sherman tank but weighed like one. Even stripped to the bare essentials, he had plenty to carry around, and flesh and bones were the least of it. There was the burdensome business of having to defend his title against all comers. There were the mangled remains of the runners-up. . . . When he tried to explain something, it was like pushing a truck uphill. His dark moods were leaden and his light moods elephantine. He considered under-arm deodorants a sign of effeminacy.

The stone from David's slingshot caught him between the eyes, and when he hit the dirt, windows rattled in their frames as far away as Ashkelon. The ringing in his ears drowned out the cat-calls of the onlooking armies and his vision was all but shot, but he could still see enough to make out the . . . figure of a boy running toward him through the scrub. . . .

As [David] straddled Goliath with Goliath's sword in his hand, the giant believed that what he was seeing was his own soul stripped of the unwieldy flesh at last for its journey to Paradise, and when David presented the severed head to Saul later, there was an unmistakable smile on its great lips.

Hearing this famous story from a different perspective illustrates how a narrator's choices affect the audiences. I've heard detached and subjective third-person accounts of the story; I've even heard a narrator take the persona of David. My sympathies, like most people's, always lay with David. Only after reading Buechner's account did I consider Goliath's viewpoint. Buechner personalized and humanized this villain, giving him understandable emotions and motivations and making him a sympathetic figure.

Determine the Nature of the Intended Audience

As part of your analysis, identify how the narrator sees the listeners and what relationship he or she has with those listeners. (Chapter 4 describes this as audience mode.) Then treat your classroom listeners as if you were addressing the intended group. (You may have to create an artificial audience, as described in Chapter 2.)

Is the narrator a teenager, the piece a confession, and the intended audience a best friend? Confide to the friend. Is the narrator explaining her actions

STOP AND CHECK: Analyze the Narrator

Here are excerpts from several texts. Analyze the narrator in each. Is the narrator an outsider or an insider? Relatively detached or subjective? Partly or wholly omniscient? Identify specific ways you could incorporate the results of your analysis into an interpretation of the story.

Excerpt #1 [from an essay about preschoolers in beauty pageants]:[16] I sit down in a chair recently vacated by one of the . . . winners of other local pageants. To my left sits a stately, composed woman who is scrutinizing the proceedings. I ask her if she is the mother of the queen whose seat I just appropriated. "No," she answers, pointing to yet another queen who is getting ready to entertain the crowd, "That's my daughter."

As we discuss pageants in general, I ask her about the cost of the clothing.

"You can't wear a sack, you know. This is based on more than talent and poise. You can put the most talented, beautiful girl up there, but if her dress is not competitive . . . well . . ." She leaves the sentence unfinished, raises her eyebrows, looks at me knowingly.

Excerpt #2 [from a Chinese story from 1929]:[17] Imagining what life would be like with a baby often became the focus of our conversation together. In those moments, my wife would appear to forget her usual depression, speaking quite cheerfully with me. But it did little to alleviate her mounting anxiety and as the extent of her physical changes grew more obvious, she could rarely forget her troubles even momentarily. She grew alarmingly dispirited and refused to do anything. . . . She would often sit alone, despondently, lost in thought, not moving for long periods of time. Once in a while when I spoke to her she would lift her head and stare up at me blankly, as if she were thinking about something else and had not clearly heard what I said. . . . Seeing her this way made me indescribably scared and upset; I began to feel that she was really suffering from some invisible, destructive force.

Excerpt #3 [from a short story in the *New Yorker* magazine]:[18] When you met Christie for the first time, it took only minutes to learn that she was from Greenwich, Connecticut, but months could go by before you got another solid fact out of her. After a couple of years in New York, she realized that she had to give people a little more information to stop them

to a parent? To a psychiatrist? Adjust your performance accordingly. Is the narrator's audience friendly or hostile? Be relaxed or wary, depending on their attitude. Are they young or old? People often address children differently than they do adults. Are they rich, poor, or middle class? Are they educated or illiterate? Are they married? Do they have children? And so on. All salient audience characteristics should inform and guide your interpretation.

Look back at *A Dog's Life* (pages 126–127) and at *Daisy Fay and the Miracle Man* (page 127). Analyze these brief cuttings to discern the narrator's intended audience and relationship with them. The dog knows that his audience, those of the human persuasion, is sometimes frustrated by doggy doings, basically likes dogs, finds them amusing, and tolerates their little foibles. He capitalizes on their goodwill and tries to humor them and just maybe alter

---

STOP AND CHECK (continued)

wondering, so once she'd mentioned Greenwich she would quickly add that she'd gone to "the high school," meaning the public one. The first time she said this, you'd find her forthrightness refreshing—disarming, even, in the midst of so many pretenders. You'd be prompted, perhaps, to admit something about yourself . . . But then you'd overhear Christie making the same confession to someone else, and it would lose its charm.

Excerpt #4 [from a British novel from 1952]:[19] [Lord Emsworth] eyed her apprehensively like some rat of the underworld cornered by G-men. Painful experience had taught him that visits from [his sister] meant trouble, and he braced himself, as always to meet with stout denial whatever charge she might be about to hurl at him. He was a great believer in stout denial and was very good at it.

For once, however, her errand appeared to be pacific. Her manner was serene, even amiable.

"Oh, Clarence," she said, "have you seen Penelope anywhere?"

"Eh?"

"Penelope Donaldson."

"Who?" asked Lord Emsworth courteously, "is Penelope Donaldson?"

Lady Constance sighed. Had she not been the daughter of a hundred Earls, she would have snorted. Her manner lost its amiability. She struck her forehead with a jeweled hand and rolled her eyes heavenward for a moment.

"Penelope Donaldson," she said, speaking with the strained sweetness of a woman striving to be patient . . . "is the younger daughter of the Mr. Donaldson of Long Island City in the United States of America whose elder daughter is married to your son Frederick. To refresh your memory, you have two sons—your heir, Bosham, and a younger son, Frederick. Frederick married the elder Miss Donaldson. The younger Miss Donaldson—her name is Penelope—is staying with us now at Blandings Castle—this is Blandings Castle—and what I am asking you is . . . Have you seen her? And I do wish, Clarence, that you would not let your mouth hang open when I am talking to you. It makes you look like a goldfish." . . .

"Ah!" he cried, enlightened. "When you say Penelope Donaldson, you mean Penelope Donaldson. Quite. Quite."

---

their perspectives a bit. Daisy Fay is a chatty girl who is entertaining her friends with stories about community happenings. She assumes they'll enjoy her tales of small-town living but seems naïve about the ridiculousness of her maternal relatives. That's part of the fun of the piece, and a good performance would capture some of her innocent charm.

Cultural Stories

Every culture has originated a set of stories that transmit the group's beliefs and values. These stories, which emerge from the group's lived experiences, include fables, folktales, parables, myths, and legends.[20]

Fables are short stories that explicitly state some aspect of cultural wisdom (their "moral" reveals the point). The characters are usually animals or inanimate objects that embody human motivations and feelings, and their characteristics are essential to the lesson. For example, in "The Tortoise and the Hare," the slower tortoise is steady, whereas the swifter hare is impulsive. In their race, the persistent tortoise defeats the easily distracted hare. The moral: "Slow and steady wins the race."

Cultural tales entertain, as well as reinforce values. Their universal or archetypal themes deal with human hopes, passions, and fears. **Folktales,** old stories passed down orally from generation to generation by the "common folk," recount strange or fabulous happenings. Truly wicked or truly good archetypal characters enact dramas in which good conquers evil. Characters are realistic (stepmothers), fantastic (fairy godmothers), or both (Goldilocks and the three bears). They are often stylized: Princesses are beautiful, stepmothers are wicked, princes are brave, soldiers are loyal, and so on. **Fairy tales** are a subset of folktales that feature fabulous characters such as genies in lamps and frogs who are really human princes. Modern tellings typically open with "Once upon a time" and close with "and they lived happily ever after."

Many folktales have variations across cultures. For example, Little Red Riding Hood is French; her German counterpart is Little Red Cap; and the Chinese version has three little girls who encounter Lon Po Po, a wolf pretending to be their grandmother. Each story features a similar plot: the girl or girls who go to grandma's house, the wolf who devours little girls, and the individual or group who foils the carnivore's evil plot.

Parables are brief stories that teach religious or moral lessons. The moral of the story is not always explicitly stated, and the story can be understood on a number of levels. According to the New Testament, Jesus commonly taught in parables; on one occasion, his disciples begged him to interpret the parable of a farmer who scattered his seed on various types of soil, resulting in different crop yields. On the surface, it was a story about farming, but Jesus indicated that the soil was a metaphor for different kinds of listeners. The seed symbolized Jesus' teachings, and the crop yield stood for good works that hearers would perform as a response to his teachings.

Myths are ancient stories that communicate deeply held beliefs that comprise a culture's worldview. They tell about heroes or supernatural beings. Each culture has its own myths, but certain patterns recur across cultures. Myths explain the creation of the cosmos, the presence of evil, and so on. This Navajo myth explains the Big Dipper (*Ursa Major*) constellation. There were seven brothers, and one of their sisters married a bear. Furious, their father killed the beast. The sister took flesh off her husband's paw and changed herself into a bear, pursuing her brothers in revenge and killing six of them before transforming back into a human. (She is known as Changing Bear Woman.) However, the youngest brother restored the others to life, and all seven escaped to the sky, where they remain to this day.[21]

Legends are unlikely stories that are associated with real people and historical events. They exaggerate their subjects' traits or their actions. For example, there may have been a Robin Hood, but many of the legends that surround him are exaggerations; there may have been a woodsman named Paul

> ### PERFORMING CULTURE: Finding Folktales, Myths, and Legends Online
>
> Folktales were originally oral, not literary, works. However, thousands of global folktales, myths, and legends are now available in written form on the Internet. If you're interested in performing a fairy tale, try the SurLaLune Fairy Tale Web site, located at www.surlalunefairytales.com. For myths or legends, search for *Bulfinch's* *Mythology* in your campus library, or find some of the classics online at www.bulfinch.org. There you can link to "Volume I: The Age of Fable, or Stories of Gods and Heroes"; "Volume II: The Age of Chivalry, or Legends of King Arthur"; and "Volume III: Legends of Charlemagne, or Romance of the Middle Ages."

Bunyan, but many of the stories about him and his Blue Ox, Babe, could not have happened. Regardless of their basis in fact, legends teach important cultural ideas such as social justice and the need to care for the poor or character traits such as loyalty and hard work.

CUTTING YOUR PIECE

If you choose to perform part of a novel or long story, you will expect to cut and edit your piece. However, even short pieces require at least some editing. You can successfully cut a text by following a few guidelines:

- First, read aloud through the short story, the chapter, or the section you want to perform, using a conversational pace. Time yourself, and record your results. Because a class performance generally will not exceed 10 minutes, which includes your introduction, you should plan to present about 9 minutes of text. If your piece takes 19 minutes to read through, you must cut about half of the original material.

- Select a cutting with a limited number of characters. Ten minutes is too short for presenting a large cast, and your audience can easily get lost if they must keep track of the motives, moods, thoughts, and actions of too many characters.

- When you must cut a very long piece, first determine one point of climax, and then cut material *into* it. This means including sections of the text the audience must know in order to understand the climax. Add sections that show how the conflict resolves. Throughout this process, eliminate details that do not forward the plot.

- Select opening material that sets up the background and introduces the characters.

- Tag lines are phrases such as "he said" and "they replied." Whenever you can, omit the tags. Instead of saying "she shouted," show how loudly she spoke by actually raising your voice.

After this initial cutting, test your piece for coherence. Do you cut in enough material to set the time, place, and characters? Do you lead to a point of climax? Will your audience feel that the conflict resolves satisfactorily? Time your piece again, making additional edits as necessary. Here's an example of a cutting from the opening chapter of C. S. Lewis's book *The Magician's Nephew*:[20]

This is a story about something that happened long ago when your grandfather was a child. . . . [*cut two paragraphs of details*] in those days there lived in London a girl called Polly Plummer.

She lived in one of a long row of houses which were all joined together. One morning she was out in the back garden when a boy scrambled up from the garden next door and put his face over the wall. Polly was very surprised because up till now there had never been any children in that house. . . . . So she looked up, full of curiosity. The face of the strange boy was very grubby. It could hardly have been grubbier if he had first rubbed his hands in the earth, and then had a good cry, and then dried his face with his hands. As a matter of fact, this was very nearly what he had been doing.

"Hullo," ~~said Polly~~.

"Hullo," ~~said the boy~~. "What's your name?"

"Polly," ~~said Polly~~. "What's yours?"

"Digory," ~~said the boy~~.

"I say, what a funny name!" ~~said Polly~~.

"It isn't half so funny as Polly," ~~said Digory~~.

"Yes it is," ~~said Polly~~.

"No it isn't," ~~said Digory~~.

"At any rate I do wash my face," ~~said Polly~~. "Which is what you need to do; especially after —" and then [Polly] stopped. She had been going to say "After you've been blubbing," but she thought that wouldn't be polite.

"All right, I have then," ~~said Digory in a much louder voice, like a boy who was so miserable that he didn't care who knew he had been crying~~. "And so would you," ~~he went on~~, "if you'd lived all your life in the country and had a pony, and a river at the bottom of the garden, and then been brought to live in a beastly Hole like this."

"London isn't a Hole," ~~said Polly indignantly~~. But the boy was too wound up to take any notice of her, and he went on—

"And if your father was away in India—and you had to come and live with an Aunt and an Uncle who's mad (how would you like that?)—and if the reason was that they were looking after your Mother—and if your

Mother was ill and was going to—going to—die." ~~Then his face went the~~
~~wrong sort of shape as it does if you're trying to keep back your tears~~.

"I didn't know. I'm sorry," ~~said Polly humbly. And then, because she~~
~~hardly knew what to say, and also to turn Digory's mind to cheerful sub-~~
~~jects, she asked:~~

"Is Mr. Ketterley really mad?"

"Well either he's mad," ~~said Digory,~~ "or there's some other mystery. He
has a study on the top-floor and Aunt Letty says I must never go up there."

Notice how this cutting sets the piece in time and place. It introduces the
characters just enough to make their actions understandable. Gone are nonverbal cues (such as Digory's facial expressions as he fights to keep back his
tears, or Polly's humility or forced cheerfulness). A performer could *show* them,
not *describe* them.

PREPARING YOUR PROSE PERFORMANCE

Use the principles identified in the section about expository prose as you prepare. First examine the general organization of the piece: its sentences, paragraphs, speech phrases. You can usually identify these through the punctuation.
Draw slashes where you will pause, and underline all the words you need to
stress or enunciate carefully. Look for transitions such as "therefore" or "as a
result," and notice contrasts that are introduced with words such as "either . . .
or." Here are some examples:

- In Penelope Layland's short story "The Death of the Fat Man," found on
  pages 138–140, the words *later, that night,* and *alone* are repeated several
  times and are very important in creating the mood of the story. For performance, highlight them in a specific color on the script, and then carefully decide how to say them in order to create the story's tension and
  sense of foreboding.

- Mayles' dog narrator speaks very conversationally, and the author uses dashes
  to indicate pauses: "Nevertheless, the bed had a definite appeal—as it would
  to you if you normally spent your nights in a basket on the floor—and so I
  hopped up." This one sentence offers the opportunity to use three variations:

  - "Nevertheless, the bed had a definite appeal . . ." (The dog is tempted;
    he'd say this slowly and thoughtfully, perhaps with a slightly faraway
    look and faint smile as if he were dreaming about a nap there.)

  - "as it would to you if you normally spent your nights in a basket on
    the floor" (Here, he'd look directly at a couple of people in the audi-
    ence and speak defensively, like a child who got caught sneaking candy
    before dinner.)

  - "and so I hopped up." (He's definite here, having decided to succumb
    to temptation.)

> **STOP AND CHECK: Create a Prose Performance**
>
> Find a prose piece that is suitable for your classroom audience. Cut it to fit the assigned time frame. Then analyze it, familiarize yourself with it so that you can look up from the text at least 80% of the time, and interpret it for your classmates.

In addition, do a modal analysis and look for lyric sections, dramatic sections, and narration. This will help you decide when to create character placement and when to use different vocal and bodily characteristics to suggest various characters. It will help you determine when to use open focus and when to use closed or semi-closed focus. For example:

> "Yes, it is."
>
> "No, it isn't."
>
> "At any rate I do wash my face. Which is what you need to do; especially after—" [*This exchange is in the dramatic mode, so "place" Digory and Polly, and use different vocal and physical characteristics for each child during the argument.*]
>
> . . . and then [Polly] stopped. She had been going to say "After you've been blubbing," but she thought that wouldn't be polite. [*Here the text breaks into the argument with narration. Look directly at the audience, switch to the adult narrator's persona, and speak confidentially about her motivations. But say "After you've been blubbing" as Polly.*]
>
> "All right, I have then." [*You're back to the character placement and dialogue; say this line in Digory's voice.*]

These are just a few suggestions for performing prose. The bottom line is this: Be mindful; approach your piece thoughtfully. Analyzing the narrator and the intended audience, examining the literature itself, and planning your performance accordingly should lead to success!

PROSE LITERATURE FOR STUDY AND PRACTICE

Here are several short prose cuttings from both nonfiction and fiction. Use them to apply the principles presented in this chapter.

Excerpt from the **Diary of Gideon Welles**[22]

Welles was Secretary of the Navy during Abraham Lincoln's administration. His diary was originally published in the Atlantic *magazine. This excerpt provides an eyewitness account of Lincoln's death.*

April 15, 1865

I had retired to bed about half-past ten on the evening of the 14th of April, and was just getting to sleep when Mrs. Welles, my wife, said some one was at our door. . . . I arose at once and raised a window, when my messenger, James Smith, called to me that Mr. Lincoln, the President, had been shot, and said Secretary Seward and his son, Assistant Secretary Frederick Seward, were assassinated. James was very much alarmed and excited. . . . I immediately dressed myself, and against the earnest remonstrance and appeals of my wife, went directly to Mr. Seward's. . . . where there were many soldiers as well as citizens already gathered.

Entering the house, I found the lower hall and office full of persons, and among them most of the foreign legations, all anxiously inquiring what truth there was in the horrible rumors afloat. I replied that my object was to ascertain the facts. Proceeding through the hall to the stairs, I found one, and I think two, of the servants there holding the crowd in check. The servants were frightened and appeared relieved to see me. I hastily asked what truth there was in the story that an assassin or assassins had entered the house and assaulted the Secretary. They said it was true. . . .

As we descended the stairs, I asked Stanton what he had heard in regard to the President that was reliable. He said the President was shot at Ford's Theatre, that he had seen a man who was present and witnessed the occurrence. . . . The President had been carried across the street from the theatre, to a house of a Mr. Peterson. We entered by ascending a flight of steps . . . and passing through a long hall to the rear, where the President lay extended on a bed, breathing heavily. Several surgeons were present, at least six, I should think more. Among them I was glad to observe Dr Hall, who . . . [said] the President was dead to all intents, although he might live three hours or perhaps longer.

The giant sufferer lay extended diagonally across the bed, which was not long enough for him. He had been stripped of his clothes. His large arms, which were occasionally exposed, were of a size which one would scarce have expected from his spare appearance. His slow, full respiration lifted the [bed]clothes with each breath that he took. His features were calm and striking. I had never seen them appear to better advantage than for the first hour, perhaps, that I was there. After that, his right eye began to swell and that part of his face became discolored.

. . . A double guard was stationed at the door and on the sidewalk, to repress the crowd, which was of course highly excited and anxious. The room was small and over-crowded. . . . and the hall and other rooms in the front or main house were full. One of these rooms was occupied by Mrs. Lincoln and her attendants. . . . About once an hour Mrs. Lincoln would repair to the bedside of her dying husband and with lamentation and tears remain until overcome by emotion.

. . . The night was dark, cloudy, and damp, and about six it began to rain. I remained in the room . . . listening to the heavy groans, and witnessing the wasting life of the good and great man who was expiring before me.

About 6 A.M. I experienced a feeling of faintness and for the first time after entering the room, a little past eleven, I left it and the house, and took a short walk in the open air. . . . Large groups of people were gathered every few rods, all anxious and solicitous. Some one or more from each group stepped forward as I passed, to inquire into the condition of the President, and to ask if there was no hope. Intense grief was on every countenance when I replied that the President could survive but a short time. The colored people especially—and there were at this time more of them, perhaps, than of whites—were overwhelmed with grief. . . .

A little before seven, I went into the room where the dying President was rapidly drawing near the closing moments. His wife soon after made her last visit to him. The death-struggle had begun. . . . The respiration of the President became suspended at intervals and at last entirely ceased at twenty-two minutes past seven. . . .

On the Avenue in front of the White House were several hundred colored people, mostly women and children, weeping and wailing their loss. This crowd did not appear to diminish through the whole of that cold, wet day . . . their hopeless grief affected me more than almost anything else, though strong and brave men wept when I met them.

"The Death of the Fat Man"[23]

BY PENELOPE LAYLAND

Here's an entire short story by an Australian journalist and poet. Analyze the narrator, using the questions that follow the story, and come to class prepared to discuss how your analysis would help you perform this piece.

The figure was still there when the party left the restaurant in a swill of hot air and cognac.

One of the party, a fat man with greedy eyes, who would have a heart attack later that night, alone in his flat, turned to stare at the figure.

"They found one of your kind last week, you know? In the Bois. Cut up in pieces and put in a suitcase. Some crazy Japanese fellow did it—told the police he was Jesus Christ." The fat man peered into the shadows. "Hear me?" Then he spat.

"Pascal, the taxi's here. What are you doing?" The woman's voice was glassy. She peered too into the shadows and swayed perceptibly on her brittle, sophisticated heels. Later, in the taxi, she would wind down the window, feel the air inflate her lungs, vow never to drink champagne again. She would go home with her husband, the sullen man who was now beckoning impatiently from the taxi. She would dream about her husband's American friend, to whom she had made sharp, insulting remarks at dinner that night.

She was not happy, and the sight of her friend, the fat man Pascal, who would die that night, alone in his rooms, disgusted her. The knowledge of that figure in the shadows revolted her.

"Come, Pascal." The woman advanced the top half of her body toward her friend.

"Come on, you two," cried the woman's husband, leaning from the taxi and burping discreetly. Later his indigestion would become more severe and he would lie beside the living wall of his wife, wishing he was dead.

He watched his wife now as she concentrated on the cobbles, her ankles absurdly thin. Pascal hobbled after her, looking ill and colourless under the fizz of street lights.

"Perhaps if we go your way first, Pascal," said the woman. "It's probably quicker. Or cheaper at least." She laughed, amused by the suggestion that they could be concerned over a taxi fare, they who had just dined in luxury. She remembered her witty, callous remarks to the poor American, the friend of her husband, and her cruel contempt of the greediness of the man beside her, Pascal, who would die tonight.

Pascal was silent as he heaved his legs into the taxi after his shapeless torso. The taxi driver demanded an address, inner-cursing these drunken people, envying their ease. Pascal gave his address and got confused with the address of a flat he had owned years before, before . . . but he couldn't remember and the woman at his side looked cruelly at him and said sweetly, "You've drunk too much, you silly old fool."

Later, before going to bed, the woman would have a fight with her husband. He would accuse her of flirting and she would grow angry as the throb of champagne ebbed to leave her cold. He would go to the bedroom, pretending to be asleep when she came in. He would be relieved when she entered the bed too far away for accidental contact and indigestion would burn pinpoint holes in his heart.

"Ten francs."

"We'll settle," said the woman and felt annoyed when Pascal refused to recognise the gesture, not that it mattered, of course. She watched him hesitate at the door of the building, groping for keys in the stuttering light, his face grey. The taxi jerked away.

The fat man, Pascal, was to wake, later that night, for no reason he could think of but with a nagging tip-of-the-tongue awareness. The pain was not to strike at first and when it did he would wonder at the mediocrity of all previous sensation, wonder how he could ever have thought he had lived, so feeble would all things seem, compared to this. The pain would be strong, embracing and overwhelmingly surprising.

So during those moments, the ones in which his life rapidly changed into merely other people's lives, he would lie quietly, as if that would help.

Later, too, the woman would wake, would say "Pierre? Did you say something?" She would sigh, move restlessly in the territory of her half of the bed. Then Pierre, her husband, would sigh.

"Perhaps if you just tried to go to sleep . . ." Pierre would roll his head to look at his wife. Her skull, leaning against the headboard would seem as fragile as a snail's shell, her hair twisted in green-brown grain across it. "If I lit a lamp behind your head," he would think, "the light would shine right through." But he would not say so, he would say instead, "Why don't you sleep?"

Her skull would appear to be trying to scale the headboard, a pulse would move in her slug-neck.

"I slept with your friend. The American," she would lie.

"I know. I don't care. Do whatever will make you happy," he would also lie.

Outside snow would begin to fall, big wet flakes rough around the edges from the heat of the city. They would melt as they hit the roads. A few blocks away the fat man, Pascal, would just be awakening, with something on his mind.

Use these questions in your analysis:

- What can you tell about this narrator's age and gender?
- What attitude does the narrator convey toward the characters? Identify specific details that give this away.
- What is the tone of this piece?
- Is the narrator detached or subjective? Self-conscious?
- What specific features of language did you especially notice?
- Do you think the narrator is credible? (Do you believe the story?) Why or why not?
- Identify the omniscience or objectivity of the narrator.
- What's the purpose for telling this story?
- Does it help you to know that the story appeared in an anthology by women writers from New Zealand and Australia? Why or why not?

From **The Piano Tuner**[24]

BY DANIEL MASON

Daniel Mason, a 24-year-old graduate of Harvard University, wrote this book before entering medical school. It is about an Englishman called to Burma to tune a piano for an eccentric officer in the British Army. On his way to the country's interior, the main character, Edgar, accompanies Captain Nash-Burnham to a traditional story-telling event, the pwè. *As they walk along, the British captain explains the ceremony.*

"A *pwè*," [said] the Captain . . . "is uniquely Burmese. . . . There are many reasons to hold a *pwè* . . . for deaths . . . when pagodas are dedicated. Or even nonreligious reasons: . . . a boxing match, when a fire-balloon is released. Anything else you can think of. . . ."

Down the street, they could see lights, movement. "There is one!" exclaimed Khin Myo, and Nash-Burnham, "Yes we are lucky, lucky indeed. We have a saying that there are but two types of Englishmen in Burma, those who love the *pwè* and those who can't bear it. . . . I have fallen in love with the art."

. . . Edgar could see a wide crowd of people seated on mats in the middle of the road. These were arranged around an empty patch of earth . . . In the center . . . stood a pole. . . . [F]lames flickered in concentrically arranged earthenware pots, lighting the faces of the first row of spectators.

They stood at the edge of the crowd. . . . one man shouted something. . . . Khin Myo answered him. "They want us to stay" . . .

"Wonderful!" The Captain stomped his cane on the ground with pleasure. . . . "That circular space is the stage . . . [t]he Burmese call it the . . . *pwè-waing* . . . and the branch in the middle is the *pan-bin* . . . The Burmese sometimes say it represents a forest, but I have a feeling that it sometimes only serves to keep the audience back.

". . . [E]veryone here [already knows the plot]; these are only retellings of the same story. . . . This one is about Prince Nemi, one of the Buddha's incarnations, who is born into a long line of Burmese kings. As a young man, Prince Nemi is so pious that the spirits decide to invite him to see heaven. One moonlit night . . . they send a chariot down to earth. . . . The Prince boards it, and it disappears. . . . The chariot takes Nemi first to the heavens where the *nats* live—*nats* are Burmese folk spirits, even good Buddhists believe they are everywhere—and then to *Nga- yè,* the underworld where the serpents called *nagas* dwell. At last he reluctantly returns to his world, to share the wonders he has seen. The finale is quite sad: it was the tradition of the kings that when they grew old and sensed that death was near, they left their homes and traveled into the desert to die as hermits. And so one day, Nemi, like his forefathers before him, wanders into the mountains to die."

There was a long silence. . . .

"It is perhaps my favorite story," said Nash-Burnham.

From The Ladies Auxiliary[25]

BY TOVAH MIRVIN

The narrators in this book use the first-person plural "we" and are wives and mothers in an Orthodox Jewish community in Memphis. Batsheva and her daughter Shira are new converts who recently moved into this close-knit neighborhood. Yosef is the beloved rabbi's popular son.

On the first night of Chanukah, we were setting up our menorahs in the front windows of our homes when we saw Batsheva, Yosef, and Shira pushing something into the front yard of Batsheva's house. . . .

We assembled at our windows, blinds pulled up, curtains pushed aside, waiting to see what was going to happen. Not content with the view from inside, our children gathered at the edge of her lawn. We didn't have the heart to stop them, and even if we had, we doubted they would listen. We felt a small itching to let everything be all right again between Batsheva and us. We remembered how nice Sukkot had been when we were all gathered in her yard. But we reminded ourselves that this time we hadn't been invited to join and we stayed in our homes.

. . . Batsheva pulled the sheets off, and there was the biggest menorah we had ever seen. It was made of wood painted silver, and on top of each of the eight branches was a lantern waiting to be lit. We tried to tell ourselves that this menorah wasn't so special. We came up with all the problems it presented: it was ostentatious, showy. Even though we were commanded to publicize the miracle of Chanukah, we were different enough from our non-Jewish neighbors, and we didn't need to stick this in their faces more than it already was. . . . We wondered if it was even in accordance with Jewish law. . . . maybe there was some sort of prohibition against such displays.

But even so, we couldn't stop staring at how tall and proud this menorah stood against the darkening blue-gray sky, and pure and simple it was. It brought this miracle from so long ago into our front yards, and we began to wish that we had thought of doing something like this ourselves. Batsheva's menorah made us feel that we no longer had to stare longingly at the Christmas decorations in the rest of the city. We finally had something of our own to look at.

"It's time to light the candles," Batsheva announced to the children around her, and . . . [they] began singing the blessings: *Blessed are you God who commanded us to light the Chanukah candles, for doing miracles for our ancestors and for us, for renewing us and sustaining us and bringing us to this time. . . .*

We would be singing these same songs in our homes as soon as our husbands came home from work, and we wondered whether our kids would sing with such gusto, if it would still feel like the first night of Chanukah. As much as we tried to convince ourselves that it would, that our own candle lightings were special no matter what Batsheva was doing, we knew that it wouldn't be the same; the uniqueness of seeing just one of the eight candles burning was over for this year.

From My Name is Red[26]

ORHAN PAMUK (TRANS. FROM THE TURKISH BY ERDAG M. GOKNAR)

A miniaturist named Effendi, one of the Sultan's artists in medieval Istanbul, has been murdered—probably by another artist. In this mystery novel by a Turkish author, different characters narrate different chapters. The narrator in this chapter is a gold coin.

Behold! I am a twenty-two-carat Ottoman Sultani gold coin and I bear the glorious insignia of His Excellency Our Sultan, Refuge of the World. Here, in the middle of the night in this fine coffeehouse overcome with funereal melancholy, Stork, one of Our Sultan's great masters, has just finished drawing my picture, though he hasn't yet been able to embellish me with gold wash—I'll leave that to your imagination. My image is here before you, yet I myself can be found in the money purse of your dear brother, Stork, that illustrious miniaturist. He's rising now; removing me from his purse and showing me off to each of you. Hello, hello, greetings to all the master artists and assorted guests. Your eyes widen as you behold my glimmer, you thrill as I shimmer in the light of the oil lamp, and finally, you bristle with envy at my owner, Master Stork. You're justified in behaving so, for there's no better measure of an illustrator's talent than I.

In the past three months, Master Stork has earned exactly forty-seven gold pieces like myself. We're all in this money-purse and Master Stork, see for yourself, isn't hiding us from anyone; he knows there's none among the miniaturists of Istanbul who earns more than he does. I take pride in being recognized as a measure of talent among artists and in putting an end to unnecessary disagreements. In the past, before we got used to coffee and our minds sharpened, these dim-witted miniaturists weren't satisfied with spending their evenings arguing about who was the most talented or who had the best sense of color, who could draw the best tree or who was the most expert in the depiction of clouds; no, they'd also come to blows over such issues, knocking out each other's teeth in the process. Now that my judgment decides everything, there's a sweet harmony in the workshop, and what's more, an air that would suit the old masters of Herat.

. . . [L]et me list the various things I might be exchanged for: . . . a good quality walnut-handled barber's mirror, edges inlaid with bone; . . . 120 loaves of bread; a grave site and coffins for three; a silver armband; one-tenth of a horse; one buffalo calf; two high-quality pieces of china; . . . one good hunting falcon with cage; ten jugs of Pahayot's wine . . . and many other opportunities too numerous to specify.

. . . As long as you promise not to tell anyone . . . I'll tell you a secret. Do you swear not to tell?

All right then, I confess. I'm not a genuine twenty-two-carat Ottoman Sultani gold coin minted at the Chemberlitash Mint. I'm counterfeit. They made me in Venice using adulterated gold and brought me here, passing me off as a twenty-two-carat Ottoman gold. Your sympathy and understanding are much obliged.

From Autobiography of a Face[27]

BY LUCY GREALY

When she was in the fourth grade, Lucy Grealy underwent surgery for cancer on her jaw, followed by five years of treatment. She recovered from the cancer, but people's reactions to her permanently scarred face created wounds of another kind.

One morning I went into the bathroom and shut the door . . . I turned on the lights and very carefully, very seriously, assessed my face in the mirror. I was bald, but I knew that already. . . . My teeth were ugly. And I noticed, they were made worse by the fact that my chin seemed so small. How had it gotten that way? I didn't remember it being so small before. I rooted around in the cabinets and came up with a hand mirror and, with a bit of angling, looked for the first time at my right profile. I knew to expect a scar, but how had my face sunk in like that? . . . Was it possible I'd looked this way for a while and was only just noticing it, or was this change very recent? . . . I was suddenly appalled at the notion that I'd been walking around unaware of something that was apparent to anyone else. A profound sense of shame consumed me.

I put the mirror away, shut off the lights, went back into the living room, and lay in the sunlight with the cats. They didn't care how I looked. I made a silent vow to love them valiantly, truly, with an intensity that would prove I was capable, worthy of . . . I wasn't sure what, but something wonderful, something noble, something spectacular. . . .

At school the taunts were becoming only harder to take. Somehow I had reasoned that if a bad thing happened often enough it would get easier. It worked with pain, so why wasn't it working with teasing? Every time I was teased, which usually happened several times a day, it seemed incrementally more painful. I was good at not listening, at pretending I hadn't heard, but I could sense myself changing . . . Before I'd been an outgoing person . . . but now meeting new people was laced with dread. Except for the one time I went to my guidance counselor to complain, I discussed this with no one. Besides, I reasoned, what could I do about it? I was ugly, so people were going to make fun of me. I thought it was their right to do so simply because I *was* so ugly, so I'd just better get used to it. But I couldn't. No matter how much I braced myself, the words stung every time they were thrown at me. It didn't seem to matter that I was doing everything I could to know the truth, to own the fact that I was ugly, to make sure I was prepared for it, to be told nothing I didn't already know.

From **Balzac and the Little Chinese Seamstress**[28]

BY DAI SIJIE (TRANSLATED FROM THE FRENCH BY INA RILKE)

Dai Sijie, who now lives in France, was a young man in China when Chairman Mao's Cultural Revolution swept the country. This excerpt tells of two young men who were sent to the countryside to be reeducated.

The village headman, a man of about fifty, sat cross-legged in the centre of the room . . . he was inspecting my violin. Among the possessions brought to this mountain village by the two "city youths"—which was how they saw Luo and me—it was the sole item that exuded an air of foreignness, of civilization, and therefore aroused suspicion. . . .

Raising the violin to eye level, he shook it, as though convinced something would drop out of the sound holes. . . . When nothing fell out of my violin, the headman held his nose over the sound holes and sniffed long and hard. . . .

"It's a toy," said the headman solemnly.

This verdict left us speechless. Luo and I exchanged furtive, anxious glances. Things were not looking good. . . .

"A stupid toy," a woman commented hoarsely.

"No," the village headman corrected her, "a bourgeois toy." . . .

"A toy from the city," the headman continued, "go on, burn it."

His command galvanized the crowd. Everyone started talking at once, shooting and reaching out to grab the toy for the privilege of throwing it on the coals.

"Comrade, it's a musical instrument," Luo said as causally as he could, "and my friend here is a fine musician. Truly."

The headman called for the violin and . . . held it out to me.

"Forgive me, comrade," I said, embarrassed, "but I'm not that good."

I saw Luo giving me a surreptitious wink. Puzzled, I took my violin and set about tuning it.

"What you are about to hear, comrade, is a Mozart sonata." Luo announced, as coolly as before. . . .

"What's a sonata?" . . .

"I don't know," I faltered. "It's Western."

"Is it a song?"

"More or less" . . .

At that instant the glint of the vigilant Communist reappeared in the headman's eyes, and his voice turned hostile.

"What's the name of this song of yours?" . . .

"*Mozart* . . ." . . .

"*Mozart* what?"

"*Mozart Is Thinking of Chairman Mao*," Luo broke in.

The audacity! But it worked: as if he had heard something miraculous, the headman's menacing look softened. He crinkled up his eyes in a wide, beatific smile.

"Mozart thinks of Mao all the time," he said.

"Indeed, all the time," agreed Luo.

As soon as I had tightened my bow there was a burst of applause, but I was still nervous. However, as I ran my swollen fingers over the strings, Mozart's phrases came flooding back to me like so many faithful friends. The peasant's faces, so grim a moment before, softened . . . and then, in the dancing light of the oil lamp, they blurred into one.

I played for some time. Luo lit a cigarette and smoked quietly, like a man.

This was our first taste of re-education. Luo was eighteen years old. I was seventeen.

From **The Autobiography of Maud Gonne:**
Servant of the Queen[29]

BY MAUD GONNE

Maud Gonne, the radical Irish activist, was the great love of poet William Butler Yeats. You can find out more about their relationship by searching for "Maud Gonne" on www.google.com or on InfoTrac College Edition. Her son, Sean McBride, was one of the founders of Amnesty International. Tim Harrington was an Irish politician.

The next morning [Tim] Harrington and I were on the boat for Liverpool and little Pat O'Brien waved us good-bye . . .

Some of the election committee met us at the station and said a meeting was in progress and Harrington was to speak at it. Harrington insisted I should come to the meeting as it would make canvassing easier if I were seen on the platform. I was soon seated on the right hand of the elderly chairman, facing an audience of 1,500 English people. The chairman asked if I would speak next. "I'm not a speaker, I have only come to help canvass." I did not know it, but he was stone-deaf, and to my horror I heard him announce in a loud voice: "Miss Gonne, a young Irish lady, will now address you." Harrington, sitting immediately behind me, gave me a poke in the back. "Go on, you'll have to speak now." I got up: "Ladies and Gentlemen," my voice, owing to my stage training, rang out alarmingly clear, then I stopped. "Tell them about the evictions you have seen," prompted Harrington, and I began. It was easy telling a straightforward story of the scenes which I had witnessed and which were so terribly in my mind. I told of the old couple driven out of the house they had built fifty years ago; of the women with their one-day-old baby left on the roadside; of the little children trying in vain to kindle a fire in the rain; of the desolation of the overcrowded workhouse and the separated families. I forgot where I was and then suddenly I remembered and I became aware of a dead silence, of thousands of eyes looking at me and my mind a complete blank. I stopped in the middle of a sentence, my knees began to shake and I sat down and began to cry; I would have given worlds to hide, to disappear. I was too confused for a long time to know what was happening and vaguely thought the meeting was breaking up because I had made a fool of myself. I did not realize that, after the intense silence which had startled me, the audience had risen to its feet and was applauding me. When I recovered enough to take my nose out of my handkerchief Harrington was speaking. The chairman patted me on the shoulder protectingly. "My dear young lady, you were wonderful . . . "

"I am sorry to have made a fool of myself." He was deaf, so did not hear my apologies. At the end of the meeting a cab was got to take me out of a crowd all wanting to shake hands.

Over eggs and bacon at breakfast next morning Harrington read me the local papers full of my speech, all interpreting my stage-fright as evidence of my emotions. "You made a great impression; I have rarely seen an English audience so thrilled," Harrington said.

SUMMARY

Prose is probably the most common form of literature because it employs everyday language. There are two types of prose: nonfiction and fiction. Nonfiction prose includes explanations, descriptions, reports, or clarification of concepts (expository prose). Essays, opinion pieces, journals, diaries, and letters also qualify as nonfiction prose, as do speeches, biographies, and autobiographies. Performing nonfiction prose requires careful analysis of the text to determine the author's bias or tone and to locate where to pause and where to place emphasis.

Fiction emerges from the creator's imagination rather than from actual events. Stories involve realistic or fantastical characters who participate in a plot. The plot is set in a somewhat stable situation that is then disturbed by a challenge. The action rises until the climax, in which things change irrevocably. In the following denouement, the action winds down.

Narrators tell the story, so getting to know the narrator will aid your interpretation. They are insiders (first person) or observers (third person). Sometimes they speak directly to listeners (second person). Narrators can be detached (neutral) or subjective (opinionated). Some know all the characters' thoughts and motivations (omniscient); others have limited omniscience, or knowledge of just one or a few characters. Narrators may be unselfconscious or very aware of the impression they are trying to create. Their style or language varies from formal to informal, from exaggerated to spare. And their ethos or credibility ranges from trustworthy to just plain evil. Knowing the narrator's characteristics provides performance clues.

It's also helpful to determine the nature of the intended audience and of the narrator's relationship with that audience. Respond to your audience as your narrator would respond to his or hers.

Several types of cultural stories, including fables, folktales, parables, myths, and legends, transmit the beliefs and values of the group. They may be unrealistic or realistic, with a varied cast of characters. Common themes transcend cultural groups.

In general, you will have to cut out some material from the original text. Choose the climax, include information that leads up to it, and resolve the conflict satisfactorily. It's also important to limit the number of characters in the piece so that the audience can remain focused on the plot. Cut tag lines when you can substitute vocal and bodily expression for the words.

Finally, try out various performance strategies. Analyze the lyric, dramatic, and epic sections of the text and adjust your focal points, vocal variations, and bodily expressions accordingly.

KEY TERMS

prose	status quo	omniscient narrator
exposition	hero or protagonist	limited omniscience
expository prose	opposition or antagonist	objective narrator
essays	inciting incident	detached narrator
opinion pieces	denouement	subjective narrator
journal	narrators	style
diary	stance	fables
biography	first person	folktales
autobiography	third person	fairy tales
fiction	second person	parables
plot	major character	myths
setting	minor character	legends

QUESTIONS AND EXERCISES

1. Working with your classmates, create a list of situations in which someone might present nonfiction prose (a valedictorian reading her speech at graduation; a father reading a "birds and the bees" book to his children). In what future career situations might you present nonfiction prose?

2. Have you ever heard a radio ad that sounds like the speaker is completely bored? Create a 30-second ad for a product you like or a CD you'd recommend. Then perform your ad so your classmates will catch your enthusiasm and want to try the product or buy the CD.

3. Clip a short news story from your local newspaper. Perform the story for your classmates as if you were a broadcast news reporter.

4. Working with other students, create a list of situations in which performers interpret fiction (members of a book club reading aloud an interesting excerpt from the book they're discussing). In what circumstances might you perform fiction?

5. A "prose poem" combines the vivid imagery of poetry with a modified prose form. To read some examples, go online to *The Prose Poem: An International Journal* at http:www.webdelsol.com/tpp/. Naomi Shihab Nye's "Hammer and Nail" in Web Issue V is a good example.

6. A good Web site for traditional myths and legends is http:www.sacredtexts.com/index.htm. Browse the links, and look for prose from your heritage and from other cultures.

7. Working with another classmate or two, analyze the narrator in Penelope Layland's short story "The Death of the Fat Man" on pages 138–140. This text provides several questions that can guide your analysis.

8. Analyze the narrator in the prose excerpt from *The Ladies Auxiliary* on pages 141–142.

8

Performing Drama

This chapter will help you:

- Understand the value of doing a solo performance of a dramatic text

- Identify characteristics of dramatic literature

- Study a script's title, cast, stage directions, acts, and scenes

- Choose a scene that advances your goals with a specific audience

- Prepare a performance

- Develop your skills of character placement and focus

The lights dim, muted cell phones return to pockets and purses, the curtain goes up, the show begins. For the next two hours, audience members will watch as a drama unfolds on the stage or screen before them, engaging and involving them, leading them through a gamut of emotional responses. On my campus, plays such as *A Shayna Maidel, Man of La Mancha,* and *Quilters* have generated much discussion; almost a year later, a friend described in great detail how *Quilters* had affected her. Films such as *Bend It Like Beckham,* the *Lord of the Rings* trilogy, and *The Passion of Christ* prompt laughter, tears, and thoughts about significant issues. *Friends, Will and Grace, The Sopranos* and other television programs all have a wide appeal.

In everyday usage, the word *drama* commonly refers to a turbulent or highly emotional event such as the trial of an accused murderer. A reporter looks into the camera and announces, "There was *high drama* in the courtroom today as the prosecutor presented graphic photographs of the crime scene." In contrast to common usage, the literary term ***drama*** refers to the genre of literature intended for the theater.[1] Dramatic literature includes scripts for plays, radio dramas, movies, and television shows.

Although most dramatic literature is staged or filmed, solo performers can successfully present a cutting from a play or screenplay. Performing a solo dramatic interpretation is rewarding and challenging for the performer and audience alike. For example, Matt, a veteran stage actor, described his classroom performance experience:

> This solo dramatic performance was different from anything I've done before as a theatre student. It was both more challenging and more frustrating than my usual process of preparing to perform.

In theatrical performances, Matt relies on other actors, props, makeup, costuming, lighting, and so on. However, in a solo dramatic interpretation, he must unlearn some strategies that worked in the theater and learn new skills that enable him to perform all the characters and suggest all the actions. The audience similarly adapts by imagining the details of each character's appearance, the stage, the costumes, and the physical actions taking place.

Given these obstacles, why would anyone undertake a solo performance of drama? There are several good reasons:[2]

- Many audiences will never have a chance to experience important plays. Although Oregon, where I live, has cultural centers in Ashland, Eugene, and Portland that stage both contemporary and classic plays, for example, even with these resources, most plays will never be staged in these places or in smaller towns across the state.

- Many college students are unfamiliar with the great plays or playwrights. Performing a scene from a relatively unknown play is a way to introduce your classmates to a literary work they might otherwise miss. An introduction to an insightful and skillful dramatist may spark a lifelong interest in that playwright and the theater.

■ A one-person performance forces listeners to focus on the *words* of the text and to become highly involved in the cocreation of meaning. Listeners engage the plot differently when they are required to imagine the spectacle that is inherent in staged or filmed performances.

This chapter will help you identify and overcome some of the challenges of performing solo drama. It first describes distinguishing features of dramatic literature. It then provides an example of the process of choosing and analyzing a selection and concludes with specific guidelines for solo performances of drama.

CHARACTERISTICS OF DRAMA

Performing drama differs from performing other types of literature because of the nature of the genre itself. Over 2,000 years ago, Aristotle[3] identified the characteristics of drama as characters, plot, theme, diction (or language), and spectacle. Chapter 7 described character and plot. This section elaborates on spectacle, dramatic language, dramatic structure, and three genres of drama: tragedy, comedy, and tragicomedy.

Spectacle

Unlike poets and short story writers who write for the solitary reader, playwrights and screenwriters intend their works to be performed by actors on stages in front of audiences, either live or through some form of media. In other words, drama involves **spectacle**—lights, action, backdrops, props, sound effects, costumes. From experience, you know the vast difference between seeing a staged performance and simply reading a play in the quiet of your room. Reading forces you to create all the scenes, imagine the scenery, the costumes, the lighting, and so on.[4] When reading drama, you can follow stage directions and other notes that supply the details a short story writer would normally describe. Playwrights include the time and place, the cast of characters, their relationships to one another, and so on so that you can understand the setting and social context in which the action takes place.

In live theater performances, printed programs or playbills provide vital information about the place and time of the action; as a solo performer, you must rely on your introduction to convey these important details. At a minimum, you must identify the time and place where the scene occurs. Some details about the setting may also be necessary to understand the scene. For example, George Bernard Shaw's play *Arms and the Man*[5] opens with these details about the set:

Night. A lady's bedchamber in Bulgaria, in a small town near the Dragoman Pass, late in November in the year 1885. Through an open window with a little balcony a peak of the Balkans, wonderfully white and beautiful in the starlit snow, seems quite close at hand, though it is really miles away. The interior of the room is not like anything to be seen in the east of Europe. It is half rich Bulgarian, half cheap Viennese.

Shaw adds specific details about curtains, furniture, wallpaper, and other objects in the "shabby chic" room. Then he describes the characters and the context:

> *On the balcony a young lady, intensely conscious of the romantic beauty of the night, and of the fact that her own youth and beauty are part of it, is gazing at the snowy Balkans. She is covered by a long mantle of furs, worth, on a moderate estimate, about three times the furniture of her room.*
>
> *Her reverie is interrupted by her mother, Catherine Petkoff, a woman over forty, imperiously energetic, with magnificent black hair and eyes, who might be a very splendid specimen of the wife of a mountain farmer, but is determined to be a Viennese lady, and to that end wears a fashionable tea gown on all occasions.*

In your preparation, identify the information that will orient your audience to the text. In *Arms and the Man*, they need to know the date and the country in which the play takes place. They would better understand the social situation if you reveal that the Petkoff family is upwardly mobile; the family members want to be counted among the rich, but many of their possessions reveal their humble origins. The audience also needs to know the characters' names, ages, and relationships to one another. The stage directions indicate that the play has comedic elements. You may not say as much to the audience, but knowing this information will enable you to perform the scene more effectively.

Minimal Narration

Although classical Greek dramatists typically used a chorus to provide information and commentary on the plot and characters, most other dramatic literature omits the narration. No character describes the psychological, social, and physical setting; no one summarizes the action or divulges the other characters' inner thoughts and motivations. Instead, theatergoers must infer these details from what the characters themselves say and do. Each character's personality, self-concept, and opinions emerge from lines of dialogue. A character may occasionally directly address the audience or think out loud in a soliloquy. More often, however, one character reveals information about another or confides personal thoughts to another, as this excerpt from Shaw's play illustrates. Catherine (the mother) has just told Raina (her daughter) that Sergius (Raina's fiancée) was heroic and valiant in battle:[6]

Raina: . . . I am so happy—so proud! [*She rises and walks about excitedly*]. It proves that all our ideas were real after all.

Catherine: [*indignantly*] Our ideas real! What do you mean?

Raina: Our ideas of what Sergius would do—our patriotism—our heroic ideals. I sometimes used to doubt whether they were anything but dreams. . . . it was treason to think of disillusion or humiliation or failure. And yet—and yet—[*Quickly*] Promise me you'll never tell him.

Catherine: Don't ask me for promises until I know what I'm promising.

Raina: Well, it came into my head just as he was holding me in his arms and looking into my eyes, that perhaps we only had our heroic ideas because we are so fond of reading Byron and Pushkin, and because we were so delighted with the opera that season at Bucharest. Real life is so seldom like that!—indeed never, as far as I knew it then. *[Remorsefully]* Only think, mother: I doubted him: I wondered whether all his heroic qualities and his soldiership might not prove mere imagination when he went into a real battle. I had an uneasy fear that he might cut a poor figure there beside all those clever Russian officers.

Catherine: A poor figure! Shame on you! . . .

In summary, we learn about Raina's doubts and fears through her confession to her mother. We glean facts about Sergius because the two women talk about him. In addition, stage directions provide information about the characters' emotions. Bracketed information tells you that Catherine is indignant; Raina is first excited, then remorseful because of her doubts about Sergius's valor. An audience will attribute these emotions to the characters only if you show indignation, excitement, and remorse as you perform these lines.

Dramatic Language

Drama, like fictional prose, presents a story and develops a plot that moves through conflict and climax to a resolution. However, drama differs from prose in that the characters in plays inevitably speak in the here-and-now of the **present tense.** Dramatic plots unfold in lines of dialogue; the action occurs directly in front of the audience. In a way, audience members peer into the private activities of the characters who unselfconsciously act out their fates and foibles, unaware of the observers. Poetry and prose, in contrast, use the past, present, and future tenses.

Dramatic language, or **diction,** varies from formal and stilted expressions to vernacular and colloquial forms. In an interview, playwright Jose Rivera ("The House of Ramon Iglesia," "The Street of the Sun"), describes how he chooses language when writing for the theater:[7]

> . . . I always teach my students that when you write a play, you are not just writing a play, you're writing a world. That world is your world. That world will have your rules. You decide how people talk. If you think people talk with an IQ of 200, great. If you think people grunt and moan, that's great, too. That's your world.

In the imaginary world George Bernard Shaw created for *Arms and the Man,* two of the main characters greet each other using melodramatic language:[8]

Raina: *[placing her hands on his shoulders as she looks up at him with admiration and worship]* My hero! My king!

Sergius: My queen! *[He kisses her on the forehead].*

Raina: How I have envied you, Sergius! You have been out in the world, on the field of battle, able to prove yourself there worthy of any woman in the world; whilst I have had to sit at home inactive—dreaming—useless—doing nothing that could give me the right to call myself worthy of any man.

Sergius: Dearest: all my deeds have been yours. You inspired me. I have gone through the war like a knight in a tournament with his lady looking down at him!

Raina: And you have never been absent from my thoughts for a moment. *[Very solemnly]* Sergius: I think we two have found the higher love. When I think of you, I feel that I could never do a base deed or think an ignoble thought.

Sergius: My lady and my saint! *[He clasps her reverently].*

You can imagine that both lovers enunciate their words carefully and use exaggerated vocal variations. In contrast to such formal language, consider these lines from *Beautiful Bodies* by Laura Cunningham, a play about six women in their 30s who are attending a baby shower. They worry about their looks and their weight. Their language is informal and conversational:[9]

Nina: *[Handing Jessie a box.]* Here. It's a chocolate mousse cake.

Jessie: Oh, a mousse cake!

Nina: Don't let me eat any of it. It's for all of you.
[Pause.]
I'll just watch.
[Pause.]
I can't eat till Thursday.
[She waves a Diet Center packet.]
I'll just mix up my little packet when you all eat. I haven't had solid food since July.

Jessie: No! You have to eat! I've stuffed five Cornish hens.
[She gestures toward kitchen.]
It looks like a Cornish hen mass murder in there.

Nina: It's okay . . . I still take pleasure in watching others eat. It's become a kind of spectator sport for me.

The use of contractions in almost every line and the use of vivid but humorous language ("a Cornish hen mass murder"; eating as a "spectator sport") shows that the play is down-to-earth and modern. The characters are recognizable, although Nina's pauses are slightly melodramatic.

Other plays feature characters who use colloquial speech or who speak in a dialect. This character is a snail who is attempting to improve her "phone voice" by taking classes to learn standard grammar and pronunciation. She has been expelled from the school:[10]

> I diduhnt quit that school. HHH. Thought: note! Mm gonna go on—go on ssif nothing ssapin yuh know? "SK" is /sk/ as in "ask".... Failed every test he shoves in my face. He makes me recite my mind goes blank. HHH. The-little-lamb-follows-closely-behind-at-Mary's-heels-as-Mary-boards-the-train. Ain't never seen no woman on no train with no lamb. I tell him so. He throws me out. Stuff like this happens every day, y know? This isn't uh special case mines iduhnt uh uhnnn.... Hate lookin for uh job.... Only thing worse n workin sslookin for work.

Dialect often is written out phonetically so that the playwright is clear about how he or she intends it to sound. In this example, words and sounds such as "ssif" and "ssapin" and "HHH" suggest that a snail both moves and speaks in a slippery, sliding manner. If you choose a piece written in a dialect, pay careful attention to the diction; sound out difficult words and phrases such as "iduhtn uh uhnnn" until you can comfortably and confidently perform them.

The Structure of Drama

Dramatic literature also differs from prose and poetry in its structure. Although one-act plays are increasingly popular, plays are typically composed of several scenes put together into larger acts, which are combined into the play itself. When you select a scene, choose one near the middle or end of the play that shows conflict, includes emotional variety, builds to a climax, and resolves the tension.

Dramatic Genres

What kind of dramatic literature do you prefer? Serious dramas that make you think? Lighthearted plays that make you laugh? Plays that have sad elements but end on a hopeful note? These represent the three major categories of drama: tragedy, comedy, and tragicomedy.

Tragedy Tragedies deal with solemn or thought-provoking themes and grave human activities such as wars, plagues, and political intrigues. The characters come to bad ends. For example, bodies litter the stage at the end of *Julius Caesar*, *Hamlet*, and *Macbeth*. Tragic heroes are generally privileged and exalted characters who inevitably fall in ways that destroy them and crush their relatives. Their tragic end is casually connected to a conflict that is triggered by an internal flaw within the character, by treachery, or by an unavoidable set of circumstances. Here are a few examples:

- *Antigone*, a classic Greek tragedy, tells the story of a young noblewoman who must choose between two equally devastating courses of action. She can obey the king (her uncle) and leave her brother's corpse unburied, but he will remain a ghost forever, never free to enter the place of the gods. Or she can bury her brother, allowing his soul to rest in peace but, in the process, forfeiting her own life. She chooses to bury her brother and suffers the consequences.

- *Othello*, a well-respected soldier, is undone by his fatal character flaw: possessive jealousy toward his beautiful wife, Desdemona. The villain, Iago, plays on Othello's weakness and convinces him that Desdemona has been unfaithful. In a rage, Othello murders his innocent wife; once he learns of Iago's trickery, he kills himself.

- *Braveheart* tells the story of William Wallace, the "Hammer of the English," who is one of the heroes of Scotland's struggle for independence. He unites several clans and fights off an invading English king, but he is ultimately betrayed and suffers an agonizing death at the hands of the English soldiers.

Comedy Comedies, in contrast, depict characters with quirky flaws who find themselves in unusual circumstances, sometimes due to errors of judgment. Reversals of fortune are common. Comedic characters are more ordinary than tragic heroes, and things work out happily in the end. In **satiric comedies,** the ridiculous character loses, to the gain of others. **Romantic comedies** feature unexpected, improbable romantic situations that end happily.

- In Woody Allen's *Death Knocks,* Death is a bumbling character who comes to get Nat Ackerman, a stereotypical Jewish businessman in New York City. During the course of their conversation, Death confesses his love for gin rummy, and Nat ropes him into a game. The bet is simple: If Death wins, Nat goes with him; if Nat wins, he buys another day of life. Of course, Nat is victorious, and Death shuffles off to find a hotel room for the night.

- *The Importance of Being Earnest* (subtitled *A Trivial Play for Serious People*) garners lots of laughs around the theme of mistaken identity. Two English friends use the pseudonym "Ernest" as a cover for some of their activities. Unfortunately, they fall in love as "Ernest" with two women who are half in love with them because of the name.

Tragicomedy Tragicomedy blends elements of both tragedy and comedy.[11] For example, the plot might move toward a dreadful climax, like a tragedy, but the story will end hopefully, as a comedy does. Although a catastrophe such as a false accusation might befall the main character, eventually fortune intervenes and things end well. In modern tragicomedies, the characters are often doomed to unpleasant fates, but they engage in humorous or lighthearted activities as their fates play out.

- The Italian movie *Life Is Beautiful* is a tragicomedy. A father and his young son are in a desperate situation: a concentration camp in Hitler's Germany. In the camp, however, the father constructs an imaginative world full of love and hope; ultimately, his son is protected through his father's love.

- The title characters in Tom Stoppard's *Rosencrantz and Guildenstern Are Dead* are two of Hamlet's friends who are charged with taking the Danish prince

PERFORMING CULTURE: Modern Chinese Theater

Log onto InfoTrac College Edition and search for Article A98831007 in the Spring 2003 edition of the *Asian Theatre Journal*.[12] This article tells about Jiao Juyin, a Chinese director who tried to integrate what he learned about theater through his studies in the West with his inherited Chinese traditions. His Theory of Mental Images calls for actors to (1) experience life, (2) develop mental images, and (3) create stage images. He also argued that "the audience and the dramatists create jointly."

Read the article and summarize Jiao Juyin's Theory of Mental Images. Then compare and contrast Chinese theater, as presented in this article, to the theater forms that are familiar to you. Discuss your findings with your classmates.

---

to England to be executed. However, Hamlet skips out on them, and they end up aboard ship, headed for England to die in his place. They are unaware of their fate, and pass the time with word games and mental sparring.

In summary, drama is a unique literary genre for many reasons. Because plays are created to be staged, each playwright includes directions that advance the spectacle. Dramatists use present-tense verbs and rely on dialogue instead of narration to reveal the characters' motivations and ideas. The language or diction is sometimes formal and stilted, sometimes colloquial or in dialect—whatever the playwrights decide as they "write a world," in Jose Rivera's terms. Dramatic genres include tragedy, comedy, and tragicomedy.

PREPARING TO PERFORM DRAMA

Begin your preparation by finding an appropriate script. Then read the play in its entirety. This will give you an idea of the overall theme and how the playwright develops it. After you are familiar with the whole, decide on the response you want from your audience, and select a cutting that best elicits that response. Finally, plan a performance that will bring about the interactions you desire between the literature, the audience, and you as the performer. This process involves script study, scene selection, and performance preparation.

Find an Appropriate Script

Lia explained some challenges she faced in finding just the right script for both herself and her audience:

> I struggled primarily in finding a piece that I could perform because there are many pieces of drama that I am familiar with and love, but very few in which I could properly fill the role of each character. I settled on a text

STOP AND CHECK: Finding Scripts

Browse through the drama section of your campus library, and jot down at least five interesting sources for scripts. Then go online and search for scripts and create a list of useful URLs. (For instance, Shakespeare's complete plays are located at www.shakespeare-online.com/plays/. Go to www.chiff.com/art/theater/scripts.htm for additional links.) Bring your lists to class and discuss them with your classmates.

that suited my interests and capabilities. I think the most important aspect of the piece was that it was fun to practice and perform, although it was a challenge to find ways to differentiate between the two women characters.

There are many sources for suitable scripts. Movies, well-written radio dramas, or television shows can provide material. Also consider specific playwrights, such as Sophocles, Shakespeare, Oscar Wilde, or the contemporary Pulitzer Prize winners Nilo Cruz and August Wilson. Look in your library's drama collection. Campus libraries generally carry collections of comedies, one-act plays, scene books, religious plays, plays by specific playwrights, anthologies such as *The Best Short Plays of 2003*, and so on. Another source is the drama section of your literature text. Finally, online sources such as www.vl-theatre.com/list4.shtml or www.scriptcrawler.com offer links to hundreds of options. Because your performance will be limited to 10 minutes, it might be wise to consider one-act plays instead of full-length plays.

Throughout much of the discussion that follows, I will use Rebecca Gilman's award-winning play *Spinning into Butter*[13] as my main example. It is about racism on a college campus. Gilman, who now lives in Chicago, is a native of Alabama. Other plays of hers have also won awards, and she was recognized in England with the *Evening Standard* Award for Most Promising Playwright. *Spinning into Butter* is especially appropriate for a college audience because it deals with a weighty national issue (racism) in a familiar context (a college campus). Complex motivations play out as the various characters search for personal and institutional solutions to racist incidents on campus.

Analyze the Script

When you have finally decided on a play, begin your analysis by examining its title. Then look at the character descriptions and initial stage directions before you select a cutting that will accomplish your goals for the performance.

Analyze the Title Begin by thoughtfully considering the play's title. Playwrights choose titles to highlight characters, their roles, the play's theme, its setting, and so on.

Many playwrights name their work for the major character or characters. These are, not surprisingly, called the **title characters.** Shakespeare often used this strategy; *Julius Caesar, Macbeth,* and *Richard IV* are examples. You also will come across *Harold and Maude, Erin Brockovich,* and *Cyrano de Bergerac* (which in the most recent version was renamed after the lead female character, *Roxanne*). A similar strategy is to title the play after the occupation, title, or role of the protagonist. Consequently, *Father of the Bride, The Godfather,* and *The Nerd* all clue you in to the major character. The title tells which character is most important, which one looms over the actions of all the others.

Another strategy is to name the play for the place where the action takes place. For example, Jose Rivera's *The House of Ramon Iglesia* features a Puerto Rican couple who have raised their family in New York; because their sons are now grown, they make plans to sell the family home and return to Puerto Rico, but the deed to their house is contested. *Graceland* takes place outside Elvis Presley's home three days before it opened to the public. Two characters are camping out beside the doors, determined to be the first one to enter the museum. Their comical jockeying for position and their reasons for wanting to be first make up the plot.

Time is a less frequently used way to title a play. Arthur Miller's *A Memory of Two Mondays* takes place in an automobile parts warehouse in New York to which a group of workers return to work after every weekend. In Mary Gallagher's one act *Bedtime,* two sisters converse about God and the afterlife just before falling asleep.

Titles may come from literary and historical allusions, and their intertextuality gives clues to the play's themes. George Bernard Shaw often used allusions. *Arms and the Man* is about a family whose lives are changed after a foreign soldier arrives at night, needing protection. Shaw took this title from the opening lines of the Roman poet Virgil's epic poem *The Aeneid,* which begins like this (as translated by John Dryden): [14]

> Arms and the man I sing, who, forc'd by fate,
>
> And haughty Juno's unrelenting hate,
>
> Expell'd and exil'd, left the Trojan shore. . . .

Shaw was a British playwright in Victorian England; at that time, every schoolboy would have been familiar with the *Aeneid.* Many people today may miss the allusion, however, so you would have to explain it in your introduction. *The War of the Roses* is a screenplay about a long-standing and ultimately deadly feud between Oliver and Barbara Rose; the title alludes to a series of wars in medieval England between the Houses of Lancaster (red rose) and York (white rose). Although the Wars of the Roses lasted about 30 years, they were ultimately more devastating to England than the Hundred Years' War.[15] Knowing about the havoc it wreaked will help you predict the outcome of the screenplay.

Spinning into Butter—what does that title mean? Surely it's not to be taken literally? But what's the metaphor? Isn't butter churned? How does one "spin" butter? I thought of an old story, rarely told now because it is considered racist.

It features Little Black Sambo, a boy who confronts several tigers after they steal the new outfit his mother made for him. Somehow he tricks them into whirling and spinning in circles until they melt into piles of butter. His mother makes pancakes and the family slathers them with tiger butter. Could Gilman possibly be referring to that old tale? If so, who are the tigers? Who is Little Black Sambo?

Act II, Scene 6 reveals that this old tale is the source for the title, as one character tells the story and explains the allusion. Thus, the title provides vital clues for interpreting the play. (To understand the play better, search on www.google.com for the exact words "Little Black Sambo." You'll find the story online, along with explanations of the controversy surrounding it.)

Examine the Cast of Characters   After studying the title, gain as much information about each character as you can. You will find information such as names, ages, occupations, and relationships listed at the beginning. Ask yourself how the cast from *Spinning into Butter* might interact. What clues to their motivations and their views of one another can you surmise? What would you expect from these characters, given the time and place for the play?

- Sarah Daniels, dean, 35 to 40 years old

- Patrick Chibas, student, 19 years old

- Ross Collins, professor, 35 to 40 years old

- Burton Strauss, dean, 55 years old

- Catherine Kenney, dean, 60 years old

- Mr. Meyers, janitor, 50 years old

- Greg Sullivan, student, 21 years old

- Belmont College, Belmont, Vermont, present day

Skim through the stage directions to glean additional information about each character. For example, Gilman opens Act I, Scene 1 by describing Sarah Daniels's office at Belmont, a small liberal arts college in Vermont. The book-lined office is "nice" and "warm" and "comfortable-looking" and "earnest." These words suggest ways to perform Sarah Daniels, but they contrast with some of the actions that go on in the office.

Read the Entire Play   Some facts about characters are revealed only as you read the play, so prepare to jot down new information you learn about each character. For example, Sarah, the white dean of students, discovers that she was hired because college officials thought she was black when reading her application materials. She befriends and defends minority students but finds that, despite years of studying and working with African Americans, she is still deeply racist. She's involved romantically with Ross, and she hates Strauss.

The two students, Patrick and Greg, are very different. Patrick is a "Nuyorican" (he will not refer to himself Hispanic or Latino; Nuyoricans are Puerto Ricans who live in New York). However, he agrees to be labeled

Puerto Rican in order to get a $12,000 scholarship that Sarah offers. Later, he thinks he sold out. Greg is white, a "Mr. Belmont College" type from a comfortable Connecticut background. He responds to a racist note directed at an African American student by forming "Students for Tolerance." However, he confesses to Sarah that his motives aren't noble; he's hoping to add an important line to his law school application. At the end of the play, he is the character who changes the most.

You may discover some characters who never appear onstage but are pivotal to the plot. For example, in Samuel Beckett's play *Waiting for Godot*, the title character never shows up, but what the characters say and do revolves around him.

Several of Gilman's characters are essential but absent from the stage. For instance, President Garvey and "the board" never appear, but their authority influences all the dean's decisions. Most importantly, Simon Brick, an African American student who is the play's pivotal character, stays out of sight. He's the one who found hate notes on his door (one containing the phrase "Little Black Sambo"), and his window was shattered when a rock was hurled through it. Simon refuses to support the administrators' "racism forums." Eventually we learn that he himself wrote the racist notes and tossed the rock that set the campus spinning. He is ultimately dismissed from Belmont.

Throughout the play, notice what people say to one another. Take note, also, of the subtext, or what they're *not* saying. In *Spinning into Butter*, Sarah, Patrick, and Greg examine their personal attitudes about race and probe their own prejudices; other characters do not.

Pay attention to the language each character uses, and look for variations in the way a character addresses different characters. Sarah speaks differently to Patrick than to Greg; they, in turn, address her in unique ways:

- She uses relatively formal language with Greg; they are obviously strangers, and their interaction is businesslike.
- With Patrick, who is also a stranger, she uses more conversational, even casual forms, as if she wants to befriend him. Why does she respond differently to the two young men? Is this patronizing?
- Patrick is not deferential; instead, he speaks directly and confrontationally to Sarah.
- Greg speaks formally and respectfully to Sarah.

These details and others like them subtly communicate the characters' attitudes toward one another, and they provide you with hundreds of clues about how to interpret the action.

Select a Cutting That Meets Your Purposes

As a result of your performance, what do you want your listeners to know? To feel? To do? Your answer to these questions will help you find the best cutting for your specific audience. Is your goal to invite a predominately white audience to examine their potentially racist views? Or is your goal to disturb a diverse but apathetic audience with a more confrontational performance? To make appropriate choices, you must know what happens in each act and scene and then select the one best scene, given your audience and your goal.

List the Major Scenes *Spinning into Butter* is composed of two acts. Act I has six scenes, and Act II has seven scenes. All the action takes place in Sarah's office. You can automatically eliminate some scenes or sections; for example, Sarah finds out that Ross and Petra are romantically involved, but this has little to do with overall theme of latent racism.

To understand each scene in context, list all the acts and outline the scenes, underlining sections that could fit your purpose, like this:

Act One

- *Scene one.*
  - Sarah calls Patrick into her office to offer him a $12,000 science scholarship designated for a minority student. He refuses to be labeled Hispanic or Latino, and he listed his race as "other," but in order to qualify for the money, he agrees to apply as a Puerto Rican.

- *Scene two: One week later.*
  - Sarah informs Kenney, Strauss, and Ross of a racist note left on Simon's, a black student's, door. They are shocked and decide on a public gesture of support. Kenney is outraged that Sarah alerted the police about what she considered an internal incident.

- *Scene three: Two weeks later.*
  - Greg Sullivan, a handsome, self-assured white senior, proposes a Students for Tolerance organization. Eventually, he confesses that founding it will look good on his resume, but he insists he would do it anyway.

As you outline, underline each scene that meets the criteria you have established for the performance. For example, the underlined sections above can be combined in a way that builds toward a climax; in addition, each has a manageable number of characters.

Match the Cutting to Your Goal Several scenes in *Spinning* have the potential to lead listeners to confront issues of racism. You might focus on Patrick's story, using cuttings from Act I, Scenes 1 or 4, to provide the perspective of someone who is not Caucasian. In contrast, Greg's story shows a white student who is initially oblivious to his racism but later realizes how deeply some of his prejudices run. The most powerful and disturbing scene appears in Act II when Sarah, who initially denies her prejudices, confronts her personal responses to racial issues.

Choosing from these options depends on both your audience and your abilities. Would your specific audience best learn from and respond to Patrick's, Greg's, or Sarah's experiences? Sarah's scene is raw and unsettling

STOP AND CHECK: Ethical Cutting

Review the ethical guidelines for cutting literature described in Chapter 3, and apply them when you select a scene to perform.

because it is so confrontational. Perhaps this is exactly what your specific audience needs. Patrick's story, on the other hand, presents more subtle aspects of racism that might better invite an audience to probe their personal responses to issues of race.

Of course, you must also consider your skill level. Some scenes are more technically challenging than others. Sarah's story requires intense analysis and subtle presentational skill; Greg's story is easier to present. Take into account the technical difficulty of the scene in light of your experience and skills.

To create the actual cutting, first identify a point of climax. Then cut in, or add, enough lines of dialogue to establish the characters and the setting, clarify the inciting incident, build to a climax point, and provide a satisfying resolution. Don't think of this process as cutting *out* material; instead, think of it as cutting *in* the material you want your listeners to hear.[16]

Prepare Your Performance

Not surprisingly, much of what you need when preparing for your drama performance you've already honed during your prose presentation, such as the following:

- Analyze your characters in depth. Get to know their psychological attitudes and motivations. Determine how demographic factors such as educational level and economic background affect their demeanor and their responses. Identify their character traits: their morals and values, their integrity or lack thereof. Analyze their personalities, and note the unique qualities you would portray for each character, such as introversion or extroversion, confidence or shyness, pride or humility.

- "Try on" each character, one at a time. Visualize that character physically, and then experiment with different ways to perform her or his vocalic characteristics, facial expressions, bodily movements, and so on. Separate out that character's lines, and perform all of them in character. When you are satisfied that your portrayal is accurate and consistent, move on to another character.

- Prepare your script, and specify where to place a **beat,** or a pause. (Playwrights often write a beat into the script.) Some performers integrate their manuscript into their performances by planning a page turn to accompany a beat or to otherwise support the meanings in the text.

- Familiarize yourself enough with the text so that you can look up from the script at least 80% of the time. You should only need to glance at your script occasionally.
- Study stage directions for performance cues. Think of the playwright as a long-distance director who cannot be present during your rehearsals and can only coach you through written stage directions. She tells you when to smile and when to stare, when to think and when to be startled. Following the stage directions is one way to assure that your performance reflects the author's intent for the play.

Although many performance skills are transferable between literary genres, dramatic interpretation presents some unique challenges or emphases. Chief among them are focal points. After observing her classmates' performances, Martha Ruth observed:

> Focal points are key; if you aren't consistent, the audience will definitely notice. In our class I saw several performances with good focal points and some with inconsistent focal points. Wobbly focal points confuse the plot line and make the performance seem less polished.

Return to the information on focal points in Chapter 5, pages 92–102. Offstage focus, closed focus, and character placement are especially important. Don't place the characters so far apart that you must turn your body when you switch from one speaker to another; instead, locate each character slightly off center. Figure 8.1 shows how to place two characters. Place additional characters only slightly farther out.

Other focus principles apply at other times. Use an inner-closed focus when a character is musing, writing a letter, or brooding. When a character is praying or addressing an absent person, use a semi-closed focus.

Sarah locates Patrick here   Patrick locates Sarah here

When Sarah is speaking   When Patrick is speaking

FIGURE 8.1 Character Placement

Because the action unfolds in lines of dialogue (or monologue), you must rely on vocabulary details to interpret the characters' attitudes and responses. Dialogues often reflect the scripts we commonly use in everyday incidents. For example, Sarah and Greg use the more formal, businesslike script that relative strangers would use.

Sarah: So what would you like me to do for you, Greg?

Greg: Well, I thought I might go ahead and call a meeting for next week.

Sarah: Do you need a space?

Greg: That would be good.

Sarah: (*Opens a three-ring binder on her desk.*) You can have Scott Auditorium, Monday at seven.

Greg: Terrific. And I'd like to put up posters announcing it.

Sarah: Go right ahead.

Greg: . . . how long would it take to get funding?

Sarah: Probably six weeks.

Greg: Man.

Sarah: I know it seems like a long time, but . . . you can get the posters yourself and the committee will reimburse you. (*Beat.*) So if I were you, Greg, I'd go see Dean Strauss first.

(*Beat.*)

Greg: This wouldn't . . . I mean, well, would it look bad if I said I was president of Students for Tolerance before the committee actually approved it?

Sarah: Bad to whom?

Greg: Well, I mean, to be perfectly honest, I'm applying to law school, and my resume is a bit thin, if you know what I mean. I mean something like this would definitely add a line.

Sarah: I see.

(*Beat.*)

Greg: So do you think it would look bad?

Sarah: I really couldn't say. Would anyone question it?

Greg: I don't know. If they did, though, if they called the college . . .

Because you're familiar with the polite demeanor and the typical vocalic characteristics that professionals use, you have many resources for portraying this scene. You know how a confident student can suddenly become tentative or shy around institutional authorities. Here's a situation where subtext is important. Greg doesn't come right out and ask Sarah to cover for him if a law school checks his resume, but he wants her implied agreement before he adds the line. Consequently, he hesitates and pauses.

Now study some lines between Sarah and Patrick. Compare them to Sarah and Greg's conversation, and then come to class prepared to talk about how you'd perform each section of dialogue:

Sarah: Did you get a letter from financial aid? I cleared up your scholarship. (*Pause. Patrick studies her.*)

Patrick: You wanted to talk to me about my editorial, didn't you?

Sarah: That was . . . yes.

Patrick: Am I not allowed to express my opinions now? Is that it?

Sarah: No. That's not it. You just raised some . . . serious allegations and I thought we should discuss them.

Patrick: So you can tell me I'm wrong.

Sarah: No. I think you're right. Even though I think some of this is about me, probably. (*Beat.*) It is about me, isn't it?

Patrick: Part of it, I guess. I mean, obviously most of it is about Dean Strauss.

Sarah: But this part . . . (*She picks up her own copy of the paper and reads*) "The discriminatory attitude of the administration, however, is not isolated to Dean Strauss and his outburst at Tuesday night's race forum. It is pandemic, as many students have come to learn the hard way. One student tells of being called upon in his sociology class to give the 'African American point of view.' Another tells of being offered a minority scholarship before the college even knew his race or ethnicity, as if any minority would do. This treatment reeks of tokenism and is an insult to the achievements of all students of color at Belmont."

(*Beat.*)

Patrick: I didn't mention you by name.

Sarah: I appreciate that, I guess.

Patrick and Greg relate very differently to Sarah—and she to each of them. What does this say about their views of one another? Identify some specific relational differences between the two scenes. Who pauses in each scene? When? why? Contrast how you could portray Greg and Patrick. How would you use vocal and physical variations to convey Sarah's different responses to each student?

After his performance, Jeremy summed up some of the more significant things he had learned:

The most challenging part of the drama performance was discovering the personalities of the characters. I found that, especially for *Richard III,* body language was essential in portraying his emotional range. Richard goes from borderline insanity and rage to deceptive kindness, and the audience needs to understand this emotional range. Vocal variation and body language helped me portray him sometimes as submissive, sometimes as impassioned. Drama really showed me the power of nonverbal changes when communicating emotions.

DRAMATIC LITERATURE FOR STUDY
AND PRACTICE

Here are some short excerpts from plays. Study the characters, and then prepare to discuss how you would perform each one. What vocal and physical characteristics would you use for each? Where would you "place" each character? If the character is performing a monologue, what focus should you use?

From Graffiti[17]

BY NILO CRUZ

Bruno (late 20s) is visiting Lucy (20s) in her apartment in New York's inner city. Her 12-year-old brother, Waldo, lives with her:

Bruno: Do I make you nervous?

Lucy: No, it's not you.

Bruno: Then be still for a while. . . .

Lucy: It just feels that way sometimes, like I never stop. Tomorrow I don't work out there but I work here. I help the owner clean her place. She's old and needs help. Then I come here and do my stuff.

Bruno: Everything looks clean to me.

Lucy: It's all dusty in here. Dust gets everywhere.

Bruno: I don't see it.

Lucy: That's because you don't live here. . . .

Bruno: You work too much. . . . I'd like to take you out somewhere where we could dance and enjoy ourselves. Do you ever go out?

Lucy: I do. . . .

Bruno: You're lying. . . .

Lucy: I go out. Except I don't go out to any particular place. Sometimes I take the public bus and I go somewhere. . . . Wherever it takes me. . . . I like doing that. I figure that all buses have a route. They go somewhere, then they come back. And I just want . . . to be taken somewhere. I don't care where. . . . I want to distract myself looking at the streets, the people, the stores. Haven't you ever felt like doing that? . . . I'd go to the moon if I could. . . . I learn by watching people, looking at a tree. I learn about myself. . . . I'm glad you get along with my brother.

Bruno: He's a good kid.

Lucy: I worry about him.

Bruno: Why?

Lucy: I don't know where he's at sometimes. . . . I'm concerned about what kind of friends he has. I feel I'm responsible for him. When my mother died, I felt she put him in my hands to take care of him. . . .

Bruno: But he's not a kid.

Lucy: I know. But he needs guidance. . . . Things are bad as they are. They've been bad enough for a while with Papi turning his back on us. A boy like Waldo needs authority . . . And he's beginning to like the streets too much. This is the second time I've had to pick him up at the police station for writing on a wall.

Bruno: Most kids do that.

Lucy: I know, but it's against the law. It's vandalism. It's wrong. . . . Why mess up the place where we live? Look at our streets. They're filthy. Is it because we hate ourselves? Each other? Is it because we hate where we live? Our neighborhood is poor. This house is falling apart. But I keep a clean house and that's what matters. Decency is what counts. The rich don't mess up their walls. Their neighborhoods are clean . . .

From Boundary County, Idaho[18]

BY TOM TOPOR

A female Manhattan reporter is interviewing a member of a militia group for a magazine article. The militia member does all the talking.

. . . It can all be on the record, I got nothing to hide. Turn on your machine right now. You need any help? You're way too pretty to be real good with mechanical stuff. Ready? Okay. First off, I want to say for the record that I'm not one of those guys who thinks there's a black chopper hovering around over my head. Second, I don't think the CIA planted a transmitter in my front tooth. Or my back tooth. Not that they don't—they just didn't with me. Look: all my own teeth.

I want you to get that down because it's really important for you to know—and I mean, you, you personally, and not just because you're a good-looking woman, but because you're the one talking to me . . . I am not crazy. Not off the wall. Not nuts. Not paranoid even a little bit. I've got certain beliefs. . . and I hold those beliefs pretty strongly. Okay?

Now, what are these beliefs? . . . Freedom. I believe in freedom. Now, what if I tell you, we don't have freedom? I saw that expression. You're saying to yourself, oh, man, this is another Christian Identity wacko who's going to tell me how the income tax amendment was never ratified, or how he can't keep an H-bomb in his freezer. Uh uh. Freedom.

You ever hear of the Tuskeegee Experiment? . . . You ever heard of the Oak Ridge Experiment? . . . Remember what they did to the Japanese. . . . Old history, right?

Look at these; these are not old history:

New York cops go on a rampage and shoot up a hotel in Washington. Who gets punished? Nobody. . . . Government auctions off 2,600 family farms in one month. . . . Out! Go! . . . [H]ow many people is 2,600 families? Ten thousand? Fifteen thousand? My dad is one of them. Fifty-eight years on the farm. Out!

You ever hear of the Communications Assistance Enforcement Act? You missed that one, right? It orders every phone company in America to re-engineer their equipment so that every single phone in the United States can be tapped by the feds. . . . By next year, every time you talk, the feds will be listening. I am not making this up. . . .

Let's get down home. When you drove up here, you remember that sign you passed on your left? Government property, no trespassing. . . . Tell me this: how can the government have property and keep the people off it? We're the government, right. They're supposed to have our consent for everything. . . .

You see what I'm getting at? There is no freedom because they never ask for our consent. We are not in charge. They are in charge . . . I mean, the pols, the bankers, and the media, and the hired guns they buy. . . . That's the they. . . .

From Judgment Call[19]

BY FREDERICK STROPPEL

During baseball's spring training, three umpires practice for the upcoming season. Harvey, the veteran, is low-key and self-assured; young Joe is flamboyant; the introspective Frank considers each call carefully before he calls it.

Joe: [*throwing his arms out wildly*] SA-A-AFE! SA-A-A-AFE!

Harvey: [*a minimalist*] Safe!

Frank: [*almost questioning*] Safe . . .

Joe: SA-A-A-AFE! [*switching now, jerking his thumb wildly*] OW-W-W-U-UT! YOU'RE OW-W-W-U-UT!

Harvey: [*a sharp thumb jerk*] Out!

Frank: [*still on safe, not sure of his hands*] Safe. Safe . . .

Joe: [*gives a strike*] STEEE-RIKE!

Harvey: [*a different strike call; he leans forward on one knee, extends his palm*] Hi-eek!

Frank: Out . . . !

Harvey: Ball four . . .

Joe: SA-A-AFE!

[*They go on like this for a few moments . . . Frank gets less confident with each call.*]

Harvey: What's up, Frank? You seem a little tentative.

Frank: I'm rusty, that's all. I haven't done this since October.

Harvey: Hey, well, you can't walk away for four months and just expect it to all come back to you on the first day. That's why I stay busy. I like to keep those umpiring juices flowing.

Joe: [*waving his arms to the side*] FOUL BALL! FOUL BALL!

Harvey: [*amused*] Look at the kid. He thinks he's gonna be a star. [*prompts Joe*] Tie goes to the . . .

Joe: [*whirls*] Tie goes to the runner! The runner! [*back to his calls*] STEE-RI-I-E-E-EKE!

[*Harvey laughs, shakes his head.*]

From Hamlet[20]

BY WILLIAM SHAKESPEARE

In this monologue, Polonius bids his son Laertes farewell and gives him some fatherly advice before he sails for France.

Yet here, Laertes! aboard, aboard, for shame!
The wind sits in the shoulder of your sail,
And you are stay'd for. There; my blessing with thee!
And these few precepts in thy memory
5   See thou character. Give thy thoughts no tongue,
Nor any unproportioned thought his act.
Be thou familiar, but by no means vulgar.
Those friends thou hast, and their adoption tried,
Grapple them to thy soul with hoops of steel;
10   But do not dull thy palm with entertainment
Of each new-hatch'd, unfledged comrade. Beware
Of entrance to a quarrel, but being in,
Bear't that the opposed may beware of thee.
Give every man thy ear, but few thy voice;
15   Take each man's censure, but reserve thy judgment.
Costly thy habit as thy purse can buy,
But not express'd in fancy; rich, not gaudy;
For the apparel oft proclaims the man,
And they in France of the best rank and station
20   Are of a most select and generous chief in that.
Neither a borrower nor a lender be;
For loan oft loses both itself and friend,
And borrowing dulls the edge of husbandry.
This above all: to thine ownself be true,
25   And it must follow, as the night the day,
Thou canst not then be false to any man.
Farewell: my blessing season this in thee!

From Tone Clusters[21]

BY JOYCE CAROL OATES

Frank and Emily Gulick's 17-year-old son Carl has been arrested for the brutal murder of a neighbor girl whose body was discovered in the Gulicks' basement. The entire play consists of the anguished parents doing an on-camera interview. Mr. Filco is their lawyer; Denny is their eldest son. Ms. Oates structured the script to show the Gulicks' confusion through hesitations and repetitions.

Voice: Frank and Emily Gulick as we wind down *our*　　time together.
　　What are your plans for the future?

Frank: . . . Oh that's hard to　　that's hard to answer.

Emily: It depends I guess on

Frank: Mr. Filco had advised

Emily: I guess it's
　　next is the grand jury

Frank: Yes: the grand jury.
　　Mr. Filco cannot be present for the session to protect our boy I don't
　　understand the law, just the prosecutor is there swaying the jurors' minds
　　Oh I try to understand but I can't,

Emily: he says we should be prepared
　　We should be prepared for a trial

Voice: You are ready for the trial　　to clear your son's name?

Frank: Oh yes . . .

Emily: yes that is a way of,　　of putting it
　　Yes. To clear Carl's name.

Frank: . . . Oh yes you have to be realistic.

Emily: Yes but before that　　the true murderer of Edith Kaminsky
　　might come forward.
　　If the true murderer is watching this　　*Please come forward.*

Frank: . . . Well we both believe Carl is protecting someone, some friend
　　another boy

Emily: the one who really　　committed that terrible crime

Frank: So all we can do is pray.　　Pray Carl will come　　to his
　　senses　　give police the other boy's name, or I believe this: if it's a
　　friend of Carl's
　　He must have some decency　　in his heart

Voice: Your faith　　in your son remains unshaken?

Emily: You would have to see his　　toes,
　　his tiny baby toes in his bath.
　　his curly hair,　　splashing in the bath
　　his yellow rompers or no: I guess that was Denny

Frank: If your own flesh and blood looks you in the eye,　　you believe

Emily: Oh yes. . . .
    This medication the doctor gave me, my mouth   my mouth is so
    dry In the middle of the night I wake up drenched in

Frank: You don't know who you are   until a thing like this happens,
    then you don't know.

Emily: It tears your brain in two, trying to remember
    like even looking at pictures
    Oh you are lost

Frank: in Time you are lost

Emily: You fall and fall,
    . . . ever since the,   the butcher shop
    he wasn't always himself   but
    who he was then, I don't know.
    It's so hard, remembering why.

Frank: Yes my wife means thinking backward the way   the way the
    police make you, so many questions you start forgetting right away it
    comes out crazy. Like now,   right here   I don't remember
    anything up to now I mean, I can't swear to it: the first time, you see,
    we just lived. We lived in our house. I am a, I am a post office
    employee   I Guess I said that?   Well, we live in our,   our
    house.   . . . I guess I'm trying to say
    Those actual people me and her   the ones you see *here* aren't them
    [*Laughs.*]
    I guess that sounds crazy,

Voice: We have here the heartbeat   of parental love and faith, it's a
    beautiful thing   Frank and Molly Gulick, please comment?

Frank: We are that boy's father and mother.
    We know that our son is not a murderer and a,   a rapist

Emily: We know that, if that girl came to harm   there is some reason
    for it to be revealed, but
    They never found the knife, for one thing

Frank: Or whatever it was

Emily: They never found the knife, the murderer could tell them
    where it's buried, or whatever it was.
    Oh he could help us so   if he just would.

Voice: And your plans for the future,   Mr. and Mrs. Gulick of
    Lakepointe, NJ?

Frank: . . . Well.
    I guess,   I guess we don't have any.
    [*Long silence, to the point of awkwardness.*]

Voice: . . . Plans for the future, Mr. and Mrs. Gulick of Lakepointe, NJ?

Frank: The thing is, you discover   you need to be protected from
your own thoughts sometimes,   but who is there to do it?

Emily: God didn't make any of us strong enough I guess.

Frank: Look: one day in a family like this, it's like the next day and the
day before.

Emily: You could say it *is* the next day, I mean the same   the same day.

Frank: Until one day it isn't.

SUMMARY

Drama is a genre of literature with enormous potential to engage audiences and evoke intense feelings. Although plays are generally staged, interpreting a cutting from a play can be satisfying for a number of reasons: It acquaints audiences with plays and playwrights they might otherwise not know; solo performances also invite listeners to focus on the text rather than on the spectacle that live theater provides.

The genre of drama is different from prose or poetry in a number of ways. Texts are meant to be staged; they are written in here-and-now language; they consist of scenes that combine to form acts within the larger play.

Although you will only perform a cutting, you should be familiar with the entire play. First, examine the title and explore the possible meanings it suggests. Then look at the cast of characters. Try to imagine how they relate to one another. Look also for the characters who never appear on stage but who advance the plot. Then read the stage directions to get an idea of the setting. Finally, read the play in its entirety, listing the acts and outlining the action in each scene. Underline the scenes that would accomplish your performance purposes. Then select a specific section to perform, cutting it to fit the allotted time and using the ethical principles for making cuts described in Chapter 3.

You'll use skills you developed in previous performances. However, because there's rarely a narrator, you will use offstage focus throughout. Carefully study the language and the characters, and develop distinct, consistent characterizations.

You can locate drama scripts in textbooks, libraries, radio, television, or movie scripts, or on the Internet.

KEY TERMS

drama	tragedy	tragicomedies
spectacle	comedy	title characters
present tense	satiric comedies	subtext
diction	romantic comedies	beat

QUESTIONS AND EXERCISES

1. Look in your local and campus newspapers to discover which plays are currently being produced in your area. What types of plays are they (classics, contemporary, comedies, etc.)? Make a list of plays that have important messages but will probably never be performed in your region. Which of these might provide a good cutting for your classroom?

2. Learn more about theater traditions in other cultures. Information about theater traditions in Kerala, India can be found online at http:www.bhasabharathi.com/. You can find an interactive drawing of Japanese Kabuki theater at http:www.dartmouth.edu/~ukiyoe/kabuki/. Then search for drama traditions in a culture that is part of your heritage, and discuss your findings with a group of your classmates.

3. Review the analysis of *Spinning into Butter*. What intertextual, paratextual, hypotextual, and architextual aspects of the script can you identify in this short excerpt? To examine the metatextual material, find an online review and discuss it with your classmates.

4. One-act plays are often good choices for classroom performances. Find a one act with few characters and read it aloud, timing it. Then decide how you would cut the play to fit within your assigned time. Talk over your choices with at least one classmate.

5. Drama has power to influence individuals and cultures. Info-Trac College Edition Article A103711705 tells about a public discussion of "The Playwright's Role in Fostering Social Change." Read it, and come to class prepared to discuss several ways that the playwrights on the panel described theater's potential to bring about social changes.

6. Chapter 1 mentioned an Info-Trac College Edition article that said acting lessons are beneficial for accountants. Read Article 55166421, "You're On!," in the June 1999 issue of *Strategic Finance*. List the advantages that can be gained through a study of acting techniques. Are there similar benefits from a course in oral interpretation? Defend your answer in a small group.

9

Performing Poetry

This chapter will help you:

- Identify and analyze poetic language

- Understand and work with a poem's rhyming and rhythmic patterns

- Describe three classifications of poetry: narrative, lyric, and dramatic

- Analyze several poems

The outlook wasn't brilliant for the Mudville nine that day;
The score stood four to two with but one inning more to play.
And then when Cooney died at first, and Barrows did the same,
A sickly silence fell upon the patrons of the game.
A straggling few got up to go in deep despair. The rest
Clung to that hope which springs eternal in the human breast;
They thought if only Casey could but get a whack at that—
We'd put up even money now with Casey at the bat.

But Flynn preceded Casey, as did also Jimmy Blake.
And the former was a lulu and the latter was a cake;
So upon that stricken multitude grim melancholy sat,
For there seemed but little chance of Casey's getting to the bat.
But Flynn let drive a single, to the wonderment of all,
And Blake, the much despisèd, tore the cover off the ball;
And when the dust had lifted, and the men saw what had occurred,
There was Johnnie safe at second and Flynn a-hugging third.

Then from 5,000 throats and more there rose a lusty yell;
It rumbled through the valley, it rattled in the dell;
It knocked upon the mountain and recoiled upon the flat,
For Casey, mighty Casey, was advancing to the bat. . . . [1]

Ernest Lawrence Thayer, a bored newspaper reporter, tossed off the words to
"Casey at the Bat" for the June 3, 1888, edition of the San Francisco *Examiner*.[2]
The poem soon appeared in newspapers across the nation, but it took a performer to make it famous. DeWolf Hopper first interpreted "Casey" at an 1888
sports banquet honoring the New York Giants. Hopper's autobiography
describes the occasion: "the house, after a moment of startled silence . . .
shouted its glee."[3] (The dramatic Hopper eventually recited "Casey" more
than 10,000 times.[4]) Although "Casey at the Bat" may not be great literature,
it is great fun, and thousands of performers have kept the tragic slugger's legend alive, so much so that a life-sized bronze in the Baseball Hall of Fame
honors this fictional character!

Poetry performances are woven into the cultural fabric of the United
States. You can hear poets in local coffee shops and bookstores. Librarians, parents, and teachers read aloud the rhymes of Shel Silverstein and Dr. Suess.
Worshippers in churches and synagogues recite the Psalms. Rappers compose
impromptu rhymes, and fearless poets compete in **poetry slams,** challenges
in which poets perform original works before live audiences, who judge them
on the spot. Poetry performances are also available online; visit www.poets.org
and link to the listening booth. You can search for a specific poem by title or
first line or for a specific poet.

To perform poetry competently, you should know several elements of its
literary genre. This chapter describes important poetic features and presents

---

PERFORMING CULTURE: International Poetry Audiences

Log onto InfoTrac College Edition, and search for Mona Molarsky's article "Spoken/Word" in the April 29, 1996, issue of *The Nation*. Here are a few of her claims:

In other societies, poetry attracts large audiences:

Russia: In the 1960s, thousands heard poets like Yevtushenko, Voznesensky, and Akhmadulina. There "poetry readings were second only to soccer as entertainment."

Japan: Japan has a long tradition of poetry writing. Today there are 5 to 10 million Japanese poets; "haiku-scribbling stars" perform on the radio and on TV.

Chile: The 20th-century poet Pablo Neruda performed before fishermen,

miners, and students. He once commented, "A poet who reads his verse to 130,000 cannot go on as before."

Central America: Born in Nicaragua but raised in El Salvador, the prize-winning poet Claribel Alegría commented, "Almost everyone writes poetry."

- Read the article to discover how spoken word performances are becoming popular in the United States. What has influenced this trend? Have you heard such performances?
- How has hip-hop popularized the performance of poetry among young people worldwide?

---

several poems for analysis and study. Come to class prepared to discuss each example and to try out possible interpretations within small groups of your classmates.

POETIC LANGUAGE

A popular college literature text says that reading poetry is somehow different than reading other types of literature. Poetry requires you to be "more attentive to the connotations of words, more receptive to the expressive qualities of sound and rhythm in line and stanza, more discerning about details of syntax and punctuation."[5] Attention to detail is vital because compression, density, implication, and suggestion are typical in poetry. In short, "poems concentrate meaning and distill feeling."[6]

Language is made up of **words,** which are "symbols for our experiences with objects and events."[7] **Pragmatic language** functions in utilitarian ways to achieve practical or useful ends. A director who shouts, "Lights! Camera! Action!" uses words to issue commands. She's not trying to evoke emotions; she's using pragmatic language to tell people what to do. **Illocutionary speech** is speech that actually does something.[8] When the jury pronounced Rubin "Hurricane" Carter "guilty," he went to jail; only after another jury in a retrial returned a "not guilty" verdict was he freed. A judge who utters, "By the authority vested in me by the State of New Mexico, I now pronounce you married" ushers the couple into a new, legally binding state of affairs. The words in a real sense create the social reality.

In contrast, **expressive language** appeals to the senses by combining images, rhymes, and rhythms in unique, vivid, and evocative ways. This section focuses on several elements of language that will help you better understand and perform poetry: denotative and connotative meanings, titles, sensory imagery, tone color, literary imagery, and repetition.

Denotative and Connotative Meanings

Words denote, or stand for, objects or abstract ideas. **Denotative meanings** are meanings found in dictionaries. I. A. Richards calls this the *sense* of the word: the plain, overt meaning.[9] For instance, *father* can denote either a thing (noun) or an act (verb). That is, a man can be a father (noun), and he can father (verb) a company. Dictionary[10] meanings include:

> 1. A male parent; human or animal. 2. A male ancestor. 3. A man who creates, originates, or founds something. 4. God, the first person of the Christian Trinity. 5. Leading men, as of a city: the town fathers. 6. A priest or clergyman in Roman Catholic or Anglican churches.

When you come across a totally unfamiliar word or one you can't actually define, think back to your elementary school teachers' advice and "Look it up!" William Wordsworth's poem "I Wandered Lonely as a Cloud," written in 1807, contains these lines:

> A poet could not but be gay,
> In such a *jocund* company . . .

If Wordsworth wrote these lines today, he might choose different words. *Jocund?* What does that mean? And how do you pronounce it? It may have been a familiar word in 1807, but I can't remember ever hearing anyone toss *jocund* into a casual conversation—or a public speech, for that matter. The dictionary tells me it means "characterized by joyful exuberance."[11] It's pronounced "JOCK-und." Knowing this, you could perform Wadsworth's line, confident in your pronunciation, perhaps smiling slightly as an additional means of helping the audience understand what *jocund* denotes.

Denotative meanings can change over time. In 1807, *gay* meant cheerful, happy, jovial. In at least one dictionary, its first meaning is "of, relating to, or having a sexual orientation to persons of the same sex."[12] If you choose to perform this poem, you must take into account what *gay* probably means to today's audiences.

Words come loaded with emotional overtones and personalized associations that interweave with and overlie the dictionary meanings. These are the **connotative meanings**, all the associations you have with a word. Consider the difference between *daddy* and *father*. Both denote a male parent, but *father* seems more formal and rigid, whereas *daddy* seems warmer and more approachable. Connotations vary from person to person, depending on each one's personality, background, and experiences.

To most people, *death* has a negative connotation. For example, both Paul Mariani ("Then Sings My Soul," pages 203–204) and John Donne ("Death Be Not Proud," page 185) resist death. Compare their reactions with Walt Whitman's response to *death*, which the sea whispers to him at the climax of his poem, "Out of the Cradle Endlessly Rocking":[13]

> A word then, (for I will conquer it,)
> The word final, superior to all,
> Subtle, sent up—what is it?—I listen;
> Are you whispering it, and have been all the time, you sea-waves?
> Is that it from your liquid rims and wet sands?
>
> Whereto answering, the sea,
> Delaying not, hurrying not,
> Whisper'd me through the night, and very plainly before daybreak,
> Lisp'd to me the low and delicious word Death;
> And again Death—ever Death, Death, Death,
> Hissing melodious, neither like the bird, nor like my aroused
>   child's heart,
> But edging near, as privately for me, rustling at my feet,
> Creeping thence steadily up to my ears, and laving me softly all over,
> Death, Death, Death, Death, Death.
>
> The word of the sweetest song, and all songs,
> That strong and delicious word which, creeping to my feet,
> The sea whisper'd me.

Few poets depict death as Whitman does: the word "superior to all," "low and delicious," "the word of the sweetest song," "the strong and delicious word." In your interpretations, identify and perform the connotations the poet suggests. That is, in performing Whitman's poem, show his fascination with and acceptance of death; use softer volume and linger on the words in a way that suggests tidal waves. In contrast, for Donne's poem, use louder volume and more defiant tones to confront the idea of death.

Titles

As Chapter 4 explained, titles are paratexts that authors choose to reveal something about the work. Analyzing titles is especially important in poetry, for they often reveal the topic or theme, which may or may not be stated in the poem itself. For example, Henley chose the Latin title "Invictus" for his meditation on his "unconquerable soul." (*Invictus* means *not vanquished* or *invincible*.) Edward Higgins called his poem "The Poetry Surgeon" (pages 204–205).

Titles can reveal information about the when or where of the poem. "Lines Written in Early Spring," "To a Young Lady: On Her Leaving the Town after a Coronation," or "Australia, 1894" provide the poem's time frame. "Dover Beach" and "London" reveal the place or the setting. Muriel Sparks's title gives the location of her characters; they are conversing "In the Orchard" (Chapter 4).

Some titles reveal the poem's classification, or genre. These include "Ode to the West Wind," "Soliloquy of the Spanish Cloister," and "Elegy in a Country Church-Yard."

Poets sometimes include a short inscription or **epigraph,** a subtitle that follows the title, sometimes in a foreign language. Study these inscriptions carefully, for they usually relate to the content and help set the tone.[14] For instance, Robert Lowell uses an epigraph from the Bible for "The Quaker Graveyard in Nantucket (for Warren Winslow, Dead at Sea)": "Let man have dominion over the fishes of the sea and the fowls of the air and the beasts and the whole earth, and every creeping creature that moveth upon the earth" (from Genesis 1:26). For his poem "The Mediterranean," Allen Tate quotes from Virgil's *Aeneid*: "*Quem das finem, rex magne, dolorum?*" ("When, great King, will you bring an end to our griefs?")

Poets occasionally explain the incidents that prompted them to write. Wordsworth prefaces his poem "Stepping Westward" with this paragraph:[15]

> While my Fellow-traveller and I were walking by the side of Loch Katrine, one fine evening after sunset, in our road to a Hut where, in the course of our Tour, we had been hospitably entertained some weeks before, we met, in one of the loneliest parts of that solitary region, two well-dressed Women, one of whom said to us, by way of greeting, "What, are you stepping westward?"

Even titles that echo the first line ("my momma moved among the days") or another line in the poem ("Suddenly I Realized I Was Sitting") clue you in to the poem's overall theme.

Sensory Imagery

A primary characteristic of poetry is the use of images that appeal to our senses of sight, smell, sound, touch, and taste. Not surprisingly, these are the channels through which we perceive and experience the world. As you analyze and perform poetry, try to mentally experience what the speaker sees and hears, smells, touches and tastes.

In this excerpt from "Dover Beach,"[16] Matthew Arnold creates sensory images related to sights, smells, and sounds:

> The sea is calm tonight.
> The tide is full, the moon lies fair
> Upon the straits;—on the French coast the light
> Gleams and is gone; the cliffs of England stand,

Glimmering and vast, out in the tranquil bay.
Come to the window, sweet is the night-air!
Only, from the long line of spray
Where the sea meets the moon-blanch'd land,
Listen! you hear the grating roar
Of pebbles which the waves draw back, and fling,
At their return, up the high strand,
Begin, and cease, and then again begin,
With tremulous cadence slow, and bring
The eternal note of sadness in. . . .

Arnold combines the look of the sea, the sound of waves, and the smell of the fresh air in vivid images. Similarly, in "Snake," D. H. Lawrence combines imagery to create a memorable character, a poisonous snake at a water trough, and his speaker watches the visitor, fascinated:[17]

[The snake] reached down from a fissure in the earth-wall in
    the gloom
And trailed his yellow-brown slackness soft-bellied down,
    over the edge of the stone trough
And rested his throat upon the stone bottom,
And where the water had dripped from the tap, in a small
    clearness,
He sipped with his straight mouth,
Softly drank through his strait gums, into his slack long
    body,
Silently.

I don't particularly like snakes, but I liked this one—as did the speaker, who wrestles with his natural urge to kill the animal and his fascination with the snake's relaxed self-assurance, brought to life by the poem's vivid sensory images.

Tone Color and Tone

The vocabulary of poetry overlaps with musical terminology. Take the term *tone color,* for example. Each instrument has its own timbre, or tone color. The sound made by a reedy saxophone contrasts with a more mellow cello or a brash trumpet. Even when they all play the same note, the difference is obvious. Composers combine different instruments to create a variety of moods and sounds. Saxophones are common in jazz; symphonies rely on violins and French horns; rock music makes use of electric guitars and drums.

In poetry, **tone color** refers to the way a poet puts together sounds to develop the poem. Different sounds convey different moods and textures. A word, when spoken aloud, often suggests the idea it represents. For example, lines 3 and 4 of "Dover Beach" read: "On the French coast, the light / Gleams and is gone." The word *gleams* invites you to extend the sounds, lingering on the vowel and on the /m/ before dropping your voice to say "and is gone;" this suggests the image of a rotating light in a lighthouse that *g-l-ea-ea-m-m-m-s-s,* then disappears.

Several literary devices contribute to tone color. Poets use **onomatopoeia** when they want a word to mirror a sound. The "his-s-s-s" of a snake, the "tlot-tlot" of horses' hooves, the "at-choo" of a sneeze are examples of onomatopoeia that actually suggest sounds. Onomatopoeia is common in children's poetry.

Assonance, the repetition of vowel sounds, adds color. For example, "The road was a ribbon of moonlight, / Looping the purple moor" includes three /oo/ sounds in close proximity. "The Windhover" includes the /aw/ sound three times in one phrase: "daylight's dauphin, dapple-dawn-drawn Falcon...." And the lines "like a dreamwalker in a field; / seemed like what she touched was hers" contain three /ee/ sounds close together.

Consonance is the repetition of consonants within words, such as, "[The snake] trailed his yellow-brown slackness soft-bellied down...." *Trailed, yellow, slackness,* and *bellied* all contain an /l/ sound. Say them aloud, letting the /l/ linger on your tongue. The combination of sounds suggests the languid way a snake actually moves. In another line, the speaker refers to water that "had dripped from a tap"; *dripped* and *tap* feature /d/, /t/, and /p/ sounds that, when pronounced crisply, suggest the sound of water plopping into a trough.

Alliteration is the repetition of beginning consonants. These lines from "Snake" use six words that begin with /s/: "He *s*ipped with his *s*traight mouth, / *S*oftly drank through his *s*traight gums, into his *s*lack long body, / *S*ilently." /S/ is a sibilant made by expelling air through your teeth. Notice how Lawrence uses the /z/ sound, also a sibilant, at the end of *his*. By putting a word that ends with a sibilant just before a word that begins with one (*his straight* and *his slack*), Lawrence doubles the intensity of the hissing sound that we commonly associate with snakes.

Don't confuse *tone color* with *tone*. **Tone** is the poem's implied attitude toward its subject. Tone is complex. In poetry, as in everyday life, our attitudes are sometimes playful and sometimes sad, sometimes rebellious and sometimes respectful, sometimes regretful and sometimes joyous. To discern the tone of a piece, pay attention to the use (or nonuse) of meter and rhyme, the details that are included and excluded, the images and figurative language, the sentence patterns and word choices.[18]

Some literary critics define tone as the persona's attitude toward the audience in light of the subject. I. A. Richards says it is "the writer's relation to the reader in view of what is being said and their joint feelings about it."[19] Poets can take a respectful or condescending tone; they can ignore or flatter their readers; they can insult or confide in their audience. Discerning the tone, in both senses of the term, will help you interpret and perform the poem.

PERFORMING CULTURE: Arab Poetry

Different cultures have different poetic traditions, and features prized in one culture can be dismissed in another. For example, the online version of *Encyclopedia Britannica* says that the Sufi poet al-Mutanabbi, regarded by some as the greatest of the classical Arabic poets, writes in a "flowery, bombastic style marked by improbable metaphors."[20] A more favorable source addresses "the intense musicality of his language," which features internal rhyme and alliteration.[21] Eric Ormsby explains that Arab poets traditionally use "abundant language." In fact, he explains, "[a]n Arab poet would have felt dishonored by writing the sort of parched and minimal verse so in favor among American poets."

- Read Ormsby's analysis of classical Arabic poetry on the Parnassus Poetry Web site at www.parnassus-poetry.com/Ormsby.htm. Be prepared to discuss two or three interesting characteristics of Arabic poetry with your classmates. How is the poetry similar to and how does it differ from some of the conventions described in this chapter?
- Listen online to one of al-Mutanabbi's poems, read in the original by Samer Traboulsi and captioned in English, at www.princeton.edu/~arabic/poetry/al_mu_to_sayf.html.

Literary Imagery

There are over 250 types of **figures of speech,** which are verbal expressions or nonliteral uses of words. Five of the most common are allusion, personification, apostrophe, metaphor, and simile.

- An **allusion** is a reference to a cultural or historical figure or event, either real or fictional. Many poets allude to Greek and Roman gods and goddesses, Biblical characters, cultural heroes and villains, or wars and other important historical events. To understand Jessie Fauset's poem "Oriflamme" (pages 201–202), you should know something about Sojourner Truth (a former slave who was a famous abolitionist) and *l'oriflamme* (the flag that French kings raised in times of war). You will understand "The Poetry Surgeon" better if you know what "triage" is or what "all hallow's" and "adam & eve" refer to. Whenever you encounter an unfamiliar allusion, do an intertextual analysis (Chapter 4, pages 70–71), and find out what you can about the character or event behind the allusion.

- **Personification** is a figure of speech that treats an animal or inanimate object as if it were human, giving it person-like qualities that may include physical features, motivations, or emotions. Here, Luci Shaw personifies the Lake of Galilee:[22]

Quietly the old lake leans
Against the land,
Rubbing a shoulder
Along the pebbles, water-worn,

Sun-warm. The lips of the waves
Mouth old secrets
Among the reeds.

- Sometimes poets address an absent person, an inanimate object, or a supernatural being. Or they personify an abstract concept (such as truth or justice) and speak to it as if it were a person. This literary device, called **apostrophe,** allows poets to express emotions forcefully. In these famous lines, John Donne defiantly addresses a personified death:[23]

Death, be not proud, though some have called thee
Mighty and dreadful, for thou are not so;
For those whom thou think'st thou dost overthrow
Die not, poor Death, nor yet canst thou kill me.

To perform such a poem, use a semi-closed focus. Locate the object or personified idea in a particular spot, and speak to that place. It's common to place a supernatural being slightly higher.

- **Metaphor** is a figure in which one thing is spoken of as if it were another. For example, the prose poem "Suddenly I Realized I Was Sitting" (page 190) likens a couple's smoldering conflict to a volcano. The narrator explains: "Suddenly I realized I was sitting on a volcano. . . . You can't name it but it's there, the volcano, the unloving or too-loving mass of situation."[24]

- An extended metaphor that encompasses much of or even the entire work is called an **analogy.** The poem "Anger" in the Stop and Check feature is a good example.

- A **simile** is a comparison that uses *like* or *as* to signal the relationship between the two things. Here's a simile by the ancient Greek poet Sappho:[25]

Without warning
As a whirlwind
Swoops on an oak
Love shakes my heart.

Look for comparisons that seem fresh and unique. Overused comparisons become so common that they become clichés, like "fresh as a daisy" or "dead as a doornail." Presenting death as "the Grim Reaper" is common; in contrast, Paul Mariani uses fresh metaphors to describe his friend Lenny's response to his approaching death:[26]

He was a toreador waving the red flag
at death itself, horns lowered now
to come hurling down on him. . . .

What does all this mean for performance? When the poet uses an analogy that's developed in some detail, experiment with bodily and vocalic variations that suggest the connection between the figurative image and the thing it stands for. Test your intuition. For instance, a performer might decide to suggest bullfighter images for the above lines, using an erect stance, with her feet angled slightly. Using an offstage focus, she could "place" the bull a bit to the

---

STOP AND CHECK: Performing Metaphors

Here's a poem that uses two metaphors to contrast two individuals' ways of dealing with anger. Linda Pastan compares "my" anger to a dangerous caged beast and "your" anger to a pet dog. Come to class prepared to discuss how the analogies themselves suggest performance strategies.[27]

Anger
You tell me
that it's all right
to let it out of its cage,
though it may claw someone,

even bite.
You say that letting it out
may tame it somehow.
But loose it may
turn on me, maul
my face, draw blood.
Ah, you think you know so much,
you whose anger is a pet dog,
its canines dull with disuse.
But mine is a rabid thing,
sharpening its teeth
on my very bones,
and I will never let it go.

---

right, above the audience's head, and watch his approach warily. (The key is to *suggest*, not *act*.) She'd use defiant vocal tones for "He was a toreador waving the red flag" then pause and slow down for "horns lowered now." She could then speed up as the bull hurtles down on Lenny.

Repetition

Repetitions of single words, longer phrases, and entire lines are common in poetry. "In the Orchard" (Chapter 4) contains several repetitions. In one line the girl repeats, "Not you! Not you!" Later, the boy asks, "Well what's to be done?" "To be done?" she echoes.

This poem by Lucille Clifton repeats exact phrases ("seemed like"), parallel phrases ("seemed like what she touched"; "seemed like what touched her"), and slightly varied phrases ("right back in"; "right back on in").[28]

my momma moved among the days

my momma moved among the days
like a dreamwalker in a field;
seemed like what she touched was hers
seemed like what touched her couldn't hold,
she got us almost through the high grass
then seemed like she turned around and ran
right back in
right back on in

Repetition offers many opportunities for interpretation. A line that repeats at intervals throughout the piece can function as a litany that audience members listen for. It's sometimes effective to use similar vocal variations each time you repeat the line. In line 3 above, you could emphasize "she" and put stress on "her" in line 4. In line 5, try pausing before and after "almost."

RHYME AND RHYTHM

The earliest childhood poetry comes in the form of lullabies and nursery rhymes. Many babies snuggle close to a caregiver and are soothed to sleep with a song, perhaps rocked in an old family rocker that squeaks out the rhythm in time with the adult's crooning voice:

Hush little baby, don't say a word
Papa's gonna buy you a mockingbird.
If that mockingbird won't sing,
Papa's gonna buy you a diamond ring.

Children thus commonly learn some forms of poetry early on, especially rhyme and rhythm.

Rhymes and Rhyme Patterns

A **rhyme** is an echo of repeating sounds that may come at the end, at the beginning, or in the middle of words. As you examine your poem, look for the following types of rhymes:

End Rhyme. Words that start differently but end in similar sounds (*true / do*; *remain / explain*). These are often used at the end of lines.

Multiple Rhymes. More than two lines in the poem that rhyme with each other (*lie, rye, sky, by*).

Closed Couplets. Two rhyming lines that contain a complete thought. Sonnets often end with a closed couplet ("But if the while I think on thee, dear friend, / All losses are restored and sorrows end.").[29]

Internal Rhymes. A rhyme that occurs within the line itself ("My heart in hiding/ *Stirred* for a *bird* . . . ").

Poets often use a distinct pattern for end rhymes. For example, Alfred, Lord Tennyson employed a multiple rhyme scheme in "The Lady of Shalott:"[30]

On either side the river lie	A
Long fields of barley and of rye,	A
That clothe the wold and meet the sky;	A
And thro' the field the road runs by	A
To many-tower'd Camelot;	B
And up and down the people go,	C
Gazing where the lilies blow	C
Round an island there below,	C
The island of Shalott.	B

The poem continues in a similar pattern. Four rhyming lines are followed by a line ending in *Camelot*; then three rhyming lines are followed by a line ending in *Shalott*. "Invictus" (pages 56–58) contains the following rhyme pattern: ABAB / CDCD / EFEF / GHGH. The poem consists of four **quatrains** (a four-line grouping), each with alternating rhymes.

One of the best known rhyme patterns is the **sonnet,** a 14-line poem that has two major variations: ABBAABBA / CDCDEE or ABBAABBA / CDECDE. A second form consists of three quatrains followed by a couplet: ABAB / CDCD / EFEF / GG. Here, the last two lines usually pack the most impact. William Shakespeare's "Sonnet 116" is a famous example:[31]

Let me not to the marriage of true minds	A
Admit impediments. Love is not love	B
Which alters when it alteration finds,	A
Or bends with the remover to remove.	B
O no, it is an ever-fixèd mark	C
That looks on tempests and is never shaken;	D
It is the star to every wand'ring bark,	C
Whose worth's unknown, although his height be taken.	D
Love's not time's fool, though rosy lips and cheeks	E
Within his bending sickle's compass come.	F
Love alters not with his brief hours and weeks,	E
But bears it out ev'n to the edge of doom.	F
If this be error and upon me proved,	G
I never writ, nor no man ever loved.	G

There are many ways to perform this poem. You can hear several interpretations at www.educeth.ch/. Link to *Englisch* and then to Shakespeare Sonnets and to Sonnet 116. Come to class prepared to compare and contrast Linda Gregerson's, Lloyd Schartz's, and Mark Doty's interpretations.

Rhythm and Meter

Rhythm is the underlying beat of an utterance, produced through stress or accent on a syllable within a word and on words within a phrase; **meter** occurs when the rhythm becomes predictable and regular. Each group of stressed and unstressed syllables that make up a pattern is called a **foot.** There are six common feet (don't worry too much about the terminology, but pay attention to the details of stresses within lines):

Iambic	stress on the second syllable in a two-syllable word or phrase NiCOLE, TyRONE
Trochaic	stress on the first syllable in a two-syllable word or phrase CARol, MAtthew
Anapestic	stress on the third syllable in a three-syllable word or phrase Mary ANN, a la MODE
Dactylic	stress on the first syllable in a three-syllable word or phrase EMily, JERemy
Spondee	two heavy beats in a row, usually in a line with other types of feet

---

STOP AND CHECK: Analyzing Rhyme and Repetition

Examine the rhymes and the rhyming pattern in this famous poem by Gerard Manley Hopkins. It's a good example of a poet's fascination with words. Label the end rhymes by using letters in alphabetical order. Some lines are already marked, and some analysis appears in brackets: [32]

The Windhover
  To Christ Our Lord
I caught this morning morning's minion, king-   [*repetition*]   A
dom of daylight's dauphin, dapple-dawn-drawn Falcon, in his riding   B
Of the rolling level underneath him steady air, and striding   B
High there, how he rung upon the rein of a wimpling wing   A
In his ecstasy! then off, off forth on swing,
As a skate's heel sweeps smooth on a bow-bend: the hurl and gliding
Rebuffed the big wind. My heart in hiding
Stirred for a bird, —the achieve of, the mastery of the thing!   [*internal rhyme*]

Brute beauty and valour and act, oh, air, pride, plume, here
Buckle! AND the fire that breaks from thee then, a billion
Times told lovelier, more dangerous, O my chevalier!

No wonder of it: shéer plód makes plough down sillion
Shine, and blue-bleak embers, ah my dear,
Fall, gall themselves, and gash gold-vermilion.

   How many alliterated words or phrases do you find? Notice the repetitions of words and sounds (e.g., *dauphin, dawn,* and *drawn* in line 2). Finally, read the poem aloud, listening to the sounds that Hopkins carefully wove together.

YOU SAY that LETting it OUT . . .

BUT LOOSE it may TURN on ME . . .

Pyrrhic   two light stresses in a row; usually in a line with other types of feet

my momma MOVED AMONG THE DAYS . . .

Each line of poetry is made up of a number of feet. As you might expect, poets often intentionally combine a specific number of feet into their lines.

Trimeter   a three-beat line

Tetrameter   four stressed syllables per line

Pentameter   five-beat line

Hexameter   six–beat line

Free verse   lines of varying length and varying rhythm

Pentameter is the most common pattern, especially iambic pentameter, which sounds more natural and less forced than some other patterns. This is probably because iambic pentameter is the most similar to typical speech patterns used in everyday English. Most sonnets are written in this pattern.

Poets often use predictably patterned **stanzas,** or sets of lines that are similar in length. For example, "Naming of Parts" on page 198 is comprised of six-line stanzas. However, poets also vary stanza length. "The Poetry Surgeon" by Edward Higgins (pages 204–205) features stanzas that vary in length from one line to five lines. In addition, Higgins uses **enjambment,** a poetic device that carries over an idea from one line to another or from one stanza to another.

Other forms include **blank verse,** in which the rhythm is predictable but the lines are not rhymed. **Free verse** is characterized by optional rhyme and rhythm patterns; "Anger" and "my momma moved among the days" are two examples. Some poets are experimenting with **prose poems,** which use some conventional poetic tools even as they break traditional notions of stanzas, lines, and other formal features. Here's a prose poem by Elizabeth Kostova:[35]

Suddenly I Realized I Was Sitting

I was entirely—let me start again. I was entirely unsure how the situation. I was entirely unsure how the situation arose out of nothing. As situations do. First, you think you know people: Rose, Phil, that other acquaintance who knows both of them. Then you're looking through them, through their quirks—like handling a pen badly, complaining about minor illnesses, tipping too little at restaurants because they can't do arithmetic. You're not only seeing through them, but hearing through them, almost not hearing them, almost not hearing what you're listening to. One is telling a story, already too long a story for a short lunch. One is telling a story you've heard before from another friend. Listening, looking, seeing through as if they are becoming transparent around the table, you are there but not present to them, you are watching. Suddenly I realized I was sitting on a volcano. First, the friends around me, then the situation looming up large and solid, bulky under or beyond their insubstantial forms. And what is it? Rose loves. No. Phil hates Rose from way back. No. You can't name it but it's there, the volcano, the unloving or too-loving mass of situation. You'd make a plot of it. Frightening, maybe, or dull or worth trying to describe, but always something. Not always volcano. Not always. In this case, however, I realized suddenly what I was sitting on.

These poems typically have a **stream of consciousness** quality; that is, they flow like the ongoing, constantly changing thoughts and impressions that reflect the inner and outer forces impinging on the speaker.[36] You can find additional examples of this genre in *The Prose Poem: An International Journal,* available online at http://webdelsol.com/tpp/.

During your analysis, be aware of **elisions,** or unstressed vowels or syllables the poet omits in order to preserve the meter. Words like *o'er, oft, e'er, e'en* are elisions of *over, often, ever,* and *even.* Elisions are less common in contemporary poetry and rarely occur in free verse; they are more common in older poems and traditional forms with strict rhythm patterns. Notice that Shakespeare elided the words *wand'ring* (wandering) and *ev'n* (even) in order to keep the rhythm in "Sonnet 116."

STOP AND CHECK: Working with Rhythm

Alfred Noyes's ballad "The Highwayman" is written in a galloping meter, suggesting the bandit's approach to the inn where his love awaits. Each stanza incorporates repetition in lines 4 and 5 (and sometimes into line 6) that breaks the meter found in lines 1 through 3 and 6.

Examine these four stanzas from the poem: (1) the highwayman gallops to the inn, (2) rouses Bess to the window and, (3) unaware that an eavesdropper is listening, (4) tells her his plans. Your first time through, play with the sounds. That is, don't say the actual words; instead, use nonsense syllables to sound out the beat, like this:

   da DUH da da DUH da da DUH da da DUH da DUH da DUH

Then begin playing around with the words, testing various ways to be true to the beat without being bound up in it. What differences will there be between the first and the third stanzas? Where might you use a heavier beat? When would you minimize the stress? In the fourth stanza, he's talking to her; how conversational can this be?[35]

The wind was a torrent of darkness among the gusty trees,
The moon was a ghostly galleon tossed upon cloudy seas,
The road was a ribbon of moonlight, looping the purple moor,
And the highwayman came riding,
    riding, riding
The highwayman came riding—up to the old inn-door. . . .

Over the cobbles he clattered and clashed in the dark inn-yard,
And he tapped with his whip on the shutters, but all was locked and barred;
He whistled a tune to the window, and who should be waiting there
But the landlord's black-eyed daughter,
    Bess, the landlord's daughter,
Plaiting a dark red love-knot into her long black hair.

And dark in the old inn-yard a stable-wicket creaked
Where Tim the ostler listened; his face was white and peaked;
His eyes were hollows of madness, his hair like mouldy hay,
But he loved the landlord's daughter,
    The landlord's red-lipped daughter,
Dumb as a dog he listened, and he heard the robber say—

"One kiss, my bonny sweetheart, I'm after a prize tonight,
But I shall be back with the yellow gold before the morning light;
Yet, if they press me sharply, and harry me through the day,
Then look for me by moonlight,
    Watch for me by moonlight,
I'll come to thee by moonlight, though hell should bar the way." . . .

Performing rhyme and rhythm effectively is vital. It's especially important when the poetry is highly patterned, which easily locks you into a rhythm pattern and eliminates many opportunities for subtle interpretations. Of course, a heavily stressed rhythm can support the poem's central theme. For example, Robert Louis Stevenson incorporates a swinging rhythm into his poem "The Swing," which opens with the lines: "How do you like to go up in a swing? / Up in the sky so blue? / Oh, I do think it the pleasantest thing / Ever a child can do!" (It a great poem to chant as you help a young child swing.)

CLASSIFICATIONS OF POETRY

There are three common classifications of poetry: narrative, lyric, and dramatic. Each is further divided into subtypes, and each requires different strategies for interpretation and performance.

Narrative Poetry

Narrative poems tell a story in verse; "The Highwayman" is one famous example. Epics and ballads are in this category. Many, even most, of the great narrative poems were originally oral.

Epics tell the life and work of a hero, mythological character, or group. They differ in scale and style from other stories told in verse: They are usually too long to read in one sitting, and the language is generally relatively formal. They deal with historical people and events and are important in educating the young.[36] You are probably somewhat familiar with one or more great epics of Western civilization such as the *Odyssey* and *Beowulf.* (The movie *O Brother, Where Art Thou* was loosely based on the *Odyssey.*)

The term **ballad** refers to anonymously composed folk songs that present a story, usually tragic, in simple meter and structure. They are somewhat like the last act of a play because they often omit elements of setting, background, and character motivation, focusing, instead, on the way things turn out.[37] Some have recurring refrains. Ballad traditions include Appalachian folk ballads, cowboy poetry, labor movement poems (especially commemorating violent events), "bush" ballads from Australia, and some Calypso traditions from the West Indies.[38] Although not all ballads are sung, they are common in country music, which traditionally narrates stories of the rural working class.

Ballads typically follow a tetrameter-trimeter pattern, such as Edgar Allen Poe's "Annabel Lee":[39]

It was MANy and MANy a YEAR aGO,
In a KINGdom BY the SEA,
That a MAIDen there LIVED whom YOU may KNOW
By the NAME of ANNabel LEE,
And this MAIDen she LIVED with NO other
    THOUGHT
Than to LOVE and be LOVED by ME.

PERFORMING CULTURE: Global Narratives

There are many great epic poems from non-Western traditions, including the longest book ever, the Tibetan *Epic of King Gesar,* which fills approximately 120 volumes. Two influential Indian works are the *Mahabharata,* the great text of Hinduism; it is four times longer than the Bible. Another, the *Ramayana,* narrates the story of the ideal hero, Prince Rama, whose wife, Siva, is kidnapped by the demon Ravana. Epic texts from other cultures include the *Shahnama,* or *Book of Kings,* by the great Persian poet Firdausi Tousi, which narrates tales of heroes from ancient Persia.[40] Epics are important in perpetuating culture. For example, when the medieval Serbian state crumbled, the Serbs used epic stories and legends, often set to music, to keep alive their religious traditions and to resist assimilation by neighboring cultures.[41]

Before you perform a narrative poem, review the sections in Chapter 7 that discuss characters and plot. Then reread the section on narrators, focusing on the narrator's perspective and attitude toward the characters and their actions. Think, also, of the storyteller's attitude toward the intended audience. Use the guidelines in that chapter to analyze and perform the poem. If you perform a ballad, work with the strong rhythm pattern, but don't let it dominate your performance.

Lyric Poetry

As Chapter 4 explains, texts in the lyric mode express the emotions and thoughts of a single persona who may or may not represent the creator. Lyric poems typically deal with common experiences; they make a significant emotional impact in a brief space; and they focus on a response to what happens, rather than on the event itself. The personae are typically agents of revelation who offer a new way of seeing or reacting to the common experiences. Because of their comparative brevity, lyric poems invite the audience to supply much of the background and context.[42]

Lyric poetry may be reflective or descriptive. **Reflective poems** use past-tense verbs and present the persona's musings on past happenings or reliving of past events. D. H. Lawrence's "Snake," excerpted on page 182, is an example. **Descriptive poems** use the present tense and describe the subject in the here-and-now. The following poem by Alfred, Lord Tennyson, is an excellent example. As is typical of lyric poetry, the title reveals the subject:

The Eagle[43]
He clasps the crag with crooked hands,
Close to the sun in lonely lands,
Ringed with the azure world, he stands.

The wrinkled sea beneath him crawls;
He watches from his mountain walls,
And like a thunderbolt he falls.

Another lyric form is the sonnet, a highly personal poem that follows a distinctive rhythm and rhyme pattern, described earlier. Sonnets can be reflective or descriptive. **Elegies** memorialize a person who has died or reflect on death itself. This genre dates back to classical Greece. Thomas Gray's "Elegy in a Country Church-Yard" is one of the most famous elegies. **Odes** praise an idea or object or celebrate a specific occasion. They can be descriptive or reflective. They are comparatively long, composed using formal language and formal style. Like elegies, they date to classical Greece. Some titles—"Ode on a Grecian Urn," "Ode to Himself," "Ode on Solitude," "To Sleep," and "To Autumn"—reveal the variety of subjects poets have explored. The 1950s saw the emergence of **confessional poetry,** which is written using the first person and confides personal details of the poet's life and emotions that were formerly considered taboo or profane. Topics include adultery (Anne Sexton's "For My Lover Returning to His Wife"), mental illness (Robert Lowell's "Skunk Hour"), rage against cultural norms (Allen Ginsberg's "Howl"), dysfunctional families (Sylvia Plath's "Daddy"), and so on, usually written about in raw, direct language. Confessional poets include Stephen Dunn, W. D. Snodgrass, and Sharon Olds.

To perform lyric poetry effectively, employ **empathy,** which *Merriam-Webster's Collegiate Dictionary* defines as "the action of or the capacity for understanding, being aware of, being sensitive to, and vicariously experiencing the feelings, thoughts, and experience of another of either the past or present without having the feelings, thoughts, and experience fully communicated in an objectively explicit manner."[44] To be an empathic performer, you need knowledge of, identification with, and the ability to express the persona's emotion.[45]

- *Knowledge.* Empathy has a cognitive dimension. This means you understand which emotions are appropriate in which situations, and you know at least some of the components of those emotions.

- *Identification.* Empathy also has an affective dimension, a feeling "with" the person. Not only do you understand the emotion intellectually, but you also vicariously experience the person's feelings.

- *Expression.* After you understand and identify with the emotion, you show it through bodily and vocalic expressiveness. Think about nonverbal expressions of various emotions; play with and test your ideas, finally choosing those that seem best for the particular character and situation.

Dramatic Poetry

Dramatic poetry features one or more characters who narrate the story or portray a situation and guide the audience's emotions. The action usually unfolds in the present tense. There are five basic subgenres: dramatic narrative, dramatic lyric, dramatic monologue, dramatic dialogue, and soliloquy.

In a **dramatic narrative,** the narrator participates in the action and is affected by the outcome. An example is "The Raven," by Edgar Allen Poe.[46] It begins like this:

> Once upon a midnight dreary, while I pondered, weak and weary,
> Over many a quaint and curious volume of forgotten lore,
> While I nodded, nearly napping, suddenly there came a tapping,
> As of some one gently rapping, rapping at my chamber door.
> "'Tis some visitor," I muttered, "tapping at my chamber door—
>   Only this and nothing more."

As the poem progresses, the narrator tells of his encounter with the raven, and we watch him progressively descend into madness over the loss of his beloved Lenore.

Dramatic lyric poetry features a narrator who describes a situation or emotion or relates his or her impressions of a thing or happening. In Elizabeth Kostova's "Suddenly I Realized I Was Sitting," the narrator is probably a woman. She is visiting with old friends when she suddenly sees their relationship for what it is—a volcano waiting to erupt. The narrator in Paul Mariani's "Then Sings My Soul" is a recognizable character—male, middle-aged or older—who confidentially reveals his feelings about his dying friend. Stephen Dobyn's "Loud Music" is narrated by a stepfather who tells of his four-year-old stepdaughter's response to his love of loud music.

In **dramatic monologues,** we overhear as one character talks to a silent other and in the process usually reveals personal information that might be better kept hidden. Although the listeners are silent, we imagine their reactions and their impressions of the speaker. Perhaps the most famous dramatic monologue is Robert Browning's "My Last Duchess" (at the end of this chapter). Shakespeare's plays also include many dramatic monologues. Performing dramatic monologues uses many of the same skills required for solo drama. You must capture the speaker's personality characteristics even as you suggest the listener's reactions. You must consider the relationship between the speaker and listener, their motivations and attitudes toward one another. Use closed focus and character placement (or open focus if the character is addressing a group).

Dramatic dialogues feature two characters speaking with one another. "In the Orchard" (Chapter 4) is an example. Use character placement and closed focus, as you would in performing solo drama.

Soliloquies contrast with monologues in that they allow us to overhear characters talking to themselves, not to another person. This genre began in the theater when the audience needed to be let in on a character's thoughts and motivations. Shakespeare uses them liberally throughout his plays. Hamlet's musing about suicide, "To be or not to be,—that is the question" is a classic example. Robert Browning's famous "Soliloquy of the Spanish Cloister" reveals the jealousy of one monk, who puts on an outward show of piety but harbors murderous thoughts toward a fellow monk. Use inner-closed focus to perform a soliloquy.

POEMS FOR STUDY AND PRACTICE

These poems illustrate the concepts presented in this chapter. The first three poems are followed by a series of discussion questions.

"Ode of Mulan" [47]

ANONYMOUS (C. 5TH CENTURY C.E.) TRANSLATED BY H. H. FRANKEL

This poem from ancient China provided the characters and plot line for the Disney movie Mulan. Answer the questions that follow, and come to class prepared to discuss how you might perform this poem:

Tsiek tsiek and again tsiek tsiek,
Mu-lan weaves, facing the door.
You don't hear the shuttle's sound,
You only hear Daughter's sighs.
They ask Daughter who's in her heart,
They ask Daughter who's on her mind.
"No one is on Daughter's heart.
No one is on Daughter's mind.
Last night I saw the draft posters,
The Khan is calling many troops,
The army list is in twelve scrolls,
On every scroll there's Father's name.
Father has no grown-up son,
Mu-lan has no elder brother.
I want to buy a saddle and horse,
And serve in the army in Father's place."

In the East Market she buys a spirited horse,
In the West Market she buys a saddle,
In the South Market she buys a bridle,
In the North Market she buys a long whip.
At dawn she takes leave of Father and Mother,
In the evening camps on the Yellow River's bank.
She doesn't hear the sound of Father and Mother calling,
She only hears the Yellow River's flowing water cry *tsien tsien*.

At dawn she takes leave of the Yellow River,
In the evening she arrives at Black Mountain.
She doesn't hear the sound of Father and Mother calling,
She only hears Mount Yen's nomad horses cry *tsiu tsiu*.
She goes ten thousand miles on the business of war,

She crosses passes and mountains like flying.
Northern gusts carry the rattle of army pots,
Chilly light shines on iron armor.
Generals die in a hundred battles,
Stout soldiers return after ten years.

On her return she sees the Son of Heaven,
The Son of Heaven sits in the Splendid Hall.
He gives out promotions in twelve ranks
And prizes of a hundred thousand and more.
The Khan asks her what she desires.
"Mu-lan has no use for a minister's post.
I wish to ride a swift mount
To take me back to my home."

When Father and Mother hear Daughter is coming
They go outside the wall to meet her, leaning on each other.
When Elder Sister hears Younger Sister is coming
She fixes her rouge, facing the door.
When Little Brother hears Elder Sister is coming
He whets the knife, quick quick, for pig and sheep.
"I open the door to my east chamber,
I sit on my couch in the west room,
I take off my wartime gown
And put on my old-time clothes."
Facing the window she fixes her cloudlike hair,
Hanging up a mirror she dabs on yellow flower powder
She goes out the door and sees her comrades.
Her comrades are all amazed and perplexed.
Traveling together for twelve years
They didn't know Mu-lan was a girl.
"The he-hare's feet go hop and skip,
The she-hare's eyes are muddled and fuddled.
Two hares running side by side close to the ground,
How can they tell if I am he or she?"

- What details does the poet provide about the characters? What do you learn about their motivations?

- How would you perform the lines that contain onomatopoeia?

- Briefly sketch the plot. Does the poet provide enough information about the setting, the rising action, the climax, and the denouement to satisfy you?

- Analyze the narrator. What is his or her attitude toward Mulan?

- Who is the intended audience?

- If you have seen the movie, compare the poem to the movie.

- What is the meaning of the last four lines?

"Naming of Parts" [48]

BY HENRY REED

War has been a topic for poets for thousands of years. There are hundreds of emotional responses to war, such as bravado, true bravery, fear, and regret. War poems provide opportunities for beginning performers to develop their skills and for experienced performers to hone theirs. This favorite British poem from World War I has two distinct personae, and you will have to decide when each one (or both) speaks. First, read the poem aloud, and then analyze it using the questions that follow. Come to class prepared to discuss how you would move from analysis to performance:

To-day we have naming of parts. Yesterday,
We had daily cleaning. And to-morrow morning,
We shall have what to do after firing. But to-day,
To-day we have naming of parts. Japonica
Glistens like coral in all of the neighbouring gardens.
　　　And to-day we have naming of parts.

This is the lower sling swivel. And this
Is the upper sling swivel, whose use you will see,
When you are given your slings. And this is the piling swivel,
Which in your case you have not got. The branches
Hold in the gardens their silent, eloquent gestures.
　　　Which in our case we have not got.

This is the safety-catch, which is always released
With an easy flick of the thumb. And please do not let me
See anyone using his finger. You can do it quite easy
If you have any strength in your thumb. The blossoms
Are fragile and motionless, never letting anyone see
　　　Any of them using their finger.

And this you can see is the bolt. The purpose of this
Is to open the breech, as you see. We can slide it
Rapidly backwards and forwards: we call this
Easing the spring. And rapidly backwards and forwards
The early bees are assaulting and bumbling the flowers
　　　They call it easing the Spring.

They call it easing the Spring: it is perfectly easy
If you have any strength in your thumb: like the bolt,
And the breech, and the cocking-piece, and the point of balance,
Which in our case we have not got; and the almond-blossom
Silent in all of the gardens and the bees going backwards and forwards,
　　　For to-day we have naming of parts.

- Who are these people, and what are they doing?
- Note when the poem changes from first-person singular (*I*) to second-person plural (*you*) to first-person plural (*we*) to third-person plural (*they*). How do these changes contribute to the poem's overall expressiveness? What vocal, facial, and postural variations would you use to express the

different personae's approaches to their tasks? Where might clipped tones be appropriate? Wistfulness?

- What words and phrases are repeated in a row? Which are repeated at several points throughout the poem? How does repetition contribute to the emotional expressiveness of the poem? How would you perform the repetitions?

- Where does the speaker's attention shift from the military drill to nature? How does that shift change the emotions? How might you use vocal variations in pitch, volume, and rate to convey the speaker's emotions regarding his situation?

- Are there two speakers in the poem or just one? How do you know?

- What's the tone of the poem? How does the double meaning of "easing the spring" support the poem's tone?

- Mark with a double slash the places where you'd use large pauses; mark smaller pauses with a single slash.

- With which character do you feel the most empathy? What do you know about the emotions he conveys? How will you express his emotions?

"Loud Music"[49]

BY STEPHEN DOBYNS

Dobyns writes about a common experience: a parent and a child who disagree about whether to turn down the volume on the music.

My stepdaughter and I circle round and round.
You see, I like the music loud, the speakers
throbbing, jam-packing the room with sound whether
Bach or rock and roll, the volume cranked up so
each bass note is like a hand smacking the gut.
But my stepdaughter disagrees. She is four
and likes the music decorous, pitched below
her own voice—that tenuous projection of self.
With music blasting, she feels she disappears,
is lost within the blare, which in fact I like.
But at four what she wants is self-location
and uses her voice as a porpoise uses
its sonar: to find herself in all this space.
If she had a sort of box with a peephole
and looked inside, what she'd like to see would be
herself standing there in her red pants, jacket,
yellow plastic lunch box: a proper subject
for serious study. But me, if I raised
the same box to my eye, I would wish to find

the ocean on one of those days when wind
and thick cloud make the water gray and restless
as if some creature brooded underneath,
a rocky coast with a road along the shore
where someone like me was walking and has gone.
Loud music does this, it wipes out the ego,
leaving turbulent water and winding road,
a landscape stripped of people and language—
how clear the air becomes, how sharp the colors.

- What type of poem is this? How do you know?

- Who is speaking? To whom?

- Try to discern the emotional tone of the poem and the persona's attitude toward the listener.

- What revelations or insights into the conflict itself does he provide?

- What emotions does the stepfather have? What do you *know* about each emotion? How could you *identify* with each one? How would you *express* the various emotions?

- What are the child's emotions? How would you show your empathy with them?

"My Last Duchess"[50]

BY ROBERT BROWNING

This classic dramatic monologue is written in iambic pentameter. In this one-sided conversation, the persona (a duke) reveals his sinister personality to a man who has come to negotiate a marriage contract. A search for "My Last Duchess" on www.google.com will give you more than 20,000 hits. Link to two or three Web pages and read what others have said about this poem.

That's my last Duchess painted on the wall,
Looking as if she were alive. I call
That piece a wonder, now; Frà Pandolf's hands
Worked busily a day, and there she stands.
5   Will't please you sit and look at her? I said
"Fra Pandolf" by design, for never read
Strangers like you that pictured countenance,
The depth and passion of its earnest glance,
But to myself they turned (since none puts by
10 The curtain I have drawn for you, but I)
And seemed as they would ask me, if they durst,
How such a glance came there, so not the first
Are you to turn and ask thus. Sir, 'twas not
Her husband's presence only, called that spot
15 Of joy into the Duchess' cheek; perhaps
Fra Pandolf chanced to say, "Her mantle laps
Over my lady's wrist too much," or "Paint

Must never hope to reproduce the faint
Half-flush that dies along her throat:" such stuff
20 Was courtesy, she thought, and cause enough
For calling up that spot of joy. She had
A heart—how shall I say?—too soon made glad,
Too easily impressed: she liked whate'er
She looked on, and her looks went everywhere.
25 Sir, 'twas all one! My favor at her breast,
The dropping of the daylight in the West,
The bough of cherries some officious fool
Broke in the orchard for her, the white mule
She rode round the terrace—all and each
30 Would draw from her alike the approving speech.
Or blush, at least. She thanked men,—good! but thanked
Somehow—I know not how—as if she ranked
My gift of a nine-hundred-year-old name
With anybody's gift. Who'd stoop to blame
35 This sort of trifling? Even had you skill
In speech—(which I have not)—to make your will
Quite clear to such an one, and say, "Just this
Or that in you disgusts me; here you miss,
Or there exceed the mark?" —and if she let
40 Herself be lessoned so, nor plainly set
Her will to yours, forsooth, and made excuse,
—E'en then would be some stooping; and I choose
Never to stoop. Oh sir, she smiled, no doubt,
Whene'er I passed her; but who passed without
45 Much the same smile? This grew; I gave commands;
Then all smiles stopped together. There she stands
As if alive. Will't please you rise? We'll meet
The company below, then. I repeat,
The Count your master's known munificence
50 Is ample warrant that no just pretence
Of mine for dowry will be disallowed,
Though his fair daughter's self, as I avowed
At starting, is my object. Nay, we'll go
Together down sir. Notice Neptune, though,
55 Taming a sea-horse, thought a rarity,
Which Claus of Innsbruck cast in bronze for me!

"Oriflamme"[51]

BY JESSIE FAUSET

Ms. Fauset, an editor and author during the Harlem Renaissance, prefaced her poem with this quotation from
Sojourner Truth: "I can remember when I was a little, young girl, how my old mammy would sit out of doors
in the evenings and look up at the stars and groan, and I would say, 'Mammy what makes you groan so?'

And she would say, 'I am groaning to think of my poor children; they do not know where I be and I don't know where they be. I look up at the stars and they look up at the stars!" (Note: Oriflamme is French for "gold flame;" l'oriflamme was the sacred banner of the Abbey of St. Denis. For centuries, French kings would go to the Abbey and raise the banner before going to war.)

I think I see her sitting bowed and black,
    Stricken and seared with slavery's mortal scars,
Reft of her children, lonely, anguished, yet
    Still looking at the stars.

5   Symbolic mother, we thy myriad sons,
    Pounding our stubborn hearts on Freedom's bars,
Clutching our birthright, fight with faces set,
    Still visioning the stars!

"In Just-"[52]

BY E. E. CUMMINGS

e. e. cummings experimented with form and sense in his poetry. The form of this free-verse poem suggests how you should perform it.

   in Just-
spring   when the world is mud-
luscious the little
lame balloon man

whistles   far   and wee

and eddieandbill come
running from marbles and
piracies and it's
spring

when the world is puddle-wonderful

the queer
old balloonman whistles
far   and   wee
and bettyandisbel come dancing

from hop-scotch and jump-rope and
it's
spring
and
     the
         goat-footed

balloonMan   whistles
far
and
wee

"Then Sings My Soul"[53]

BY PAUL MARIANI

This poem deals with the topic of death, specifically, the death of a comparatively young person. It includes lyrics from a song that may be familiar to you or to someone in your class. Discuss with a small group of classmates ways you might perform song lyrics that are part of a text.

Who can tell a man's real pain
when he learns at last the news
that he must die? Sure we all know
none of us is going anywhere

5   except in some pineslab box or its fine
expensive equal. But don't we put it off
another day, and then another and another,
as I suppose we must to cope? And so

with Lenny, Leonardo Rodriguez, a man
10 in the old world mold, a Spaniard
of great dignity and a fine humility,
telling us on this last retreat for men

that he had finally given up praying
because he didn't want to hear
15 what God might want to tell him now:
that he wanted Lenny soon in spite

of the hard facts that he had his kids,
his still beautiful wife, and an aged
mother to support. I can tell you now
20 it hit us hard him telling us because for me

as for the others he'd been the model,
had been a leader, raised in the old Faith
of San Juan de la Cruz and Santa Teresa
de Avila, this toreador waving the red flag

25 at death itself, horns lowered now
to come hurling down on him. This story
has no ending because there is still life,
and life means hope. But on the third day,

at the last Mass, we were all sitting
30 in one big circle like something out of Dante—
fifty laymen, a priest, a nun—with Guido
DiPietro playing his guitar and singing

one of those old Baptist hymns in his rich
tenor and all of us joining in at the refrain,
35 *Then sings my soul, my Savior God to Thee,*
How Great Thou art, how great thou art,

and there I was on Lenny's left, listening
to him sing, his voice cracked with resignation,
how great thou art, until angry glad tears
40 began rolling down my face, surprising me. . . .

Lord, listen to the sound of my voice.
Grant Lenny health and long life. Or,
if not that, whatever strength and peace
he needs. His family likewise, and

45 his friends. Grant me too the courage
to face death when it shall notice me,
when I shall still not understand why
there is so much sorrow in the world.

Teach me to stare down those lowered horns
50 on the deadend street that will have no alleys
and no open doors. And grant me the courage
then to still sing to thee, *how great thou art.*

"The Poetry Surgeon"[56]

BY EDWARD HIGGINS

Higgins, an English professor, uses a metaphor that compares a poet to a surgeon. Poems are his instruments for cutting into his audience's inner thoughts and feelings. Has a poem ever worked on your "head and heart" in a way that let light into a painful personal situation?

Don't misunderstand me, but I must plot against you like this,
seize opportunity, so to speak, by the vital organs.

Perhaps you may suspect my gauze-masked smile,
but we've already begun the preliminaries you and I—
Note, for example, how easily you're confined here,
so desperate your need or idle curiosity.

Well, now I'll confess: I am an unlicensed poetry surgeon.
Ha, ha! that freaked you out of your Frank & Stein sneakers, eh?
A disarming technique, paralyzing humor and horror at once.
But otherwise you'd never patiently allow me
this triage I am about to practice on your head and heart.

I must first sever your wits with these demon-edged words,
then slit up dull resistance, spill you all hallow's adam & eve
scalpel-wide open, steadily probing, shining
ruby tinged laser-eerie, hey look out! light heading in:

A triple klieg-bright sun disk, salty-sweet with fear,
tainting the darkness there, revealing wolf shadows
& the slush of red unmelted snow.

So you see I know, I know, too,
speaking of our pain cloistered everywhere.

& my mischief is to carry terrible light lovingly there.

"Yun'er's Bell"[57]

BY YUN'ER (C. 500 C.E.), TRANSLATED BY CONSTANCE A. COOK

According to Professor Cook, few facts are available about Prince Yun'er. Originally from a small state in eastern China that was conquered by another state, he probably fled west to the state of Chu, where his bell was found. The poem's style reflects an ancient Chinese performance tradition.[58]

The first month, Early auspicious, Dinghai day
I, Yun'er, the younger son of King Kang of Xu,
chose these Auspicious Metals
to cast myself a harmonious bell:
Endlessly peal and toll!
Primarily call the Resounding Brilliant One!
Resounding celebrate the Primal Achiever!
Drinking wine from a basin,
in harmony the Hundred Nobles meet:
Skilled in Awesome Deportment.
Charitable in Luminous Sacrifice.
I feast, please, and entertain
the celebrated guest
and our fathers, brothers, and clan sons:
Brilliant! Brilliant!
Glittering! Glittering!
Extended longevity limitless!
Sons and grandsons eternally
Protect and strike this bell!

SUMMARY

Poetry is characterized by expressive language that appeals to the senses. The denotative meanings of words are those you'd find in a dictionary; their connotations are the emotional overtones and personalized associations that interweave with and overlie the dictionary meanings. Poets choose linguistic devices such as onomatopoeia, alliteration, assonance, and consonance to give tone color to a poem; this differs from tone, which is defined as the poet's attitude toward the topic or toward the audience.

There are more than 250 types of figures of speech, including metaphors, similes, personification, allusion, and apostrophe. Skillful poets avoid clichéd comparisons, choosing instead unexpected and creative wording. Repetitions may occur with single words, longer phrases, or entire lines, all of which offer many opportunities for interpretation.

Poetry's rhymes and rhythm patterns distinguish it from prose. Rhymes, the echoing of repeating sounds, combine with rhythm patterns that result from the underlying beat, stress, or accent on syllables and on words within phrases. Meter occurs with predictable and regular rhythm. Lines are made up of feet; traditionally, each line has three to six beats. Iambic pentameter is the pattern closest to the typical speech patterns of English. Poets often organize their work into stanzas, or sets of lines that are similar in shape or length. Elisions are omitted vowels or syllables that preserve the rhythm. It's important to study carefully the rhyme, repetition, and rhythm patterns in order to interpret the text effectively. Contemporary poets experiment with free verse and prose poems, in which rhyme and rhythm are optional.

There are three basic types of poetry: narrative, lyric, and dramatic. Narrative poetry predates writing; subtypes include epics and ballads. Analyze a narrative poem like you would a story, and use your analysis to perform the characters and the situation. Lyric poetry expresses the emotions and thoughts of a single persona who takes a particular tone toward the subject. It can be either descriptive or reflective. Subgenres include sonnets, elegies, odes, and confessional poetry. When performing lyric poetry, it's important to employ empathy, which requires that you understand the appropriate emotions, identify with the emotion, and express the emotion through bodily and vocal expressiveness. Dramatic poetry features a character who is involved in the action and invested in its outcome. Types include dramatic narrative, dramatic lyric, dramatic monologue, dramatic dialogue, and soliloquy.

KEY TERMS

poetry slams	metaphors	prose poem
words	analogies	stream of consciousness
pragmatic language	similes	elisions
illocutionary speech	rhyme	narrative poetry
expressive language	end rhymes	epics
denotative meanings	multiple rhymes	ballads
connotative meanings	closed couplets	metrical verse
epigraph	internal rhymes	lyric poetry
tone color	quatrains	descriptive lyric poetry
onomatopoeia	sonnet	reflective lyric poetry
assonance	rhythm	elegies
consonance	meter	odes
alliteration	foot	confessional poetry
tone (two meanings)	pentameter	dramatic poetry

figures of speech

allusion

personification

apostrophe

blank verse

stanzas

enjambment

free verse

dramatic narrative poetry

dramatic lyric poetry

dramatic monologues

dramatic dialogues

soliloquies

QUESTIONS AND EXERCISES

1. Aaron Shepard formatted "Casey at the Bat" for Readers Theatre. Log onto www .aaronshep.com/rt/RTE23.html; read through his version, and decide if you like it as is or if you'd change it. If so, tell how.

2. Use InfoTrac College Edition to find and read the article, "From Poetry to Rap: The Lyrics of Tupac Shakur," by Walter Edwards. Describe the two sides of Shakur's upbringing. How did his poetry differ from his rap lyrics? Why do you think this might have been?

3. http://wiredforbooks.org/ poetry/ has dozens of audio clips of poems as well as interviews with poets. Link to Bonnie Proudfoot, and listen to "News from the Edge of the World" and "Picking Them," following along on the text version. Identify the unique repetition pattern in the first poem, and notice her performance of enjambment in both poems.

4. Bring to class a children's book that is written in rhyme (for example, *Horton Hatches an Egg* by Dr. Suess or *The Giving Tree* by Shel Silverstein). Perform a

section of that text for a small group of your classmates.

5. The "Favorite Poem Project" was instituted in 1997 by Robert Pinsky, Poet Laureate of the United States. More than 18,000 people between ages 5 and 97, from diverse backgrounds, education, and occupation, volunteered their favorite poems. The project recorded 50 Americans reading their favorite poems, including a young boy reciting "Casey at the Bat." You can find videos at www.favoritepoem.org/. Browse through them, looking for both familiar poems and those from a new perspective. Watch at least three videos, and come to class prepared to discuss them with your classmates.

6. Poetry often inspires people at important stages of their lives. Log onto www.favoritepoem .org/ and watch the videos featuring Rev. Michael Haynes and Jayashree Chatterjee. Then describe how a particular poem spoke to their situations at a specific time.

7. Log onto InfoTrac College Edition and search for the

words "Igede AND praise AND poetry." Read the book review of *Art, Society, and Performance: Igede Praise Poetry* in the 1999 issue of *Research in African Literatures*. How do the performers reinforce cultural values? What specific performance skills are valued? How does performance enhance the poet's reputation?

10

Performing in Groups

This chapter will help you:

- Select and perform unison readings

- Select and perform responsive readings

- Format choral readings

- Choose and perform texts with a partner

- Format, block, and perform a Readers Theatre production

I pledge allegiance to the flag
Of the United States of America . . .

Have you ever stood alone in the quiet of your room and recited the Pledge of Allegiance? Of course not. The pledge is just one of many texts intended to be performed by a group. Playground chants are in this category, as are group chants at athletic events and group prayers in religious settings.

Participating in a group presentation provides you with opportunities to analyze your audience, plan a performance, and practice your overall presentational skills. This chapter discusses several contexts in which group performances occur. It also gives tips for effective performances in various group genres.

UNISON READINGS

In **unison** performances, everyone reads or says memorized words together, which can result in a meaningful group experience. For example, scouts recite their oath during meetings; members of churches and synagogues participate in unison readings at services; schoolchildren chant nursery rhymes as part of their literacy education. As you can imagine, it's important for the entire group to stay together; 300 people, each reading at his or her own personal rate and pausing whenever, can take the participants' focus off the words and put them onto the technique itself. Needless to say, this detracts from the group experience.

Preschool classrooms and elementary school programs regularly feature unison performances, and future teachers are wise to collect a number of potential readings. Here's an example of a unison reading that is appropriate for young children when they are learning to read and spell the *-ck* sound. The humor and playfulness of the language itself make the poem fun to perform, and it illustrates rhyming words as well as onomatopoeia, or language that resembles the sound that the thing itself makes. Here, the recurrent "pickety-pickety-pickety-pick" phrase actually resembles the sound a stick makes as it's dragged along a picket fence.

Read it aloud with your classmates:

The Pickety Fence[1]
    BY DAVID McCORD

The pickety fence
The pickety fence
Give it a lick it's
The pickety fence
Give it a lick it's
A clickety fence
Give it a lick it's
A lickety fence
Give it a lick

> ### STOP AND CHECK: Select and Perform a Unison Reading
>
> Bring to class an appropriate short piece to use as a unison reading. (Children's literature, especially poetry, works well.) Either transfer your chosen text to a transparency or make enough copies to distribute to each person in the class. Perform it with the class.

> Give it a lick
> Give it a lick
> With a rickety stick
> Pickety
> Pickety
> Pickety
> Pick

The following tips are important when you participate in a group reading.

- Read phrases rather than individual words, and pause after each phrase.

- Pay close attention to punctuation, including commas, colons, dashes, and end punctuation.

- Listen to the people around you and stay in sync with them; the goal is not to be the first person to say the final word but to read along with other people as they say the same words you are saying.

RESPONSIVE READINGS

Responsive readings are texts in which a leader reads a section alone, followed by the group reading the next section in unison. Like unison readings, responsive readings are common in worship settings. Responsive performances can also be heard at events such as rallies:

> **Leader:** What do we want?
>
> **People:** *Equal rights.*
>
> **Leader:** When do we want 'em?
>
> **People:** *Now.*

A modified example occurs in the movie *Kindergarten Cop*, when Arnold Schwarzenegger's character leads his class in a group rendition of "The Gettysburg Address." Different kindergartners recite a phrase, the rest of the class echoes it, and they perform the final phrase responsively.

Here's an American folk song formatted as a responsive reading. Perform this text with members of your class. Have a soloist read the first and third lines of each stanza, and have everyone read the second and fourth lines. Adapt the rhythm of the sung version into your group performance.

PERFORMING CULTURE: Call and Response

In the African American tradition of call and response, a speaker (or leader) and an audience together create a performance. In 1871, the student choir from one of the first African American universities, Fisk University, toured the United States and introduced "Negro" spirituals to many who had never heard them. The choir was so popular that it was invited to tour England. Queen Victoria requested the song "Go Down, Moses," which features a call and response interaction. This anti-slavery spiritual is based on an Old Testament story in which God freed Israel from slavery.[3] Research the story of this spiritual and others online. One source for information is www.negrospirituals.com/.

You can easily adapt spirituals as responsive readings. In "Go Down, Moses," a soloist reads the narrative lines and the others respond with "Let my people go." Everyone recites the chorus, as this excerpt illustrates:

Go Down, Moses

Leader: When Israel was in Egypt's land,
Response: Let my people go;
Leader: Oppressed so hard they could not stand,
Response: Let my people go.

All: Go down, Moses, way down in Egypt's land, Tell ol' Pharoah,
Response: Let my people go.

Down in the Valley[2]

Leader: Down in the valley, the valley so low,
All: Hang your head over, hear the wind blow.
Leader: Hear the wind blow, dear, hear the wind blow,
All: Hang your head over, hear the wind blow.

Leader: Writing this letter, containing three lines,
All: Answer my question, will you be mine?
Leader: Will you be mine, dear, will you be mine?
All: Answer my question, will you be mine?

Leader: Write me a letter, send it by mail,
All: Send it in care of the Birmingham jail,
Leader: Birmingham jail, dear, Birmingham jail,
All: Send it in care of the Birmingham jail.

Leader: Roses love sunshine, violets love dew,
All: Angels in Heaven know I love you,
Leader: Know I love you dear, know I love you,
All: Angels in Heaven know I love you.

Tips for effective responsive reading are similar to those for effective unison readings. This is not an occasion to race to the finish; the point is to experience

---

STOP AND CHECK: Prepare and Perform a Responsive
Reading

Working alone or in a small group, *ballads work well. Either transfer the*
analyze your classroom audience, and *text to a transparency, or make*
then bring to class a short piece of *enough copies for everyone in the*
literature that you've formatted as a *class to have one. Perform these*
responsive reading. Folk songs or *readings in class.*

---

the meaning of a passage with a group of like-minded people. Consequently, read in phrases, pausing slightly after the punctuation. Listen to your fellow readers, and stay in sync with them.

CHORAL READINGS

Choral readings are planned performances in which a group of readers present a piece of literature that has been formatted for several voices. Formats include solos, duets, trios, quartets, and whole-group sections. Some sections may be formatted for male voices, others for female voices. The text may include a refrain.

In elementary school classrooms, choral readings enable children with various reading skills to participate meaningfully and effectively in reading experiences. Everyone can perform literature, not just the "good" readers.

Choral readings can help listeners derive more meaning from a text than from simply listening to a solo reader. For example, my university's speech team compiled, formatted, and performed a choral reading on September 11, 2002, the first anniversary of the attack on the World Trade Center and the Pentagon. Have one person read the following excerpt aloud. Then select five soloists and read it as it is formatted. Compare the two readings:

Reader	Text (from *Time Magazine*)[4]
1	An anniversary can be sweet or solemn,
1,2	But either way, it is only the echo,
3	Not the cry.
All	From this distance, we can hear whatever we are listening for.
Men	We can argue that Sept. 11 changed everything—
3	Or nothing.
All	The country is more united,
4	And less;

All	More fearful
3	And more secure,
All	More serious
5	And more devoted to *American Idol*.

All	To say we have changed feels like rewarding the enemy,
Men	But to deny it risks losing the knowledge for which we paid a terrible price—
Women	Knowledge about who we become under pressure,
2,5	In public and private.

Here are some tips for creating effective choral readings.

- Find subtle meanings within your piece of literature; emphasize those meanings by using a single voice or groupings of voices for those words or phrases.

- Use vocal ranges to advantage; have higher-pitched voices read some parts and lower-pitched voices read others.

- Format lines or phrases creatively: use solo, duet, trio, quartet, all male, all female, and unison groupings. Here's an example from a reading about a family trip. It is formatted in such a way that Risa, the narrator, describes her dad (solo); he joins her in the description (duet) and finishes in his own words (solo). Have two members of your class read it aloud:[5]

Risa	Dad had a unique sense of direction. He could get lost sliding from one side of the couch to the other.
Risa + Dad	The only way he was able to read a map was to sit at the kitchen table and maneuver a penny.
Dad	Slowly, speaking aloud the exit numbers, he'd move the coin along the route. Every time he had to make a turn, he'd rotate the map and say, "Let's see. North is . . . ?"

- Choral readings are especially useful for performing poetry. When you format a poem, incorporate rhythmic elements of the piece to enhance the overall effectiveness of the reading.

This poem was formatted for a group with at least six male and six female voices. Rehearse it with a group of your classmates, and then perform it for the rest of your class.

Curiosity[6]

ALASTAIR REID

1	ALL:	Curiosity may have killed the cat.
2	Men:	More likely the cat was just unlucky
3	Women:	or else curious to see what death was like
4	Men:	having no cause to go on licking paws, or fathering litter on litter of kittens,

5	Woman #1:	predictably.
6	Man #1:	Nevertheless,
7	Man 2, 3	to be curious is dangerous enough.
8	Woman 2,3,4:	to distrust what is always said,
9	Woman 5	what seems,
10	Man 2	to ask odd questions,
11	Man 1 & 3	interfere in dreams,
12	Woman 1 & 5	leave home,
13	Woman 4	smell rats,
14	Woman 2	have hunches
15	Women:	do not endear cats to those doggy circles Where well-smelt baskets,
16	Woman 1,3,5	suitable wives,
17	Woman 2, 4, 6	good lunches
18	Woman 6	Are the order of things,
19	Men	and where prevails Much wagging of incurious heads and tails.
20	ALL:	Face it. Curiosity will not cause us to die—
21	Man 3	Only lack of it will.
22	Woman 1	Never wanting to see the other side of the hill
23	Woman 2	or that improbable country where living is an idyll
24	Man 2	(although a probable hell)
25	Woman 2	would kill us all.
26	ALL	Only the curious have,
27	W 1 & M 1	if they live,
28	ALL	a tale worth telling at all.
29	Women	Dogs say
30	Man 1, 3	cats change too much,
31	Man 2	are irresponsible,
32	Man 3	are changeable,
33	Man 2, 3	marry too many wives,
34	Man 1	desert their children,
35	Man 2	chill all dinner tables with tales of their nine lives.
36	Women:	Well, they are lucky. Let them be nine-lived and contradictory,
37	Woman 1,3,5	Curious enough to change,
38	Woman 2,4,6	Prepared to pay the cat price,
39	Woman 6	Which is to die

40	Woman 2	And die
41	Woman 1,3,4	again and again,
42	Woman 6	Each time with no less pain.
43	ALL	A cat minority of one is all that can be counted on to tell the truth.
44	Men	And what cats have to tell On each return from hell Is this:
45	Man 1 & 2	That dying is what the living do,
46	Man 1 & 3	That dying is what the loving do,
47	Man 2	And that dead dogs are those who do not know
48	ALL	That dying is what,
49	M 2 and W 2	To live,
50	ALL	Each has to do.

When you perform in a choral reading, highlight all the lines you personally will read. Then practice with other readers until the piece is smoothly connected into a unified whole.

In "Curiosity," I'd guess that the transition from lines 14 to 15 might need practice, as would lines 22 to 24. Lines 30 to 35 call for "doggy" voices on the part of the readers. Women 2, 3, and 4 may need to work on line 8 to make sure that they all emphasize *always* similarly. Women should pronounce *nine-lived* similarly, and woman 2 needs to make sure she pronounces *idyll* (line 23) correctly. And the men, as well as the entire group, need to coordinate the way they emphasize *dying* in lines 45, 46, and 48.

DUO INTERPRETATIONS

In **duo interpretations** (such as university speech team competitions), two interpreters stand side-by-side and interpret a dialogue cut from a play. They use offstage focus and *suggest*, rather than act out, the characters. Some limited movement is allowed. Although you may never participate on a speech team, doing a piece with another person is a lot of fun for both the performers and the listeners. And if you are not performing in a competition, you can use a prose or poetry cutting instead of a play. There are some tips for effective duo performances.

- Choose a cutting in which both characters speak approximately the same amount of time. If one character dominates the interaction, the other will be forced to react during most of the performance.

- Choose a cutting in which most of the lines are relatively short, which results in a more lively dialogue. This allows the performers to interact and work on perfecting their timing.

- You may want to block a few movements. (**Blocking** is deciding how, when, and where the characters move.) For example, the two characters might change positions to indicate the passage of time; they could turn their backs to one another to indicate an argument.

- Coordinate with your partner how you will use your manuscripts. If you are using a notebook, open your books together; turn pages together; coordinate other script work that adds to the performance. For instance, a couple toasting one another might close their books (marking their place with a finger), extend them at goblet height, and "clink" the books together in a toast. They'd then draw their books back toward their lips briefly before dropping them into position and reopening them at precisely the same time. I've even seen participants exchange notebooks when one character gives the other an object. Of course, this calls for script coordination!

- The most successful duos choose a piece that fits both partners' talents. Often a text features characters with opposite traits: one emotional, the other more rigid; one flighty, the other steadier; one comic character, the other more straight-faced. As you choose a partner, take into account your personalities, and match your personalities to your characters.

David Ives's play *Sure Thing*[7] is a good example of the type of short, snappy dialogue that works well in duo performances. Here are its opening lines:

Bill: Excuse me. Is this chair taken?

Betty: Excuse me?

Bill: Is this taken?

Betty: Yes it is.

Bill: Oh. Sorry.

Betty: Sure thing. (*A bell rings softly.*)

Bill: Excuse me. Is this chair taken?

Betty: Excuse me?

Bill: Is this taken?

Betty: No, but I'm expecting somebody in a minute.

Bill: Oh, thanks anyway.

Betty: Sure thing. (*A bell rings softly.*)

Many university speech teams provide additional information about duo interpretation on their Web sites. The University of Illinois at Springfield's team site even includes video clips of duo performers introducing their pieces. Go to www.uis.edu/forensics/What_We_Do/oral_inter_lit_desp_fra.html.

READERS THEATRE

Readers Theatre (RT) requires a text (originally prose or poetry, although performers now choose dramatic scripts as well), formatted for a group of readers. The readers plan and rehearse a minimally staged theatrical performance. Its roots are in ancient Greece, but the modern genre of Readers Theatre celebrated its 50th birthday on October 22, 2001.[8] College students originally made modern RT popular; you will also find it in elementary schools, where teachers format texts to help children learn to read and appreciate literature and cultural diversity. Working with a text from another culture is a great way to learn about that culture.[9]

Some examples of Readers Theatre might help. A three-person group (a narrator, a man, and a woman) compiled a script made up of love letters between Robert Browning and Elizabeth Barrett Browning. Three readers presented "The Bear, the Balloon, and the Bees" from A. A. Milne's *Winnie the Pooh*. Two men and one woman performed "A Hen or a Horse," a Jewish folktale.

Readers Theatre has several distinct characteristics:

- Readers hold the text throughout the performance. This keeps the focus on the literature itself. This also means that the performers don't have to memorize the text, but the group should coordinate page turns.

- RT is presentational, not representational. This means there's no attempt to create a sense of reality onstage by using specific makeup and clothing (**representational**); the readers present a text by suggesting characters and actions through vocalizations, body language, and optional props (**presentational**). It's up to the listeners to create the characters and actions mentally. The benefit is that an RT production can suggest images that could never be staged realistically. Readers can shrink or stretch space and time, create fantasy worlds, and enact marvelous journeys.[10]

- Staging is very simple; in fact, performers often sit on stools or ladders. They sometimes incorporate a minimal amount of blocking.

- Performers don't wear costumes; in fact, it's customary for all the performers to wear black. One or more might use a prop to suggest a character. For example, a female character might wear a string of pearls or carry a fan; a young male character might wear a baseball cap turned backward.

- Participants generally use an offstage focus.

- Each reader can portray a number of characters. A prop can help the audience detect which character the reader is portraying at a given time. For instance, the woman might open the fan when she's portraying a young woman and close it when she's a schoolteacher.

- Readers who are not performing in a particular scene often turn their backs to the audience.

- The performance typically includes one or more narrators who introduce and provide transitions between several dramatic scenes.

For an excellent discussion of RT, including tips and scripts, visit Aaron Shepard's Web site at www.aaronshep.com.

Preparing the Script

If you are assigned to do a readers theater, plan to meet a number of times with your entire group. During these meetings, select a script, format that script into a Readers Theatre format, make performance decisions, and rehearse.

- At the first meeting, decide on a piece of literature you'd like to perform together. For this assignment, choose a piece of prose that contains several characters. Consider your audience, and choose something that meets a need within those listeners. Look for universal themes, vivid and unique imagery, and significant topics. (See Chapter 3 for further discussion.) Find a piece that is emotionally evocative, one you can all enjoy analyzing and performing.

- At the second meeting, distribute copies of the script to each group member. Go over it together, and mark it up as you identify the various reading parts. What will the narrator read? Where are the dramatic scenes in which one or more characters interact? Ideally, one member will bring a laptop computer with the script in an electronic file so that you can make edits during the meeting. Assign the various parts. Then assign one person to type up the formatted script and distribute a copy to each person in the group *before* the next meeting.

- At the third meeting, go over the formatted script and make decisions about staging the performance. During the first couple of read-throughs, identify areas that need specific work. Set aside some time to work on troublesome lines. Take a playful attitude during this stage. Try things out. Experiment. Then choose vocal variations and bodily movements, including focal points that best communicate the message. At this point, decide on props. Will you use them? Which props? When? Where? By whom? Discuss coordinated bookwork such as opening and closing the script books, coordinating page turns, and so on.

- At the fourth meeting, rehearse again. Implement all the choices you've made regarding blocking (which is described below), vocal variation, physical movements, focal points, props, bookwork, and so on. Make sure that everyone is familiar with the text. Agree to meet again, if necessary.

Staging the Performance

Readers Theatre does not require the elaborate makeup, costumes, lighting, and sets of a theatre production, but some blocking can enhance your group's performance. As noted earlier, blocking involves how, where, and when the participants move; it also involves the placement of simple props such as tables or stools.

Simple staging uses stools (or chairs) that are placed in aesthetically pleasing relationships to one another. You can add variety in head heights by using adjustable stools or by adding ladders. Some performers may stand; when appropriate, some might even recline on the floor. This visual variety makes the performance more artistically interesting and pleasing.

The narrator is often placed in a position that separates him or her from the action. Here are some examples:

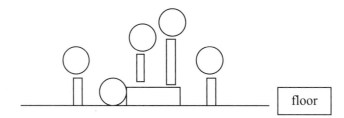

FIGURE 10.1 Blocking

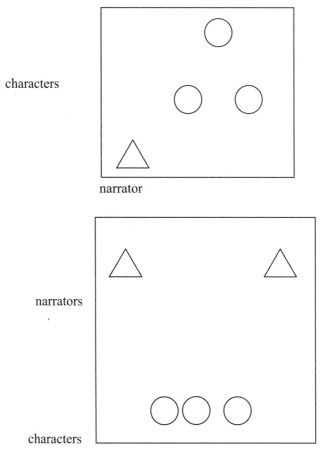

FIGURE 10.2 Narrator Placement

STOP AND CHECK: Perform a Readers Theatre

Follow the guidelines in this section to find and format a piece of prose that has a message suitable for your classroom audience. Format and block it to create maximum impact. Rehearse it with your group, and present it in your class.

You can see several examples of blocking, by searching for "readers theater" in the images feature on either www.yahoo.com or www.google.com.

SUMMARY

Some texts were created for group performances; other texts can be formatted and presented by a group. A group performance enables audiences to experience the text differently than if performed by one person. Performers can deliver lines in unison, responsively, in duos, and in Readers Theatre groups. Each type of presentation must be planned and rehearsed carefully so that the various performers can coordinate their lines. Both hearing and presenting group performances can be a rewarding experience.

KEY TERMS

unison readings	choral readings	representational
onomatopoeia	duo interpretations	presentational
responsive readings	Readers Theatre (RT)	blocking

QUESTIONS AND EXERCISES

1. Divide your class into small groups, and have each group format a choral reading script containing poetry that would be suitable for children to perform. (Children's poets such as Shel Silverstein or John Ciardi are just two of the many poets who provide amusing material.) Rehearse the text with your group (and others in your class if necessary), and perform it for your classmates. Assess each group's work. Was the text appropriate? How effective was the formatting? What was the best thing about the performance? How could it be improved?

2. Go to http:www.io.com/f1bus/RRMLKJrDream.htm, and print out the responsive reading of Martin Luther King's "I Have

a Dream" speech. Bring a copy to class. First, have a solo reader read through the text, and then read it responsively with your classmates. Compare and contrast the impact of listening to a solo reader with that of hearing a responsive reading of the same material.

3. Teachers commonly use choral reading and Readers Theatre in the classroom. Read the information at http:www.pbs.org/ wnet/americanmasters/ education/general.html. Then discuss the benefits of group performance and additional guidelines for effective group presentations with your classmates.

4. For more information on selecting and formatting a text for Readers Theatre, go to Aaron Shepard's Web site, "Readers on Stage," at http:www.aaronshep .com/rt/Tips.html. Aaron is primarily a children's author, but he provides excellent online resources for storytelling and for Readers Theatre performances. Another excellent source that includes several sample scripts is at http:www.stemnet.nf.ca/ CITE/langrt.htm.

5. Watch an example of a duo or a Readers Theatre performance on the Web site that supports this text. What ideas does that performance give you for your own group performances?

Appendix: Speech Team Competitions

Many colleges and universities host a speech team, sometimes called a forensics team. *Forensics* does not require a dead body; the term derives from the Latin *forum* and has to do with evidence that is appropriate for public discussion or legal argumentation. Speech team members typically compete in a number of interpretation events.

Competitive Speech Events

My university competes in the Northwest Forensics Conference, but there are several other leagues around the country, and each one follows somewhat different conventions. If you join a team, your coach will guide you through the expectations that are common in your league. Here is a description of the interpretation events at the American Forensic Association's National Individual Events Tournament. All performances require use of a manuscript; all require an introduction (similar to the type of introduction explained in Chapter 6); all are limited to 10 minutes, including the introduction.

- *Prose.* You may use fiction or nonfiction prose taken from one or more sources. Although the rules don't require this, winning competitors in the northwest league tend to perform selections that feature first-person narrators.

- *Poetry.* Select one long poem or put together two or more poems that develop a common theme.

- *Drama.* Perform one or more characters from a play or plays written for the stage, film, or radio. Material may be serious or humorous.

- *Dramatic Duo.* Work with another competitor to perform a cutting from a play (stage, screen, or radio) that features two or more characters. Material may be serious or humorous. Use offstage focus. Some blocking is acceptable.

- *Program Oral Interpretation (POI).* Develop a program of thematically linked material chosen from at least two of the three genres (prose, poetry, and drama), each from a separate literary text. Allot substantial amounts of the total time to each genre.

Winning competitors select fresh material and interesting themes. This is not to say that you can't perform classic texts; however, as one judge put it, "I have heard this piece so often that I have dozens of other performances in my head to compare with it—including performances by professionals." For this reason, the balcony scene from *Cyrano de Bergerac* might succeed in the classroom but fail to win in intercollegiate competition. However, a skillful competitor might incorporate it into a program by interspersing cuts from *Cyrano* with poetry or prose on the same theme.

A good place to search for contemporary prose and poetry is in literary journals. Some are affiliated with universities; the *Colorado Review* comes out of the Department of English at Colorado State University. Published three times annually, it features texts about unconventional responses to universal dilemmas. Others come from literary associations; the Spoon River Poetry Association publishes the *Spoon River Poetry Review* twice annually. Still others, such as the *Apalachee Review*, are published by nonprofit corporations.

Additional current materials that have passed the scrutiny of many editors can be found in "best of" anthologies. For example, each year there are collections of "the best American" writing in the following categories: short stories, short plays, poetry, sports writing, travel writing, essays, science and nature writing, and so on. You can also find works such as *Scribner's Best of the Fiction Workshops* series.

Bookwork

Competitors must use a manuscript and follow a number of conventions that have developed over the years. This is called **bookwork,** and bookwork in competition is much more detailed than script handling in most other performance settings. Many a competitor has been criticized by the judges for having "sloppy bookwork" or failing to make "crisp page turns." Here are some suggestions for using your performance notebook in ways that will enhance your competitiveness.

Prepare the manuscript so that it fits into a standard performance notebook. These are small three-ring black binders that measure $7\frac{1}{2}" \times 9" \times 1"$. Type or write out the manuscript, mount it on black construction paper, and slip it into plastic sleeves for protection and stability. Put all the pages into the binder. Keep all your texts for all your events in the same binder.

When it's your turn to perform, go to the front of the room and pause for a few seconds with your notebook closed. Then open your notebook and begin. It is most common to start with a teaser, a short excerpt from the text that gains the listeners' attention. (See Chapter 6.) Close the book at the end of the teaser, being sure to keep your finger in place for a smooth reentry to the text. (Note: Follow the norms in your league; although a teaser is not technically required, everyone in my district starts with one, and judges typically mark down the rare competitor who omits it.)

After the teaser, give your introduction. Then, extend your book toward the audience, state the author and title, open the notebook crisply, and continue your performance. Some general guidelines for bookwork include the following:

- Cup the book. Hold it with one hand during the performance, and cup it in such a way that the pages do not show.

- Make crisp page turns. Just before each turn, slip a finger of your free hand beneath the page, lift it slightly, then turn the page with a precise, quick movement. Release it immediately after the turn.

- End forcefully. At the end of the performance, close the book purposefully and pause for a second before returning to your seat.

- If you participate in a Readers Theatre or duo performance, coordinate your bookwork with your partner or partners.

Because you will be using a manuscript, you will not be totally free to use both arms and hands (unless you use a podium or stand). This can be both a drawback and a blessing. You cannot rub your hands together when a character might do so, for example. And if you want to extend both arms, the manuscript will be very visible. But performers sometimes incorporate their manuscripts into their performances, with good and poor results; some bookwork is overly dramatic and detracts from the performance. Here are a few things students have done:

- Cradled the book protectively to their chests, or rocked it as if it were a child.

- Used it to suggest a shield against an enemy.

- Put it in front of their face and peeked over or around it.

- Held it over their head as an umbrella or roof.

- Traded books with a duo partner as part of a transition in the text.

Although practicing bookwork may seem tedious, the way you hold and manage your notebook often makes the difference between a sloppy and a polished performance.

Judging

At a typical speech tournament, you'll find yourself competing on a panel with six other performers. You'll repeat your performance during three different rounds throughout the tournament. In each round, a judge will mark your ballot with a group ranking (from 1–5; the bottom two competitors are each ranked 5) and an individual rating (from 1–25). You're competing for a low rank and a high rate. You'd love a 1/25 (top in the group; most number of points possible).

Judges vary in what they look for in a performance, so don't put too much store in any one ballot. Judges in the Northwest Forensics Conference created a booklet in which they stated their judging philosophies. They provide good insights into the mind of a judge:[1]

- Brent Northup (Carroll College) prefers subtle, understated, complex, slow, deliberate performances. "Interp[retation] is a gift—a student allowing me to experience the emotions of an author. Hand me that gift gently."[2]

- Jim Hanson (Whitman College) likes interpretations "that have an interesting plot, an insightful point to make, and delivery that is like I would hear from a real person in the real world."[3]

- Ed Inch (Pacific Lutheran University)[4] believes that the introduction should set the scene and theme and tie the program together. He likes creative pieces that develop interesting, unique themes. He bases his final judgment on how well an interpretation develops an important thesis.

- Amanda Feller (Pacific Lutheran)[5] wants the interpreter to answer this question in the performance: Why out of all the available stuff to interpret is this THE piece?

- Molly Mayhead (formerly of Western Oregon State University) prefers selections that have a definite climactic build. She judges on the level of difficulty in the selection. "Variety of emotions and responses and sophisticated language would impress me. Ostentatious bookwork (dramatic page flapping or book snapping) is distracting and unrealistic."[6]

Always keep in mind that performing competitively is an educational activity. If you read your ballots carefully and adapt your performance from tournament to tournament, you will better understand your literature, your audiences, and yourself.

References

Chapter 1

[1]Ngugi, w. T. (1997, Fall). Enactment of power: The politics of performance space. *TDR, 41(3),* 11–31. Retrieved March 30, 2005, from InfoTrac College Edition.

[2]See the National Communication Association–sponsored journal *Text and Performance Quarterly* for scholarly articles about current performance theories and practices.

[3]Pelias, R. J., & Van Oosting, J. (1987). A paradigm for performance studies. *Quarterly Journal of Speech, 73,* 219–231.

[4]Campbell, P. N. (1971). Performance: The pursuit of folly. *The Speech Teacher, XX,* 263–274.

[5]Fine, E. C., & Speer, J. H. (1977). A new look at performance. *Communication Monographs, 44,* 374–388.

[6]Owsen, D. M., Kreuze, J. G., & Woodworth, A. (1999, June). You're on! *Strategic Finance, 80(12),* 56–61. Retrieved March 30, 2005, from InfoTrac College Edition.

[7]Schechner, R. (2000, Summer). Mainstream theatre and performance studies. *TDR, 44(2),* 4. Retrieved March 30, 2005, from InfoTrac College Edition.

[8]Bahn, E., & Bahn, M. L. (1970). *A history of oral interpretation.* Minneapolis, MN: Burgess.

[9]Collins, D. (2001). Improvisation in rhapsodic performance. *Helios, 28(1),* 11–29. Retrieved October 30, 2004, from InfoTrac College Edition.

[10]Markus, D. D. (2000, April). Performing the book: The recital of epic in first-century C.E. Rome. *Classical Antiquity, 19(1),* 138–179. Retrieved October 6, 2003, from InfoTrac College Edition.

[11]Armistead, S. G. (1999). *The 700-year oral tradition of the pan-Hispanic ballad: A case study.* Faculty Research Lecture, University of California, Davis. Retrieved October 4, 2003, from http://flsj.ucdavis.edu/home/sjjs/lecture/lecture3

[12]The American star speaker and model elocutionist. (1902). Quoted in

Johnson, N. (2002). *Gender and rhetorical space in American life, 1966–1910* (p. 32). Bloomington: University of Southern Illinois Press.

[13]These pictures come from the following sources: Caldwell, M. (1845). *A manual of elocution: Embracing voice and gesture.* Campbell, H. (1897). *Voice speech and gesture.* Retrieved June 3, 2004, from www.google.com, Images.

[14]Pace, P. (1998). All our lost children: Trauma and testimony in the performance of childhood. *Text and Performance Quarterly, 18(3),* 233–247.

[15]Evans, N. (1998). Games of hide and seek: Race, gender and drag in *The Crying Game* and *The Birdcage. Text and Performance Quarterly, 18(3),* 199–216.

[16]Fuoss, K. W. (1999). Lynching performances, theatres of violence. *Text and Performance Quarterly, 19(1),* 1–37.

[17]Hale, T. A. (1998). Griots *and* griottes*: Masters of word and music.* Bloomington: Indiana University Press.

[18]Haley, A. (1976). *Roots.* Garden City, NY: Doubleday.

[19]Moon, S-J. (2002). *Pansori: Traditional Korean singing.* Retrieved October 6, 2003, from Ajou University, Department of English and College of Humanities Web site: http://madang.ajou.ac.kr/~moon/pansori.htm. See also Bailor, P. (2003). *Pansori at the Lincoln Center Festival 2003.* Retrieved October 6, 2003, from www.nytheatre-wire.com/pb03074t.htm

[20]Lutgendorf, P. (1997). *The oral tradition and the many "Ramayanas."* Retrieved October 4, 2003, from Syracuse University Institute Web site: www.maxwell.syr.edu/maxpages/special/ramayana/Intro.htm

[21]Canadian Museum of Civilization, Aboriginal Training Programme Interns. (n.d.). *Cree storytelling.* Retrieved October 6, 2003, from www.civilization.ca/aborig/storytel/crme3eng.html

[22]University of California Santa Barbara: Archserve, NATlink. (1996). Lakota oral traditions. Retrieved May 26, 2004, from http://id-archserve. ucsb.edu/natlink/old_natlink/NATraditions/Lakota/HTML/OralTraditions.html

[23]Cigar stars. (1995–1996, Winter). Cigar kings: The Rolando Reyes family relies on time and traditional techniques to make Cuba Aliados Cigar. *Cigar Aficionado Online.*

[24]Smith, J. (2001, June 11). A Cuban cigar primer. Message posted to www.epinions.com/fddk-topic-Cigars-Background_Info-What_Should_You_Know_About-Cuba

[25]Mohor, D. (2002, April). A town that time forgot: An example of socialism in Cuba's tobacco industry. In *Cuba 2001: Hustling, breaking rules, making waves.* Retrieved September 22, 2003, from http://journalism.berkeley.edu/projects/cubans2001/story-town.html

[26]Weiss, H. (2003, Sept. 16). Smoke signals from a Pulitzer Prize winning playwright. *Chicago Sun-Times.* Retrieved September 30, 2003 from http://suntimes.com/output/weiss/cst-ftr-cruz16.html

[27]Juliano, V. (1997, September). *A history of reading:* A review by Vince Juliano. *Looking at Books Online, 39(8).* Retrieved September 30, 2003, from the Connecticut Libraries Web site: http://cla.uconn.edu/reviews/hisread/html

[28]Ngugi. (1997). Op cit.

[29]Jacobson, L. (1994, January). What is performance studies? NYU and Northwestern define an elusive field. *American Theatre, 11(1),* 20–23. Retrieved April 12, 2004, from InfoTrac College Edition.

[30]Bowman, M. S., & Ristenberg, C. J. (1992). "Textual power" and the subject of oral interpretation: An alternate approach to performing literature. *Communication Education, 41,* 287–299.

[31]School Improvement in Maryland. (2000, March 19). Standards: English literature. Retrieved June 3, 2003, from www.mdk12.org/mspp/standards/english/literature. html#top

[32]McGuire, M., & Slembek, E. (1987). An emerging critical rhetoric: Hellmut Geissner's *Sprechwissenschaft. Quarterly Journal of Speech, 73,* 349–400.

[33]Campbell, P. N. Op. cit.

[34]MacFarquhar, L. (1997, October 20). Slim chance. *The New Yorker,* 77–78.

[35]Rafkin, L. (1998). *Other people's dirt: A housecleaner's curious adventures* (pp. 12–13). Chapel Hill, NC: Algonquin Books of Chapel Hill.

[36]Key, F. S. (1814). The star spangled banner. Retrieved October 15, 2003, from http://www.bcpl.net/~etowner/anthem.html

[37]Ayers, J., & Hopf, T. (1989). Visualization: Is it more than extra-attention? *Communication Education, 38,* 1–5.

[38]Brownell, W. W., & Katula, R. A. (1984). The Communication Anxiety Graph: A classroom tool for managing speech anxiety. *Communication Quarterly, 32,* 243–249.

Chapter 2

[1]Montgomery, L. M. (1908). *Anne of Green Gables.* Retrieved April 8, 2004, from www-2.cs.cmu.edu/People/rgs/anne-table.html

[2]Berlo, D. (1960). *The process of communication.* New York: Holt, Rinehart and Winston.

[3]Fadiman, A. (1997). *The spirit catches you and you fall down: A Hmong child, her American doctors, and the collision of two cultures.* New York: Farrar, Straus, and Giroux.

[4]Wright, J. (n.d.). The bora ring. Retrieved June 25, 2004, from www.oldpoetry.com/poetry/33235. Reprinted by permission.

[5]Amphibian Research Center. (n.d.) Project Corroboree. Retrieved June 25, 2004, from http://frogs.org.au/corroboree/index.html

[6]Pongweni, A. (2000, July). Voicing the text: South African oral poetry and performance. *Critical Arts, 14(2),* 175–223. October 28, 2004. InfoTrac College Edition.

[7]Anaya, R. (1995). *The Anaya reader.* New York: Warner Books.

[8]Rudolfo Anaya. (n.d.). *Home page.* Retrieved May 13, 2004, from the University of New Mexico Web site: http://www.unm.edu/~wrtgsw/anaya.html

[9]Pearce, W. B. (1989). *Communication and the human condition.* Carbondale: Southern Illinois University Press.

[10]Paul, M. R. (2003, September 12). A powerful film not for everyone. Message posted to www.imdb.com/title/tt0257850/usercomments

[11]The Bellwether Prize for Fiction. (n.d.). *Defining a literature of social change.* Retrieved November 12, 2003, from www.bellwetherprize.org/change.html

[12]Evers, L., & Pavich, P. (1998). *A literary history of the American West.* Fort Worth: Texas Christian University Press.

[13]Quoted in Barba, E. (Ed.). (2002). *Towards a poor theatre* (p. 237). New York: Routledge. For information about Artaud, explore the Web site www.theatrehistory.com/french/artaud001.html, or read the chapter about him in Fowlie, W. (2001). *Dionysus in Paris* (pp. 203–209). New York: Meridian Books. (Original work published 1960).

[14]Ngugi. Op. cit.

[15]Aristotle. Op. cit.

[16]Ibid.

[17]Maslow, A. H. (1987). *Motivation and personality* (3rd ed.) San Francisco: Harper & Row.

[18]Packard, V. (1957). *The hidden persuaders.* New York: Simon & Schuster.

[19]Pelias. R. J., & Van Oosting, J. (1987). A paradigm for performance studies. *Quarterly Journal of Speech, 73,* 219–231.

[20]The Mothers of Plaza de Mayo. (n.d.). The vanished gallery. Retrieved May 27, 2004, from www.yendor.com/vanished/madres.html

[21]Johnson, S. (2004, July 20). Bethel College. Personal communication.

Chapter 3

[1]Nafisi, A. (2003). *Reading Lolita in Tehran: A memoir in books.* New York: Random House.

[2]Bowman, M. S., & Ristenberg, C. J. (1992). "Textual power" and the subject of oral interpretation: An alternate approach to performing literature. *Communication Education, 41,* 287–299.

[3]There are many sources for lists of American values. See, for example, Rokeach, M. (1972). *Beliefs, attitudes, and values.* San Francisco: Jossey-Bass; van der Veen, E. W. (2001, August 29). *US values list: American ethos (Based on Robin Williams, Jr., 1970).* Retrieved December 3, 2003, from University of Alaska Anchorage, Introduction to Sociology Web site: http://hosting. uaa.alaska.edu/afewv/Class_relations/ US_values_ list.htm; Welker, E. (n.d.). *Appreciating other cultures.* Ohio State University Extension Fact Sheet, HYG-5202–96. Retrieved December 3, 2003, from http://ohioline.osu.edu/hyg-fact/5000/5202.html

[4]Mathur, I., quoted in Howard, M. (n.d.) Arranged marriage and the Holi Festival. Retrieved November 19, 2003, from Haverford College, English Department Web site: www.haverford.edu/engl/engl277b/Contexts/arranged.htm

[5]Longfellow, H. W. (1838). "A psalm of life." In H. W. Longfellow, *Favorite poems* (pp. 2–3). New York: Dover Publications.

[6]Kilmer, J. (1913). Trees. Retrieved December 4, 2003, from http:// hometown.aol.com/l6898/poem.html

[7]Rich, A. (1993). "The trees." In G. McMichael, F. Crewes, J. C. Levenson, L. Marx, & D. E. Smith. (Eds.). *Concise anthology of American literature* (2nd ed., pp. 1961–1962). New York: Macmillan. (Original work published 1963). Copyright © 2002 by Adrienne Rich. Copyright © 1966 by W. W. Norton & Company, Inc., from The Fact of a Doorframe: Selected Poems 1950–2001 by Adrienne Rich. Used by permission of the author and W. W. Norton & Company, Inc.

[8]Bitzer, L. F. (1999). The rhetorical situation. In J. I. Lucaites, C. M. Condit, & S. Caudill (Eds.). *Contemporary rhetorical theory: A reader* (pp. 217–223). New York: Guildford Press. (Original work published 1968)

[9]Austerlitz, S. (2000, March 2). Ye olde theatre of penzantial pirates, samurai. *Yale Herald Online.* Retrieved November 18, 2003, from www. yaleherald.com/archive/xxix/ 2000.03.02/ae/p16topsy.html

[10]Twain, M. (1994). *Adventures of Huckleberry Finn* (pp. 77–78). New York: Dover Publications. (Original work published 1885)

[11]Calvino, I. (2005). *Why read the classics?* Retrieved November 12, 2003. www.emory.edu/EDUCATION/mfp /calclassics.html (Original work published 1947)

[12]Ibid.

[13]Stack, P. F. (2003, December 13). Scholars see Christian values in Tolkien's "Lord of the rings." *The Salt Lake Tribune.* Retrieved December 13, 2003, from http://www.sltrib.com/2003/dec/ 12132003/saturday/saturday.asp

[14]Pratt, J. (1998, November 23). *Something should be done.* Paper presented at the National Communication Association. Retrieved December 14, 2003, from www.phirhopi.org/prp/spkrpts5.2/ pratt.htm

[15]Jensen, J. V. (1997). *Ethical issues in the communication process.* Mahwah, NJ: Lawrence Erlbaum.

[16]Northwest Forensics Association. (2002, September). Ethical use of literature. Retrieved December 11, 2003, from www.tinytall.com/nfc/bylaws/ 2002.PDF

Chapter 4

[1]Hunsinger, P. (1967). *Communicative interpretation.* Dubuque, IA: Wm. C. Brown.

[2]Thompson, D. W. (1973). Teaching the history of interpretation. *The Speech Teacher, XXII,* 38–40.

[3]Barbauld, A. L. (2003). To a little invisible being who is expected soon to

become visible. Representative Poetry Online. Retrieved October 24, 2004, from http://eir. library.utoronto.ca/ rpo/display/poem118.html (Original work published 1825).

[4]Burgess, G. (2004). On digital extremities. In L. Untermeyer (Ed.) *Modern American Poetry*. Retrieved October 24, 2004, from www.bartleby.com/ 104/37.html (Original work published 1919)

[5]Wassef, W. (1990). Hasan's wives. In M. Badran & M. Cooke (Eds.), *Opening the gates: A century of Arab feminist writing* (p.100). Bloomington: Indiana University Press. (Originally published 1970)

[6]Nansen, O. (1957). Diary entry, June 4, 1944. In P. Dunaway & M. Evans (Eds.), *A treasury of the world's great diaries* (p. 562). Garden City, NY: Doubleday & Company.

[7]Shaw, L. (1981). Signal. In L. Shaw. *The sighting* (p. 18). Wheaton, IL: Harold Shaw Publishers. Reprinted by permission of the author.

[8]Blake, W. (1967). The tyger. In A. J. M. Smith (Ed.), *Seven centuries of verse: English & American from the early English lyrics to the present day* (3rd ed., p. 284). New York: Charles Scribner's Sons. (Original work published 1794)

[9]Bradstreet, A. (1678). The author to her book. Retrieved October 9, 2004, from www. scribbling.net/the_ author_to_her_book

[10]Bradstreet, A. (1678). To my dear and loving husband. Retrieved October 9, 2004, from www.scribbling.net/ to_my_dear_and_loving_husband

[11]Housman, A. E. (1967). Terence, this is stupid stuff. In A. J. M. Smith (Ed.), *Seven centuries of verse: English & American from the early English lyrics to the present day* (3rd ed., p. 553). New York: Charles Scribner's Sons. (Original work published 1896)

[12]Moore, M. (1981). An octopus. In *Marianne Moore: Complete poems* (p. 71). New York: MacMillian Publishing. (Original work published 1935) Copyright © Marianne Moore, ©

renewed by the Estate of Marianne Moore. Reprinted by permission.

[13]Housman, A. E. (1922). Eight o'clock. Retrieved October 23, 2004, from http://oldpoetry.com/poetry/13058

[14]Henley, W. E. (1875). Invictus. Retrieved October 12, 2001, from www.sk2k.com/invictus.htm

[15]Fletcher, R. (n.d.). William Ernest Henley. Retrieved October 12, 2001, from West Chester University, Robert P. Fletcher Web site: http://courses. wcupa. edu/fletcher/henley/project. htm

[16]Ballantine, P. (1998). The blue devils of Blue River Avenue. In G. Keillor (Ed.), *The best American short stories 1998* (p. 21). New York: Houghton Mifflin.

[17]Cruz, N. (2003). *Anna in the tropics*. New York: Theatre Communications Group.

[18]Diaz, J. (2001). Drown. In L. Watkins-Goffman & R. W. Goffman (Eds.), *Many voices: A multicultural reader* (p. 153). Upper Saddle River, NJ: Prentice Hall.

[19]McBride, J. (1996). *The color of water: A black man's tribute to his white mother* (pp. 165–166). New York: Riverhead Books.

[20]Burke, K. (1973). *The philosophy of literary form* (3rd ed.). Berkeley, CA: University of California Press.

[21]Burke, K. As cited in Golden, J. L., Berquist, G. F., & Coleman, W. E. (Eds.). (1976). *The rhetoric of Western thought* (3rd ed., p. 318). Dubuque, IA: Kendall Hunt.

[22]Ibid.

[23]Wheeler, K. L. (2004). *Literary vocabulary terms*. Retrieved October 8, 2004, from Carson-Newman College Web site: web.cn.edu.kwheeler/ lit_terms.html

[24]Hale, D. M. (2003). *Subtext: What lurks beneath*. Retrieved October 23, 2004, from http://members.aol.com/ hrwdebhale/subtext.htm

[25]Stuart, M. (1923). In the orchard. Retrieved November 10, 2003, from http://www. theotherpages.org/ poems/bestof1923b.html#32

[26]Landwehr, M. (2002). Introduction to literature and the visual arts; questions of influence and intertextuality. *College Literature, 29(3),* 1–17.Retrieved March 15, 2004 from InfoTrac College Edition database.

[27]Dalgaard, R. (n.d.) *Genette's theory of transtextuality.* Retrieved March 8, 2004, from National University of Singapore Web Site: www.comp.nus.edu.sg/~renlian/ hypertext/scholarl-yarchive/genette.htm

[28]Landwehr, M. (2002). Op cit.

[29]Alenier, K. L. (2004). Anna in the tropics: Nilo Cruz. Retrieved October 25, 2004, from www.culturevulture.net/Theater7/AnnaintheTropics.htm

[30]Pelias, R. J. (1992). *Performance studies: The interpretation of aesthetic texts.* New York: St. Martin's Press. (p. 64).

Chapter 5

[1]Chevalier, T. (1999). *Girl with the pearl earring.* New York: Dutton Books.

[2]Williams, J. R. (1998). Guidelines for the use of multimedia in instruction. In *Proceedings of the Human Factors and Ergonomics Society: 42nd annual meeting* (pp. 1447–1451). Retrieved July 2, 2004, from www.humanfactors.com/downloads/aug002.htm

[3]Grahame, K. (1999). *The wind in the willows.* (Original work published 1908) Retrieved July 5, 2004, from University of Virginia Library, Electronic Text Center Web site: http://wyllie.lib.virginia.edu:8086/perl/toccer-new?id = GraWind. sgm&images = images/ modeng&data = /texts/english/modeng/parsed&tag = public&part = 1&division = div1

[4]Venkatajiri, H. S. (2000). *Definition of stuttering: What are the characteristics of stuttering? Fluency tutorial.* Retrieved July 17, 2003, from Iowa State University Web site: www.public.iastate.edu/~cmdis476/tutorials/ fluency tutorials/definition_of_stuttering.html

[5]Glaspell, S. (1963). Suppressed desires. In Weiss, M. J. (Ed.), *10 short plays* (pp. 81–104). New York: Dell. (Original work published 1920)

[6]Lokeshwar, P. (2001). *Voice disorders.* Retrieved June 20, 2003, from www.medivisionindia.com/speechtherapy/vd.phtml

[7]Patchett, A. (2001). *Bel canto* (p. 35). New York: Perennial Books.

[8]Seaton, M. (2001, September 21). Word up. *The Guardian Unlimited.* Retrieved April 23, 2004, from www.guardian.co.uk/g2/story/0,3604,555379,00.html

[9]Orozco, D. (1995). Orientation. In Smiley, J. (Ed.), *The best American short stories 1995* (p. 1). Boston: Houghton Mifflin.

[10]Kidd, S. M. (2002). *The secret life of bees* (p. 7). New York: Viking.

[11]Joseph, J. (1961). Warning. Retrieved December 10, 2003,from www.wheniamanoldwoman.com

[12]*Red hat society.* (2003). Retrieved March 7, 2004, from www.redhatsociety.com

[13]Garcia, C. (1992). *Dreaming in Cuban: A novel* (pp. 138–139). New York: Ballantyne Books.

[14]Blunt, J. (1967). *Stage dialects.* New York: Harper & Row.

[15]Horvat, A. (2000). *Japanese beyond words: How to walk and talk like a native speaker.* Berkeley, CA: Stone Bridge Press. Retrieved July 14, 2003, from www.cic.sfu.ca/tqj/GettingRight/womencomedown.html

[16]Schisgal, M. (1992). Extensions. In Stein, H., & Young, G. (Eds.), *The best American short plays 1991–1992* (pp. 209–228). New York: Applause Theatre Book Publishers.

[17]Twain, M. (1994). *Adventures of Huckleberry Finn.* New York: Dover Publications. (Original work published 1885)

[18]Packer, ZZ. (2000). Brownies. In Doctorow, E. L. (Ed.), *The best American short stories 2000* (p. 282). Boston: Houghton Mifflin.

[19]Shear, C. (1995). *Blown sideways through life* (p. 13). New York: The Dial Press.

[20]Williams, J. (1995). Honored guest. In Smiley, J. (Ed.), *The best American short*

[20] *stories 1995* (141–155). Boston: Houghton Mifflin.

[21] Cisneros, S. (1992). *Bien pretty.* In *Woman hollering creek and other stories* (pp. 137–165). New York: Random House.

[22] Levinson, A. (1970). Socrates wounded. In Oleson, L. (Ed.), *50 great scenes for student actors* (p. 268). New York: Bantam Books. (Original work published 1959)

[23] Bradbury, R. (1996). At the end of the ninth year. In *Quicker than the eye* (pp. 175–181). Avon: New York.

[24] Craig, J. P. *Tips for improving delivery.* Retrieved July 14, 2003, from University of Iowa, Rhetoric 10:02:24 Web site: www.uiowa.edu/~c100298/anxiety.html

[25] Allende, I. (1995). *Paula.* New York: HarperCollins Publishers.

[26] Ekman, P., & Friesen, W. V. (1969). The repertoire of non-verbal behaviours: Categories, origins, usage, and codings. *Semiotics 1,* 45–98.

[27] Gurney, A. R. (1992). The open meeting. In Stein, H., & Young, G. (Eds.). Op. cit. (p. 92).

[28] Wilder, C. (1997). Dr. Tilmann's consultant: A scientific romance. In Dozois, G. (Ed.), *The year's best science fiction: Fourteenth annual collection* (pp. 486–487). New York: St. Martin's Griffin.

[29] Chevalier, T. (1999). Op. cit.

[30] Oates, J. C. (1988). Where are you going, where have you been? In Eagleton, S. (Ed.), *Women in literature: Life stages through stories, poems and plays* (pp. 84–96). Englewood Cliffs, NJ: Prentice Hall.

[31] Galyan, D. (1996). The incredible appearing man. In Wideman, J. E. (Ed.), *The best American short stories 1996* (pp. 126, 127, 130). Boston: Houghton Mifflin.

[32] Huddle, D. (1996). Past my future. Op. cit. (p. 174).

[33] Vest, G. G. (1869). *Tribute to the dog.* Retrieved June 28, 2004, from http://dogpage.mcf.com/misc/TributeTo The-Dog.html

[34] Chestnut, M. B. (1957). Excerpts from *A diary from Dixie.* In Dunaway, P., & Evans, M. (Eds.), *A treasury of the world's great diaries* (pp. 239–257). Garden City, NY: Doubleday. (Original work written 1864)

[35] Mora, P. (2001). Remembering Lobo. In Watkins-Goffman, L., & Goffman, R. (Eds.). Op. cit. (p. 60).

[36] Smilow, D. (1997). Brights. In Land, E., & Shengold, N. (Eds.), *Take ten: New 10-minute plays* (pp. 277–288). New York: St. Martin's Griffin.

[37] Simard, D. (1997). Tallulah at your feet. In Hoffman, A. (Ed.), *Scribner's best of the fiction workshops 1997* (p. 118). New York: Scribner Paperback Fiction.

[38] Carver, R. (2000). Call if you need me. In Doctorow, E. L. (Ed.). Op. cit. (p. 76).

[39] Deans of Girls of Chicago High Schools. (1921). *Manual of conduct in school and out.* Retrieved July 24, 2003 from University of Oregon Web site: http://darkwing.uoregon.edu/~joe/digilib/

Chapter 6

[1] Jaffe, C. I. (2003). *Public speaking: Concepts and skills for a diverse society.* Belmont, CA: Wadsworth.

[2] Lamott, A. (1994). *Bird by bird: Some instructions on writing and life.* New York: Anchor.

[3] Winfield, C. M. (n. d.) Oral interpretation of literature: A discipline or an event. Retrieved September 10, 2004, from http://debate.uvm.edu/NFL/rostrumlib/interpwinfield0697.pdf

[4] Cronn-Mills, D., & Golden, A. (1997). The "unwritten rules" in oral interpretation: An assessment of current practices. *SpeakerPoints, 4.* Retrieved September 9, 2004, from www.phirhopi.org/prp/spkrpts4.2/cmills.html

Chapter 7

[1] Prose. (2005). *Merriam-Webster Online.* Retrieved March 31, 2005, from www.m-w.com/cgi-bin/dictionary

[2]Exposition. (2005). *MSN Encarta — Dictionary*. Retrieved March 31, 2005, from http://encarta.msn.com/diction-ary_/exposition.html

[3]Cambrensis, G. (1949). Celtic music and music in general. In Ross, J. B. & McLaughlin, M. M. (Eds.), *The portable medieval reader* (pp. 552–556). New York: The Viking Press.

[4]Adams, L. (1997). The Holly Pageant. In Gould, C. V. & Byington, E. (Eds.), *Critical issues in contemporary culture* (pp. 186–192). Boston: Allyn and Bacon.

[5]Jackson, S. (2002, July 17). Def Poetry Jam: Lame audience, tight poets. *Youth Outlook*. Retrieved December 15, 2003, from www.youthoutlook.org/stories/2002/07/17/def.poetry.jam.lame.audience.tight.poets.html

[6]Welles, G. (1957). Diary excerpt, April 15, 1865. In Dunaway, P., & Evans M. (Eds.). Op. cit. (pp. 289–291).

[7]Clemens, S. ([1887] 1946). To Jeannette Gilder [Not mailed]. In DeVoto, B. (Ed.), *The portable Mark Twain* (pp. 764–765). New York: The Viking Press.

[8]Clemens, S. ([1879] 1946). Letter to William Dean Howells. In DeVoto, B., Op. cit. (p. 758).

[9]Muggeridge, M. (1986). *Something beautiful for God*. San Francisco: HarperCollins.

[10]Sedaris, D. (2000). *Me talk pretty one day*. Boston: Little Brown and Company.

[11]Hillebrand, L. (2001). *Seabiscuit: An American legend*. New York: Ballentine Books.

[12]Mayle, P. (1995). *A dog's life*. New York: Vintage Books.

[13]Flagg, F. (1992). *Daisy Fay and the miracle man*. New York: Warner Books.

[14]Cisneros, S. (1968). Eleven. In *Woman hollering creek and other stories* (pp. 6–9). New York: Random House.

[15]Buechner, F. (1993). *Peculiar treasures: A Biblical who's who*. San Francisco: Harper.

[16]Adams, L. (1997). Op. cit.

[17]Chen, Y. (1929). Woman. In Dooling, A. D., & Torgeson, K. M. (Eds.), *Writing women in modern China: An anthology of women's literature from the early twentieth century*. New York: Columbia University Press.

[18]Macy, C. (2003, March 10). Christie. *The New Yorker*, 73.

[19]Wodehouse, P. G. (1984). *Pigs have wings*. New York: Penguin Books. (Work originally published 1952)

[20]Mays, C. B. (n.d.). Folktale, myth, legend and fable. Retrieved October 20, 2001, from Internet School Library Media Center Web site: http://falcon.jmu.edu/~ramseyil/tradmays.htm

[21]Lewis, C. S. (1955). *The magician's nephew*. New York: Harper-Collins.

[22]Welles, G. Op. cit. (Work originally published 1911)

[23]Layland, P. (1985). The death of the fat man. In Falkiner, S. (Ed.), *Room to move: The Redress Press anthology of women's short stories* (pp. 196–198). Sydney, Australia: Unwin Paperbacks. Reprinted by permission.

[24]Mason, D. (2002). *The piano tuner* (pp. 133–136). New York: Random House.

[25]Mirvin, T. (1999). *The ladies auxiliary* (pp. 183–185). New York: Ballantine Books.

[26]Pamuk, O. (2001). *My name is red* (E. M. Goknar, Trans., p. 102). New York: Vintage International.

[27]Grealy, L. (1994). *Autobiography of a face*. Boston: Houghton Mifflin.

[28]Sijie, D. (2002). *Balzac and the little Chinese seamstress*. (I. Rilke, Trans.). New York: Random House.

[29]Maud Gonne. (1994). *The autobiography of Maud Gonne: Servant of the queen* (pp. 120–121). Chicago: University of Chicago Press. (Work originally published 1938)

Chapter 8

[1]Drama. (n.d.). In *Free dictionary*. Retrieved December 17, 2003, from www.thefreedictionary.com/drama

[2]DiYanni, R. (2002). *Literature: Reading fiction, poetry, and drama* (5th ed.). Boston: McGraw-Hill.

[3]Aristotle. Op. cit.

[4]DiYanni. Op. cit.

[5]Shaw, G. B. (2003). *Arms and the man* (Act I, Scene i). Retrieved October 14, 2004, from www.gutenberg.net/etext/3618 (Work originally published 1894)

[6]Ibid.

[7]Wassberg, T. (n. d.) Enlightenment, discovery and a bit of fun: The difference between writing with your eyes and with your ears. Retrieved October 2, 2004, from http://www.wga.org/ craft/inter-views/rivera.html

[8]Shaw, G. B. Op. cit.

[9]Cunningham, L. (1997). Beautiful bodies. In Lane, E., & Shengold, N. (Eds.), *Plays for actresses* (pp. 158–159). New York: Random House.

[10]Parks, S-L. (1992). Snails. In Stein, H. & Young, G. (Eds.), *The best American short plays 1991–1992* (p. 196). New York: Applause Theatre Books.

[11]Tragicomedy. (2004). *Encyclopedia Britannica*. Retrieved October 28, 2004, from *Encyclopaedia Britannica* Premium Service. www.britannica.com/eb/article?tocId = 9073149

[12]Su, M., & Zuo, L. (2003). A Chinese director's theory of performance: On Jiao Juyin's system of directing. *Asian Theatre Journal, 20(1),* 25–43. Retrieved January 6, 2004, from InfoTrac College Edition.

[13]Gilman, R. (2000). *Spinning into butter.* New York: Faber and Faber.

[14]Virgil. (1869.) *The Aeneid* (J. Dryden, Trans.). Retrieved October 2, 2004, from Massachusetts Institute of Technology, Internet Classics Archive Web site: http://classics.mit.edu/Virgil/aeneid.1.i.html

[15]Wars of the Roses. (2004). In *eHistory.com*. Retrieved October 2, 2004, from www.ehistory.com/middleages/warsoftheroses/overview.cfm

[16]Shineman, K. A. (1996, November). *The utilization of conceptual and geometric forms for oral interpretation performances.* Paper presented at the Speech Communication Association National Convention, San Diego, CA.

[17]Cruz, N. (1996). Graffiti. In Ellis, R. (Ed.), *Multicultural theatre: Scenes and monologs from new Hispanic, Asian, and African-American plays* (pp. 55–61). Colorado Springs, CO: Meriwether Publishing.

[18]Topor, T. (1999). Boundary County, Idaho. In Young, G. (Ed.), *The best American short plays 1998–1999* (pp. 203–205). New York: Applause Theatre Books Publishers.

[19]Stroppel, F. (1997). Judgment call. In Lane, E. & Shengold, N. (Eds.). Op. cit. (pp. 55–61)

[20]Shakespeare, W. (n.d.). *Hamlet* (Act I, Scene 3). Retrieved July 13, 2004, from Massachusetts Institute of Technology, Internet Classics Archive Web site: http://classics.mit.edu/Shakespeare/Tragedy/hamlet/hamlet.1.3.html. (Work originally published 1600–1608)

[21]Oates, J. C. (1992). Tone clusters (Scene 9). In Stein, H., & Young, G. (Eds.). Op. cit.

Chapter 9

[1]Thayer, E. L. (1888, June 3). Casey at the bat: A ballad of the republic. *San Francisco Examiner.* Retrieved December 1, 2003, from www.sportingnews.com/archives/baseball/94640.html

[2]Twombly, W. (1975, July 5). Mighty Casey haunted author. *The Sporting News.* Retrieved December 1, 2003, from www.sportingnews.com/archives/baseball/4794.html

[3]As cited in Gergen, J. (1987, June 15). Casey is still striking out – but not as a classic. *The Sporting News.* Retrieved December 1, 2003, from www.sportingnews.com/archives/baseball/94786.html

[4]Ibid.

[5]DiYanni, R. (2002). *Literature: Reading fiction, poetry, and drama* (5th ed., p. 670). Boston: McGraw-Hill.

[6]Ibid.

[7]Zerkovitz, J. (n.d.). Pragmatics: Lecture notes. Retrieved December 1, 2003, from http://ludens.elte.hu/~deal/AN-261/4.rtf

[8]Austin, J. L. (1975). *How to do things with words* (2nd ed.). Cambridge: Harvard University Press. (Work originally published 1962)

[9]Richards, I. A. (1960). *Practical criticism: A study of literary judgment.* New York: Harcourt Brace. (Work originally published 1929)

[10]Father. (2001). *The American heritage dictionary of the English language, 4th ed.* Retrieved October 8, 2001, from www.bartleby.com.

[11]Ibid.

[12]Ibid.

[13]Whitman, W. (1999). Out of the cradle endlessly rocking. In *Leaves of grass.* Retrieved August 20, 2004, from www.bartleby.com/142/212.html (Work originally published 1900)

[14]Epigraph. (2004). In *DocBook: The definitive guide.* Retrieved August 21, 2004, from www.oreilly.com/catalog/docbook/chapter/book/epigraph.html

[15]Wordsworth, W. (1969). Stepping westward. (From *Memorials of a Tour in Scotland, 1803*). In A. J. M. Smith (Ed.), *Seven centuries of verse: English & American from the early English lyrics to the present day* (3rd ed., p. 303). New York: Charles Scribner's Sons. (Original work published 1803)

[16]Arnold, M. (2001). Dover Beach. In *English poetry III: From Tennyson to Whitman: The Harvard classics. 1909–1914.* Retrieved August 20, 2004, from www.bartleby.com/42/705.html (Work originally published 1867)

[17]Lawrence, D. H. (1969). Snake. From *The Complete Poems of D. H. Lawrence,* edited by V. de Sola Pinto and F. W. Roberts. Copyright © 1964, 1971 by Angelo Ravagli and C. M. Weekely, Executors of the state of Frieda Lawrence Ravagli. Reprinted by permission of Viking Penguin, a division of Penguin Group (USA), Inc.

[18]DiYanni, R. Op. cit.

[19]Richards, I. A. Op. cit. (p. 197)

[20]Al-Mutanabbi. (n. d.). In *Encyclopedia Britannica.* Retrieved March 10, 2004, from Encyclopedia Britannica Premium Service.

[21]*Al-Mutanabbi to Sayf-al-Dawla.* (n. d.) Retrieved March 10, 2004, from Princeton University Web site: www.princeton.edu/~arabic/poetry/al_mu_to_sayf.html

[22]Shaw, L. (1981). Galilee, Easter 1979. *The sighting* (p. 17). Wheaton, IL: Harold Shaw Publishers. Reprinted by permission of the author.

[23]Donne, J. (1967). Holy sonnets, X. In A. J. M. Smith (Ed). Op. cit. (p. 135) (Work originally published 1572–1631)

[24]Kostova, E. (1997). Suddenly I realized I was sitting. In J. Tate (Ed.), *The best American poetry 1997* (p. 125). New York: Scribner Poetry.

[25]Sappho. (2001). Without warning. Retrieved July 13, 2004, from www.pddoc.com/poems/without_warning_sappho.htm

[26]Mariani, P. (1990). Then sings my soul. In *Salvage operations: New and selected poems* (pp. 184–185). New York: W. W. Norton.

[27]Pastan, L. (1985). The seven deadly sins: Anger. In *A fraction of darkness.* New York: W. W. Norton. Copyright © 1985 by Linda Pastan. Used by permission of W. W. Norton & Company, Inc.

[28]Clifton, L. (1969). my momma moved among the days. In *Good woman: Poems and a memoir 1969.* New York: BOA Editions. www.BOAEditions.org. Reprinted by permission.

[29]Shakespeare, W. (1967). Sonnet 30. In A. J. M. Smith (Ed), Op cit.

[30]Tennyson, A. (1967). The lady of Shalott. In A. J. M. Smith (Ed). Op. cit. (p. 404)

[31]Shakespeare, W. (1967). Sonnet 116. In A. J. M. Smith (Ed). Op. cit. (p. 206)

[32]Hopkins, G. M. (1967). The windhover. In A. J. M. Smith (Ed.). Op. cit. (p. 539) (Work originally published 1918)

[33]Kostova, E. (1997). Suddenly I realized I was sitting. In J. Tate (Ed.). Op. cit.

[34]James, W. (2004). *The stream of consciousness*. Retrieved August 23, 2004, from York University, Classics in the History of Psychology Web site: http://psychclassics.asu.edu/James/jimmy11.htm (Original work published 1872)

[35]Noyes, A. (1913). The highwayman. Retrieved July 13, 2004, from www.potw.org/archive/potw85.html

[36]Epic poetry. (2004). In *Wikipedia: The free encyclopedia*. Retrieved August 23, 2004, from http://en.wikipedia.org/wiki/Epic_poetry

[37] Poetry. (1998). In *Microsoft Encarta 98 Encyclopedia*. Retrieved August 23, 2004, from litera1no4.tripod.com/form_frame.html#ballad

[38]Filreis, A. (1977). *Ballad*. Retrieved March 3, 2004, from University of Pennsylvania, English Department Web site: http://www.english.upenn.edu/~afilneis/88/ballad.html

[39]Poe, E. A. (1849). Annabel Lee. Retrieved August 25, 2004, from http://eserver.org/ books/poe/annabel_lee.html

[40]Epic poetry. (2004). In *Wikipedia: The free encyclopedia*. Op. cit.

[41]Milosevic-Djordjevic, N. (2004). The oral tradition. Retrieved August 23, 2004, from www.suc.org/culture/history/Hist_Serb_Culture/chi/ Oral_Tradition.html?Suc_ Session = e45423478d244d66037bb9d00b25b62b

[42]Reading lyric poetry. (2004). *A guide to the study of literature: A companion text for Core Studies 6, Landmarks of Literature*. Retrieved July 13, 2004, from Brooklyn College, English Department Web site: http://academic.brooklyn.cuny.edu/english/melani/cs6/read_1yr.html

[43]Tennyson, A. (1967) The eagle. In A. J. M. Smith. (Ed) op. cit. (p. 433) (Work originally published 1851)

[44]Simic, C. (2005). Preface: *The Battle of Kosovo: Serbian epic poems*. Retrieved April 1, 2005, from www.kosovo.com/sk/history/battle_of_kosovo.html

[45]Cotton, K. (2001). Close-up #13: Developing empathy in children and youth. School Improvement Research Series (SIRS). Portland, OR: Northwest Regional Educational Laboratory. Retrieved September 20, 2003, from http://www.nwrel.org/scpd/sirs/7/cu13.html

[46]Poe, E. A. (1845). The raven. Retrieved August 23, 2004, from www.everypoet.com/archive/poetry/Edgar_Allen_Poe/edgar_allen_poe_the_raven.htm

[47]Frankel, H. H. (1976). *The flowering plum and the palace lady: Interpretations of Chinese poetry*. New Haven, CT: Yale University Press. Retrieved March 3, 2004, from http://www.chinapage.com/mulan-e.html. Reprinted by permission.

[48]Reed, H. (2000). Naming of parts. In H. P. Guth & G. L. Rico (Eds.), *Discovering literature: Compact edition* (p. 525). Upper Saddle River, NJ: Prentice Hall. (Work originally published 1946)

[49]Dobyns, S. (1988). Loud music. From Cemetery Nights. Copyright © 1987 by Stephen Dobyns. Reprinted by permission of Viking Penguin, a division of Penguin Group (USA), Inc. Retrieved June 25, 2004, from www.loc.gov/poetry/180/100.html

[50]Browning, R. B. (1842). My last duchess. Retrieved June 25, 2004, from www.victorianweb.org/authors/rb/duchess.html

[51]Fauset, J. (2002). Oriflamme. In J. W. Johnson. (Ed.), *The Book of American Negro poetry*. Retrieved July 12, 2004, from www.bartleby.com/269/95.html (Work originally published 1922)

[52]Cummings, E. E. (1918). in Just-. *Representative Poetry Online*. Copyright © 1923, 1951, © 1991 by the Trustees for the E. E. Cummings Trust. Copyright © 1976 by George James Frimage, from Complete Poems: 1904–1962 by E. E. Cummings, edited by George J. Frimage. Used by permission

of Liveright Publishing Corporation. Retrieved July 12, 2004. http://eir. library.utoronto.ca/rpo/display/poem607.html

[53]Mariani, P. (1990). Then sings my soul. In *Salvage operations: New and selected poems* (pp. 184–185). New York: W. W. Norton. Used by permission.

Chapter 10

[1]McCord, D. T. W. (1967). The pickety fence. From Every Time I Climb a Tree by David McCord. Copyright © 1952 by David McCord. Reprinted by permission of Little, Brown and Company, Inc. Retrieved October 2, 2001, from http://webbschool.com/ rhood/ creativewriting/verbal_music.htm

[2]Down in the valley. (n.d.). American folksong. Retrieved September 6, 2003 from www.niehs.nih.gov/ kids/lyrics/valley.htm

[3]Spiritual Workshop. (n.d.). History. Retrieved April 1, 2005, from www.negrospirituals. com/ history/htm

[4]Gibbs, N. (2002, September 9). One year later: What a difference a day makes. *Time Magazine.*

[5]Wallberg, L. (2001, September). Hell on wheels. The last page. *Smithsonian Magazine, 32* (6).

[6]Reid, A. Curiosity. Retrieved October 1, 2001, from www.geocities.com/ Paris/Lights/4231/curiousity.html

[7]Ives, D. (1995). Sure thing. In *All in the timing.* New York: Vintage Books.

[8]Chernova, J. (1997). Introduction to readers theatre. Retrieved September 20, 2002, from www.comm. unt.edu/histofperf/kellyrt.htm

[9]Shepard, A. (1997). Readers' on stage: tips for reader's theater. Retrieved September 20, 2002, from www.aaronshep.com/rt/Tips.html

[10]Education Resources, Springfield Museum of Art. (2001). Art's unique contribution to culture: Fifth grade lessons. Retrieved September 22, 2002, from www.sma.shs.nebo.edu/ swap/5lessons.html

Subject Index

Bold indicates where the key term is defined.

Author, Selections, and Excerpts Index